Vaughan Williams in perspective

Other Books written or edited by Lewis Foreman

Havergal Brian: a collection of essays (1969)

The British Musical Renaissance: a guide to research
[thesis] (1972)

Discographies: a bibliography (1973)

Archive Sound Collections (1974)

Systematic Discography (1974)

Factors Affecting the Preservation and Dissemination of Archive Sound Recordings
[thesis] (1975)

British Music Now (1975)

Havergal Brian and the performance of his orchestral music (1976)

Edmund Rubbra: composer (1977)

Dermot O'Byrne: poems by Arnold Bax (1979)

Arthur Bliss: catalogue of the complete works (1980)

The Percy Grainger Companion (1981)

Bax: a composer and his times
(1983; 2nd ed 1988; 3rd ed in preparation)

Oskar Fried: Delius and the late romantic school
[whole issue of Delius Society Journal] (1984)

From Parry to Britten: British music in letters (1987, 1988)

Farewell, My Youth and other writings by Sir Arnold Bax (1992)

Lost and Only Sometimes Found: a seminar on music publishing and archives (1992)

British Music 1885–1921 (1994)

FRONTISPIECE:

*Vaughan Williams at an Ealing
Studios recording session, late 1940s.*

Vaughan Williams in perspective

studies of an English composer

edited by
LEWIS FOREMAN

Albion Press
for
The Vaughan Williams Society
1998

Contents

List of Plates

(between pages 112–113)

1. Ralph Vaughan Williams by Herbert Lambert (1923)
2. Ingrave Rectory today. *Photograph by Tony Kendall.*
3. Charles Potiphar's cottage, Ingrave. *Photograph by Tony Kendall.*
4. "The Bell" Willingale Doe. *Photograph by Tony Kendall.*
5. Samuel Child's Cottage, Willingale. *Photograph by Tony Kendall.*
6. "The Olde [Old] Dog" Inn, East Horndon. *Photography by Tony Kendall.*
7. Sir Adrian Boult minutes his successor as BBC Director of Music, Sir Arthur Bliss, complaining about the allocation of repertoire and artists. *(BBC Written Archives centre.)*
8. Vaughan Williams presents a book of tributes to Sir Henry Wood at the Royal College of Music on the occasion of Wood's 75th birthday, 2 March 1944.
9. Vaughan Williams conducts massed local choirs at the Leith Hill Festival.
10. Elizabeth Maconchy.
11. Patrick Hadley, Kendall Taylor and Vaughan Williams at Heacham, 1952.
12. Ina Boyle.
13. Grace Williams.
14. Gerald Finzi by Herbert Lambert.
15. Ursula Wood and Vaughan Williams on the steps of Epsom Parish Church.
16. Mary Haberfield, Ernest Irving and Vaughan Williams recording the music for the film The Loves of Joanna Godden. *(Courtesy Huntley Film Archives.)*
17. Muir Mathieson, Vaughan Williams and Michael powell at the music recording session for the film 49th Parallel. *(Courtesy Huntley Film Archives.)*

Introduction and Acknowledgements

My experience of getting to know Vaughan Williams's music must be typical of many. I first came to love it while at school, when, with the aid of Hammersmith Public Libraries, I was able to explore a wide range of Vaughan Williams's output, even then available on LP. Appreciation of the lesser-known works was triggered by a concert conducted by the late Dr William Cole with the People's Palace Choral Society at Queen Mary College in 1960, even now the only time I have heard live performances of such scores as the *Six Choral Songs* and the *Suite Story of a Flemish Farm*. I was hooked: Vaughan Williams was clearly rewarding in a wide range of music, not merely one or two popular works.

But it was Michael Kennedy, Vaughan Williams's most effective and long-lasting champion, who, with his book *The Music of Ralph Vaughan Williams*, provided the body of knowledge which underpinned all subsequent exploration and research. All later writers on British music have cause to thank him for the standards he set, and for the scale of his achievement. In nearly 35 years since that book first appeared Vaughan Williams's position has been consolidated, and his music disseminated internationally by an enormous discography of recordings, a process now given new focus by the RVW Society.

The essays in the present volume first appeared as spoken presentations at the Vaughan Williams Symposium that Leslie Olive invited me to organise at Reigate Summer Music in July 1996. The articles by Tony Kendall and John Huntley, in fact, originated as separate one-man shows during the festival, John Huntley in one of his admirable and now familiar programmes of historical musical films.

My own chapter brings together material from a talk given at the 1995 annual general meeting of the RVW Society, with my remarks before and during the sessions at Reigate and from pre-concert talks at the festival.

I give most cordial thanks to all involved, both for supporting my invitation to participate and in bringing both the conference and this volume to completion. While the contributions were all first written for oral presentation, they have been here adapted as written papers.

The musical examples have been specially prepared by Andrew Herbert, and to him special thanks for resolving difficult sizing problems at the paste-up stage.

As ever in preparing a book-length study for publication there are many who have contributed to the finished product, and who I must thank for assistance, and for permission to reproduce copyright material. First, thanks are due to Leslie Olive of The English Arts Chorale, promoter of Reigate Summer Music, who first commissioned the Vaughan Williams Seminar, and to Stephen Connock and the RVW Society for asking me to prepare the book for publication. Inevitably, when preparing a series of spoken papers for publication, there are problems of consistency – and by and large I have tried to retain the character of each contributor. In particular this is reflected in Duncan Hinnells's pioneering study of the *Piano Concerto*, where I have, a-typically, retained his extensive separate bibliography as an appendix, in order to avoid increasing the notes in an already heavily footnoted article.

All books on music need the goodwill of the publishers of the music they discuss if some of the music is to be reproduced in music type. Thanks for permission to reproduce copyright music is due as follows: an extract from Edmund Rubbra's *Second String Quartet* is reprinted by kind permission of Alfred Lengnick & Co [a division of Complete Music Ltd] (Score and Parts available from William Elkin Music services, Station Road Industrial Estate, Salhouse, Norwich, Norfolk NR13 6NY tel 01603 721302 fax 01603 721801); *Toward the Unknown Region* and *A Sea Symphony* are reproduced by kind permission of Stainer & Bell Ltd; five bars from Vaughan Williams's *Sancta Civitas* is reproduced by permission of Faber Music; extracts from the Fifth and Ninth symphonies and the Piano Concerto are reproduced by kind permission of the Oxford University Press. All other examples from unpublished sketches, and particularly from the surviving sketch for *The Steersman* are reproduced by kind permisson of Ursula Vaughan Williams, and must not be performed or further reproduced without her agreement. The extract from Cyril Scott's *Lilac-time* appears by permission of Marjorie Hartshorne Scott.

Thanks are also due to the Oxford University Press in respect of quotations from the writings of Vaughan Williams, Gustav Holst and the books by Michael Kennedy on Vaughan Williams, in particular: from *National Music and Other essays* by Ralph Vaughan Williams (2nd ed 1987); from *RVW: a biography* by Ursula Vaughan Williams (1964); from *Heirs and Rebels* by Ralph Vaughan Williams and Gustav Holst, edited by Ursula Vaughan Williams and Imogen Holst (1959); and from *The Works of Ralph Vaughan Williams* by Michael Kennedy (2nd ed 1980). I am also most grateful to Michael Kennedy for his permission to reproduce his writings published both by Oxford University Press and elsewhere. A brief extract from H G Wells's Tono-Bungay is reproduced with acknowledgements to the estate of H G Wells.

I must also thank the Department of Manuscripts, British Library, for the use of material (here set by Andrew Herbert) from Additional Manuscripts in the British Library. The facsimile of an internal BBC minute is reproduced by permission of the BBC and courtesy the BBC Written Archives Centre. To Richard Mason special thanks for assistance with copyright issues.

The plates are largely taken from the editor's collection, with the exception of Tony Kendall's photographs of places in Essex, the late Christopher Palmer, and John Huntley who supplied the jacket photograph, the frontispiece, and the photographs of Vaughan Williams at recording sessions in the 1940s. To all my sincere thanks.

Tony Kendall, Duncan Hinnells, Jennifer Doctor and

Stephen   Banfield   make   individual   thanks   and
acknowledgements in their articles for the use of copyright
material, with which the editor and publisher wish to be
associated.

LEWIS FOREMAN
Rickmansworth

January 1998

I

Lewis Foreman

Restless Explorations

articulating many visions

I F THE CURRENT DISCOGRAPHY OF A COMPOSER IS ANY guide to the health of his musical fortunes, Vaughan Williams may be said to have enjoyed a rising trend for much of the period since his death in 1958, albeit at first fairly slowly. In the 1990s this appreciation is well established internationally. But other than in the UK and to a lesser extent in the USA, this is a recognition resulting largely from recordings rather than from public performances. Though he was widely recorded on LP, the medium of the compact disc has been signally more successful in disseminating this music outside the UK than any previous medium.

In 1972 in the American magazine *The American Record Guide*, the American critic Gerald S Fox declared: "Having spent many, many hours with the symphonies of Ralph Vaughan Williams in the past several months, I must begin by confessing that my deep affection has now exploded into a passionate love affair. What an extraordinary oeuvre! Does any other 20ᵗʰ-century symphonist have a higher 'batting average? What a range of emotions and styles!'[1]" The language in which performances and recordings of Vaughan Williams's symphonies are discussed is indicative of his

1. Gerald S Fox: 'Previn's Vaughan Williams: a triumph of phonographic art' *The American Record Guide,* October 1972, pp 690–694.

acceptance. No longer are reviewers writing in terms to justify RVW as a composer, these are discussions of accepted works open to a variety of interpretations. A typical example is Michael Kennedy's *Gramophone* review of Bryden Thomson's recording of the Ninth Symphony:

Although VW was not the man to say conscious farewells in music, there is inescapably something valedictory about this work, composed when he was 85. It is known to have had a programme associated with Hardy's Tess, Salisbury Cathedral and other Wessex features, such as Stonehenge; but anyone not knowing this would still sense that it is a symphony about an England – perhaps a world – beyond recall. It is not so much tragic as resigned ... the two middle movements are gripping, preparing the way for the great finale, overwhelming in its sombre impact.[2]

Thus far there have been 12 commercially issued versions of *A Sea Symphony*, 18 of *A London Symphony*, 8 of *A Pastoral Symphony*, 11 of No 4, 14 of No 5, 17 of No 6, 10 of the *Sinfonia Antartica*, 9 of No 8 and 6 of No 9. What is more these recordings have been issued and reissued and almost all are available at the time of writing. Five integral sets have been packaged together, with at least three more cycles in progress. New recordings still appear. This is a remarkable achievement and when similar statistics can be assembled for his other music, which in a recent catalogue consists of 102 works in currently available recordings excluding individual songs, short piano pieces and hymn tunes, comprising a total of 432 recordings, we have evidence of a considerable figure.

However, unlike many composers who have a recorded currency, in the UK at least, Vaughan Williams is also one of the most widely performed twentieth-century composers, only Britten and Walton among British post-Elgarian composers enjoying similar success. In the UK this is to a considerable extent the result of the wide acceptance of Vaughan Williams's choral works in the regular repertoire of local choral societies all over the country. This is music which choirs have taken to their hearts and find to be both performable and of intrinsic worth, and it enjoys wide acceptance.

Other contributors to the present volume explore how his reputation was built and the cultural politics that went into the

2. MK *Gramophone*, July 1991, pp 70–71.

establishment of Vaughan Williams as a significant figure. It was certainly clear to Adrian Boult in the 1930s, then Director of Music at the BBC, that Vaughan Williams was pre-eminent, as may be seen in this internal memo written when, in 1935, the *Radio Times* had asserted Bax and Sibelius to be the greatest living symphonists:

I think there are plenty of people inside the BBC who would consider that Vaughan Williams is a far greater symphonist than either Bax or Sibelius. I feel that some communication should go to Vaughan Williams, though personally he does not care in the least about these things ...[3]

That was written in March, a little over a month before the first performance of the Fourth Symphony.

Vaughan Williams was a product of his times, but he also transcended them by developing a language to which a wide spectrum of music lovers could respond. His appeal is surely a melodic one, for the basis of his work is the line: a melody with a visionary quality and a broad humanity. As Michael Kennedy has remarked: "its appeal at several levels makes it a remarkable expression of the national spirit in music."

Perhaps we have tended to have a rather homespun view of Vaughan Williams, and one gets the feeling that he was not unhappy with this image. In fact he was a highly educated, musically experienced, and remarkably sophisticated artist. A member of the Wedgwood family on his mother's side and also related to Charles Darwin, his education at Charterhouse and Cambridge was that of a leader both intellectual and artistic. His Cambridge degree was in history and as well as being a pupil of Parry and Stanford at the Royal College of Music he studied widely, not only with English teachers such as Charles Wood and Alan Gray, but also on the continent with Max Bruch and Ravel (as he put it to "acquire a little French polish").

Folk-song collector, editor of *The English Hymnal* and later *Songs of Praise*, editor of Purcell, organist and conductor, he, whether consciously or unconsciously, managed a synthesis of what we now see as archetypical national elements. He was the

3. Adrian Boult to M H Gorham. BBC Written Archives Centre, Vaughan Williams composer file. Quoted in Lewis Foreman: *From Parry to Britten – British Music in Letters 1900-1945*. Batsford, 1987 p 184.

complete musician, and although he took longer than many to acquire his mature voice, the progress of his music over an active life spanning more than 60 years is quite remarkable, yet always informed by his personal voice and with something distinctive and arresting to say. He wrote in every genre from songs to opera, choral music to symphonies, chamber music to ballet. His enormous integrity and liberal humanist spirit in the tradition of Sir Hubert Parry, his mentor, gave him a commanding position in our music.

Vaughan Williams acknowledged folk song as his most significant influence, yet it is one not to be overplayed in the climate of the 1990s. His discovery of folk song certainly came with the force of a revelation, and yet it did not immediately enable him to build a technique and a language that would allow him to achieve his most far-reaching ambitions. His final mature expression was complex, "taking over little or nothing from the final versions of folk song, nevertheless firmly founded on these folk-song structures, and following methods of 'expansion' which are either suggested by, or which are at any rate compatible with, the tunes themselves. It is an eminently 'melodic' expression. The whole is an 'expansion' of 'melodic' detail, and is such that the 'melody' maintains its integrity against the total effect."[4] That was Elsie Payne, writing while Vaughan Williams was still alive. She reminded us that he "did not at first deem folk song capable of sustaining full-scale composition, so that, during the time he was collecting and making simple arrangements of folk tunes, he was also experimenting to evolve a personal textural style for his more ambitious work."[5]

Vaughan Williams's strengths were always seen: invention, consistency and a massive integrity. He had the mental energy to maintain a relentless and inexorable stream of work. This productivity encompassed a constant delight in the new. In contrast to his received reputation as a reactionary, the truth was far from the case. "I don't know if I like it, but it's what I meant", his widely quoted remark after the first performance

4. Elsie Payne: "Vaughan Williams and folk-song" *Music Review* May, 1954, p 103.
5. *ibid.*

of his Fourth Symphony in 1935, could be taken as his watchword when producing so many pioneering works.

The over-riding theme of his work is a constant searching for a mystical or quasi-mystical truth, from *Toward the Unknown Region* of 1907, 'On the Beach at Night Alone' from *A Sea Symphony* in 1910, to the concerns of the late Blake Songs and the Ninth Symphony. His publisher Hubert Foss wrote: "Vaughan Williams has … developed a technique out of an ardent desire to express truths".[6] Like Benjamin Britten after him, here we have a remarkable rapprochement with the trappings of established religion on the part of a self-declared agnostic. As Jeremy Dibble shows (see p 45), this was early articulated through such works as *Toward the Unknown Region*, the composer taking his cue from Parry. Yet Vaughan Williams was very much of his time and we only have to read the reviews of the premieres at the 1907 Leeds Festival to find, alongside Stanford's *Stabat Mater*, two thrusting young modernists: Vaughan Williams and Granville Bantock. Vaughan Williams with *Toward the Unknown Region* and Bantock with *Sea Wanderers*, were both addressing the same theme, though Vaughan Williams, with his stronger text by Whitman, has proved the more direct and lasting.

Vaughan Williams used actual folk-song formations in works as varied as the early String Quartet in G minor, to such later scores as *Job* and *Dona Nobis Pacem*. Elsie Payne traced the two East Anglian tunes *Bushes and Briars* (and its variants) and *The Captain's Apprentice* as those most frequently used, "but for the most part, and where they are most vital, they have influenced his work subconsciously."[7] It is surely these elements that form a significant point of reference for many of his admirers, informing his religious or mystical moments.

It goes without saying that a composer's selection of his text is pre-eminently important. Vaughan Williams was particularly successful at this, and he found a rich vein in the American poet Walt Whitman. Whitman (1819–92) appealed to many composers at about this time, and notable examples of music based on his poetry include Delius's *Sea Drift*, Harty's *Mystic*

6. Hubert J Foss: *Music in My Time*. Rich & Cowan, 1933, p 181.
7. Elsie Payne *op cit*, p 109

Trumpeter, Holst's *The Mystic Trumpeter* and *Dirge for Two Veterans*.
Even the Austrian composer Franz Schreker set Whitman in
his *Vom ewigen Leben* ("Everlasting Life"). Whitman's personal
brand of humanism, questioning philosophy of life, and first-
hand reporting of the horrors and pity of conflict in the
American Civil War, certainly found a ready response in many
composers. Not least of these was Vaughan Williams, who was
not the first or the last young man to have Whitman's *Leaves of
Grass* as his constant companion. Before the First World War,
perhaps triggered by the Boer War, Whitman was all the
vogue, and as early as 1899 W H Bell wrote an orchestral *Walt
Whitman Symphony*, and in the same year Vaughan Williams's
friend Gustav Holst (or von Holst as he was then still known)
wrote a *Walt Whitman* Overture. But most works ascribed to
Whitman were actually settings of his words, Vaughan
Williams's teacher Charles Villiers Stanford being among the
first with his *Elegiac Ode* in 1884. Later Charles Wood set his
Darest thou Now O Soul and *By the Bivouac's Fitful Flame*, as early
as 1891 and 1897 respectively, both subsequently set by
Vaughan Williams. Between the wars, Whitman featured both
in works lamenting the First World War (such as Bliss in
Morning Heroes) and in others warning of the approaching
storm clouds (such as RVW in *Dona Nobis Pacem*). Delius,
looked to Whitman for his *Songs of Farewell* and *Idyll*. It was no
accident that the stricken Delius should rely on Whitman for
songs of affirmation and joy in life, leaving behind the
resignation and defeatism of his earlier *Songs of Sunset*.

Vaughan Williams's achievement should not only be
measured in the music he wrote, but in the way in which he
found his words to set. The development of the anthology text
in vocal and choral music, juxtaposing varied texts from
English literature, or rather literature in English, was
developed very significantly by Vaughan Williams, albeit, as
we have already noted, taking his cue from Parry. Vaughan
Williams's usage presented a ready model for later composers
that still has currency today.

This central place of words in his aesthetic is important, and
when in his late works we find that the cinema has now taken
a significant role in the development of his new sound palette,

words are still important. The quasi-religious thrust of the earlier vocal works is now represented in purely orchestral terms, using the striking new sound-world developed for film, but also having a musical appeal far removed from the specific pictorial imagery of the film.

Vaughan Williams's career revolved around a succession of "big" works which are not only a significant achievement in themselves, but also each constitute a technical or orchestral advance over his previous achievements. Spaced across these peaks are his nine symphonies, constituting a series of signposts to his music. The first of these milestones was first heard on their composer's 38th birthday; the others followed at the ages of 41, 49, 62, 70, 75, 80, 83, and 85. Two thirds of them were the work of a composer over the age of 60. Yet he was a composer with a remarkably youthful interest in the new and with a freshness of invention that he sustained to the end.

Vaughan Williams had a sure feeling for striking images, something particularly true of his excursions into the theatre, in his ballet – or rather "masque for dancing" – *Job*, his operas, particularly *The Pilgrim's Progress*, and his film music. It is this ability to find a unique response to a celebration that makes his occasional works outstanding, with memorable music for events as different as the thanksgiving for victory in 1945, the Coronations in 1937 and 1953 and the Jubilee of Sir Henry Wood. These have unexpectedly become permanent features of the repertoire.

Vaughan Williams emerged slowly as a composer of stature, though he became known at the turn of the century as a composer of memorable songs, including *Linden Lea* and *Songs of Travel*, very significant straws in the wind of his later achievement. But it was only after he had became a folk-song collector, and been editor of *The English Hymnal*, that he began to be seen as a commanding figure in the years before 1914.

A Sea Symphony was one of several major turning points which were performed between 1909 and 1912. It was a work gradually growing in his mind over seven years before being successfully committed to paper in what was more or less its final version. The sketches were completed in 1907 and revised and scored over the next two years. Having been

accepted for performance by the Leeds Festival (doubtless as a
result of Stanford's influence) the composer reported that "it
had another clean-up" and he finally revised the full score,
which meant that he re-copied most of it (Vaughan Williams
had a notoriously illegible hand).

Vaughan Williams was a composition pupil of Stanford at
the Royal College of Music, and the examples of the choral
works of Stanford and Parry (which he always championed)
were before him throughout his young manhood as the music
of the leading British composers of the day. The idea of a fully-
fledged symphony for soloists, chorus and orchestra was new
in 1910.

Long before, in 1867, the now forgotten British composer
Alfred Holmes had written a "Dramatic Choral Symphony"
about Joan of Arc which was produced in St Petersburg in
1867 and at Crystal Palace in 1875. But even in VW's day that
was forgotten. Of Vaughan Williams's contemporaries, Edgar
Bainton, also a pupil of Stanford, completed *Before Sunrise* in
1907, a choral symphony on words by Swinburne. Although
VW may have known of that score, its first movement was
purely orchestral, and it was not performed or published until
after the First World War. Another example was Holbrooke's
"Dramatic Choral Symphony" *Homage to E A Poe*, dating from
1906. Mahler's Eighth Symphony is also of similar date but it
would not have been known to Vaughan Williams. Perhaps
more germane was the example of Berlioz's *Romeo and Juliet*,
which was revived by Stanford at the turn of the century.

But Vaughan Williams's models, if he had any, were much
more likely to have been Parry's choral works *The Love that
Casteth Out Fear* (1904) and *The Soul's Ransom* (1906) – Parry
called them 'Sinfonia Sacræ' – together with Brahms' *Requiem*
and Elgar's *The Dream of Gerontius*. "With regard to the name
'symphony' " VW wrote "I use the word because the
treatment of the words is symphonic rather than dramatic –
that is to say the words are used as a basis on which to build
up a decorative musical scheme. I have therefore felt justified
in repeating the words a good deal – especially in the 1st
movement".[8]

8. Vaughan Williams to Herbert Thompson IN Foreman, *op cit,* p 42.

A Sea Symphony was given its first performance at the 1910 Leeds Festival. During the Victorian and Edwardian periods the great provincial music festivals provided a constant demand for new works, largely choral, and were the route by which many turn-of-the-century composers, including Elgar, came to fame. Stanford was the moving spirit behind Leeds in 1910, and in the same programme as *A Sea Symphony*, Rachmaninov was the soloist in his own Second Piano Concerto which Stanford himself conducted. The Festival also included Rachmaninov conducting his Second Symphony and Stanford his *Songs of the Fleet*. That this nautical feast should be created by two notable landlubbers is an inexplicable enigma of musical history.

If Vaughan Williams's first movement creates a positive, even epic, self-confidence in launching its expedition upon the sea of life, the slow movement, a haunting nocturne rises to a brief but incandescent climax as he muses on the sea as a metaphor of the human spirit, just as earlier Matthew Arnold had seen it as a metaphor of faith. In contemplating the secrets of the infinite he launches a dream of the universe, and of the ultimate fate of "all souls". These are concerns later further addressed in his *London Symphony* which would be performed in 1914. In such moments he is uniquely successful, and always very much himself.

A Sea Symphony succeeded from the beginning, owing to its fertile invention and driving purpose, characteristics heard in the first three movements. When we come to the finale its character changes, and we have a less closely-knit invention. In launching into an extended sectional piece which would indeed stand comparison as a separate work beside the "ethical" cantatas of Parry, Vaughan Williams at once shows himself as being of his time as well as providing the seeds of development from it. In his essay on Beethoven's *Choral Symphony*, VW wrote "no composer can speak out of his period ... the great artist uses the conventions as his tools and bends them to his will".[9] After Vaughan Williams's success at Leeds,

9. Ralph Vaughan Williams: *Some Thoughts on Beethoven's Choral Symphony ...* Oxford University Press, 1953 p 3.

Parry remarked "Big stuff, but full of impertinences"[10] and it has to be remembered that some of its harmony caused difficulties for his first audiences. It is emphatically not a backward-looking work.

Thus in the finale, "The Explorers", he reflects more of the traditional narrative elements of the British choral music of his day. Inevitably the treatment is episodic, and the movement falls into two parts. First we have a compact opening passage for the chorus which, dramatically, appears thrice to lose its way in unaccompanied writing before arriving at an affirmative climax on the words

> Shall come the Poet worthy that name.
> The true son of God shall come singing.

However, far from being the end the music seems to take a second breath and Vaughan Williams launches his soloists into a series of philosophical appeals. From the first this is a quest – "O we can wait no longer" – underlined by constant changes as the composer explores the "tackless seas" of the spirit. It is necessary to follow the words more closely here than in the earlier movements.

The two or three years immediately before the outbreak of the Great War was a high point for British music. Elgar had by then been in his mature stride for well over a decade, and the music of a new generation of younger composers was beginning to appear on concert programmes: music by Holst, Bax, Percy Grainger, Balfour Gardiner, Cyril Scott and many others. Slightly older than the rest, Vaughan Williams was building on the splash he had made with *On Wenlock Edge, A Sea Symphony* and the *Tallis Fantasia*. So, when in March 1914 his *A London Symphony* was first heard, it crowned the emergence of a vibrant new voice, a distinctive composer of considerable achievement.

There were few opportunities for young composers to gain a hearing in 1914, and therefore the series of concerts that figures such as Balfour Gardiner, Edward Mason and F B Ellis organised are of particular interest for their attention to the works of the younger generation of composers who were their

10. Kennedy *op cit*, p 131.

friends. F Bevis Ellis, a member of the de Walden family, had only recently come down from Christ Church, Oxford. He was a close friend of the composer and folk-song collector George Butterworth and through him of Vaughan Williams. [Terrible to remember that soon after, during the war, both Ellis and Butterworth were to die.] Vaughan Williams's symphony appeared in the second concert, followed by Balakirev's *Thamar* and Ravel's *Valses Nobles et Sentimentales* (both then new), and was conducted by Geoffrey Toye. Holst immediately noted "how futile and tawdry Ravel sounded"[11] after Vaughan Williams's *Epilogue*! It is well-known that at the beginning of the war the score of *A London Symphony* was lost, but as Stephen Lloyd recounts (see p 94), the circumstances are still far from clear.

What is particularly notable about the symphony at the time it appeared, is its scale and distinctive style. Only Elgar in his Second Symphony, first played two years earlier, could compare. At the time the Elgar did not meet with the success of its predecessor, in that there had not been repeat performances on anything like the same scale as there had been of the First Symphony. We may recognise Vaughan Williams's achievement today, but at the time it must have seemed a groundbreaking work.

Vaughan Williams was always ambivalent about his programmatic intentions in his orchestral music. Yet it is surely undeniable that the River Thames flows through this music, and when, later, Gustav Holst was to remark that his *Hammersmith* was set against "the background of the river, that was there long before the crowd and will be there presumably long after" he could have been referring to Vaughan Williams's music as to his own.

The symphony emerges from the mists with a slow brooding introduction – and at the end the vision dissolves in the quiet pages of the *Epilogue* as the idea first heard at the beginning gradually fades from view. This is a powerful vision developing the concerns and layers of meaning expressed in *A Sea Symphony* in even more certain a manner.

11. Holst to Vaughan Williams 29 March 1914 IN Ralph Vaughan Williams and Gustav Holst: *Heirs and Rebels*. Oxford University Press, 1959, p 43.

The music is, of course, bold and colourful and virtuosic in its own way. The first movement proper begins with a great outburst and presents us with a kaleidoscope of melodic fragments which certainly evoke the spirit of the capital, crowded with diverse cameos and incidents. Here, during the development we come to a quiet passage which, by its inner serenity, is paradoxically the climax of the movement, the still heart before the recapitulation rises to a grand climax, the emotion underlined by the main theme combining with itself in augmentation. However, we surely find Vaughan Williams's spiritual heart, at least in these early and middle-period works, in his more reflective passages.

This is true of the slow movement, and even the scherzo is described by Vaughan Williams as a "Nocturne". Again we are standing at the tide's edge, now on the Thames Embankment. All about are the noise and bustle of the great city. The distant sounds of the Strand and its great hotels on one side and across the water the cruder, perhaps more virile, echoes of the "New Cut" with its thronged streets and flaring lights, the crowd that Holst would celebrate, albeit a few miles up the river, in his *Hammersmith*. The conductor Albert Coates envisaged the composer sitting on the quiet Embankment hearing the far off noises of the slums across the river. "We seem to hear distant laughter", he wrote, "also every now and then, what sounds like cries of suffering. Suddenly a concertina breaks out above the rest; then we hear a few bars on a hurdy-gurdy organ".[12] Here Vaughan Williams first explored the device of *Epilogue* as a kind of spiritual and musical summation of the whole work. When the *Epilogue* comes we feel we have come full circle, the calm and the silent river's inexorable flow and the veiling mists acting as metaphors for some profound spiritual truth. At the very end a muted violin plays a last soaring reminiscence of the theme over soft strings. Muted cornets, trumpets and horns sound a soft chord and then, like the westering sun breaking through, the brass all remove their mutes for the final chord and the strings gradually fade to nothing. Such eloquence not only requires imagination of a high order but a knowledge

12. Robert Bagar and Louis Biancolli: *The Concert Companion*. New York and London, McGraw-Hill, 1947, pp 779–781.

of practical orchestration based on first-hand experience. Towards the end of his life Vaughan Williams told Michael Kennedy that the end of H G Wells' novel *Tono-Bungay* should be read in the context of the closing pages of this symphony. The passage that commentators often cite is:

Light after light goes down. England and the Kingdom, Britain and the Empire, the old prides and the old devotions, glide abeam, astern, sink down upon the horizon, pass – pass. The river passes – London passes, England passes ... .[13]

As Anthony Arblaster has pointed out, if one reads Wells' final chapter "Night and the Open Sea" it is clear there are other even more far-reaching parallels. "Images of the river and the sea, central to Wells' final chapter, are clearly evoked in the symphony's Epilogue – but also in the Scherzo ... It hardly needed Wells to suggest the use of the chimes of Big Ben, but here too it may be significant that at the end of the symphony they are heard immediately before the music of the river which begins the Epilogue, just as Wells' narrator sees Westminster from the river."[14] Wells' final sentence is: "We are all things that make and pass, striving upon a hidden mission, out to the open sea". Clearly it could be Vaughan Williams speaking, setting out a vision that he also articulated in later works, particularly the Sixth and Seventh Symphonies.

To appreciate the scale of Vaughan Williams's achievement and place it in context we need to view the composition of the symphonies against the tide of symphonies produced by other composers. Vaughan Williams's symphonies were first heard in 1910, 1914, 1922, 1935, 1943, 1948, 1953, 1956 and 1958. And moreover between 1922 and 1935 there were at least two orchestral works of quasi-symphonic scale, the Piano Concerto (composed 1926–31, performed 1933) and *Job* (1930). All these works were distinctive, contrasted in style and treatment, and all are indisputably a high point of their composer's style. In a sense each started a new phase, and yet all were individual achievements, works of unique character in a way unprecedented by almost any other British composer, and by

13. H G Wells: *Tono-Bungay and A Modern Utopia*. Odhams Press, nd p 305.
14. Anthony Arblaster: " 'A London Symphony' and 'Tono-Bungay' " *Tempo* No 163, December 1987, pp 21–25.

very few of any nationality. It was an *oeuvre* to stand beside
Sibelius, Shostakovich and Prokofiev as the giants of the
twentieth-century symphony.

To set the symphonies in context we need to review the
principal new symphonies heard over the period of Vaughan
Williams's lifetime from *A Sea Symphony* in 1910 up to, say, his
Fourth Symphony, to see to what extent the models provided
by other composers may have suggested a context. But it has
to be said that there were very few. The symphony as a form
was not championed by the leading younger composers post-
First World War, at least until later, and for most of this time
in the English-speaking world, Sibelius was pre-eminent in his
critical reception, with composer-disciples both in the UK and
the USA. Indeed, Vaughan Williams's own Fifth Symphony is
dedicated to him.

It is instructive to list the first London performances of non-
British symphonies between 1910 and 1936. Elgar apart, the
only precedent for a symphony on the scale of *A London
Symphony* is Rachmaninov's Second, unless one looks back to
Mahler's First and Fourth, and the earlier symphonies of
Sibelius, which reached London during the mid-1900s. To a
London audience Vaughan Williams's symphony would have
appeared as an original and forward-looking work.

LONDON FIRST PERFORMANCES

19/5/1910	RACHMANINOV: Symphony No 2
18/1/1913	MAHLER: Symphony No 7
13/3/1913	SCRIABIN: Symphony No 1
20/3/1920	SIBELIUS: Symphony No 4
12/2/1921	SIBELIUS: Symphony No 5
11/6/1921	PROKOFIEV: Symphony No 1
22/6/1923	NIELSEN: Symphony No 4
20/11/1926	SIBELIUS: Symphony No 6
8/12/1927	SIBELIUS: Symphony No 7
20/4/1928	BLOCH: *Israel Symphony*
22/2/1930	MAHLER: Symphony No 9
15/4/1930	MAHLER: Symphony No 8
16/4/1931	MAHLER: Symphony No 2
24/1/1932	HONEGGER: Symphony No 1
5/2/1932	SHOSTAKOVICH: Symphony No 1
20/1/1933	ROUSSEL: Symphony No 3
26/1/1934	MIASKOVSKY: Symphony No 7
20/8/1934	TOCH: Symphony for piano and orchestra

19/10/1934 PROKOFIEV: Symphony No 3
29/10/1934 SZYMANOWSKI: *Symphonie Concertante* (Symphony No 4)
21/12/1934 HINDEMITH: Symphony *Mathis der Maler*
9/2/1936   ROUSSEL: Symphony No 4

In this context it is interesting to see how much of its time Vaughan Williams's Piano Concerto was, appearing at the same time as quasi-symphonic concertante works for piano and orchestra by Bax (*Winter Legends*, first heard 10 February 1932), Szymanowski (*Symphonie Concertante*, first heard in 1932, in London in October 1934) and Toch's *Symphony for Piano and Orchestra* (first heard in August 1934). The symphony was not a form widely accepted by composers writing during and immediately after the First World War, even by those who later produced symphonies. Doubtless in the UK, the two Elgar symphonies were at once an impossible act to follow for most composers, and in an idiom rejected by the young.

To view the principal British symphonies from the year of Elgar's Second to the end of the Second World War, we find that the idea of the symphony was only slowly accepted, with Vaughan Williams established from the first as the form's pre-eminent practitioner when his *Pastoral Symphony* was premiered on 26 January 1922, and repeated at the Royal College of Music on 17 February 1922. *A London Symphony* was by then already launched on its pre-eminent inter-war run as the leading British symphony of the day, with, for example, both Sir Henry Wood and Dan Godfrey programming it many times, and both recording it on 78s.

Although Bax's First Symphony and Bliss's *A Colour Symphony* both also made quite a splash in 1922, neither achieved the frequency of performance of Vaughan Williams, and as a popular symphonist Bax was really a Thirties figure. It would be Vaughan Williams's Fourth and Walton's [First] Symphony in 1935 that would finally set the seal on the public's acceptance of the "modern" symphony as a vital living form, a fact underlined by the speed with which both were recorded.

We may see from the following table how, with few exceptions, Vaughan Williams's symphonies represent milestones both in his own output and in the history of the symphony in the UK between the wars.

SOME BRITISH SYMPHONIES FROM ELGAR TO 1945
(unless stated, performances given were first in London)

1911 ELGAR: Symphony No 2 (perf: 24/5/1911)
1911 PITT: Symphony in G minor (perf: 8/2/1912)
1911 WALFORD DAVIES: Symphony in G
1911 BANTOCK: *Atalanta in Calydon* (unnac chorus)
1912 STANFORD: Symphony No 7 (perf: 22/2/1912)
1912 SOMERVELL: *Thalassa Symphony*
1913 AUSTIN: Symphony in E (perf: 18/3/1913)
1913 **VAUGHAN WILLIAMS**: *A Sea Symphony* (first London performance: 4/2/1913)
1913 **VAUGHAN WILLIAMS**: *A London Symphony* (perf: 27/3/1914)
1914 VAN DIEREN: Symphony Op 6, Chinese (perf: 9/4/1936)
1915 TOVEY: Sympony in D (perf: 31/5/1915)
1916 BANTOCK: *Hebridean Symphony*
1917 BAINES: Symphony (not performed until 1991)
1918 BELL: Symphony No 2 (Bell went to South Africa)
1919 BELL: Symphony No 3
1921 **VAUGHAN WILLIAMS**: *A Pastoral Symphony* (perf: 26/1/1922)
1922 BLISS: *A Colour Symphony* (perf: 7/9/1922)
1922 BAX: Symphony No 1 (perf: 4/12/1922)
1922 DUNHILL: Symphony in A minor
1923 McEWEN: *A Solway Symphony* (perf: 22/2/1923)
1923 GOOSSENS: Sinfonietta
1924 HOLST: Choral Symphony (perf: [Leeds] 7/10/1925)
1926 BAX: Symphony No 2 (perf: 20/5/1930)
1926 BOUGHTON: *Dierdre Symphony* [No 2]
1927 MERRICK: Symphony in D minor
1927 BELL: *A South African Symphony* [No 4]
1927 HAVERGAL BRIAN: *Gothic Symphony* (not performed until 1961)
1928 BANTOCK: *Pagan Symphony* (perf: 8/3/1936)
1929 BAX: Symphony No 3 (perf: 14/3/1930)
1930 HADLEY: Symphonic Ballad *The Trees So High* (perf:12/1/1934)
1931 BAX: Symphony No 4 (perf: 5/12/1932)
1931 HAVERGAL BRIAN: Symphony No 2 (not performed until 1973)
1932 BAX: Symphony No 5 (perf: 15/1/1934)
1932 LLOYD: Symphony No 1
1932 HAVERGAL BRIAN: Symphony No 3 (not performed until 1974)
1933 LLOYD: Symphony No 2
1933 HAVERGAL BRIAN: Symphony No 4 *Das Siegeslied* (not performed until 1967)
1933 MORRIS: Symphony in D
1934 BAX: Symphony No 6 (perf: 21/11/1935)
1934 **VAUGHAN WILLIAMS**: Symphony No 4 (perf: 10/4/1935)
1934 WALTON: Symphony [No 1] (3 mvts perf: 3/12/1934; complete perf: 6/11/1935)
1935 LLOYD: Symphony No 3

1935 DYSON: Symphony in G (perf: 1938)
1937 HAVERGAL BRIAN: *Wine of Summer* (not performed until 1969)
1937 RUBBRA: Symphony No 1
1937 MOERAN: Symphony in G min (perf: 13/1/38)
1937 BOUGHTON: Symphony No 3
1938 CHISHOLM: Symphony No 1
1938 RUBBRA: Symphony No 2
1939 BAX: Symphony No 7 (perf: Bristol 21/6/1940; London 22/8/1943)
1939 CHISHOLM: Symphony No 2
1939 RUBBRA: Symphony No 3
1939 DARNTON: Symphony No 1
1940 BANTOCK: *Celtic Symphony*
1940 BRITTEN: *Sinfonia da Requiem*
1940 BUSH: Symphony No 1
1940 BATE: Symphony No 3 (not performed until 1954)
1940 GOOSSENS: Symphony No 1 (perf: 3/5/44)
1940 HUBERT CLIFFORD: Symphony
1940 BERKELEY: Symphony No 1
1941 RUBBRA: Symphony No 4
1943 **VAUGHAN WILLIAMS**: Symphony No 5 (perf: 24/6/1943)
1944 GOOSSENS: Symphony No 2 (perf: 2/11/1946)
1945 GIPPS: Symphony No 2
1945 BENJAMIN: Symphony
1945 STEVENS: Symphony No 1
1945 TIPPETT: Symphony No 1

While the symphonies provide us with a continuity across his career, the power and originality of Vaughan Williams's imagery may be typically seen in those well-known works of genius which successively established him an individual name before 1914. Possibly the most striking of these are the settings of A E Housman in his cycle *On Wenlock Edge*, first performed by Gervase Elwes at London's Aeolian Hall on 15 November 1909. It is difficult now to realise how "modern" it must have seemed then. This and the First String Quartet were the works he wrote after returning from studying with Ravel during the first three months of 1908. Both were heard in public at the same concert and one may imagine that their impressionistic textures, concern with instrumental sonorities, and the song cycle's elastic sense of tonality must have been particularly striking. Although not the first work for solo voice to be accompanied by piano quintet, the ensemble must have contributed to its impact. The seemingly naïve and immediate impact of the cycle is actually achieved by remarkably sophisticated means, and it would have sounded uncompromisingly modern to many in his first audience; one would love to know what Stanford thought of it all.

The range of textures Vaughan Williams conjures from his small group of players is remarkable, each movement having the impact of a miniature tone-poem, wonderfully dramatic and evocative in their contrasted textures. Indeed, the work was later very successfully orchestrated, where Vaughan Williams more explicitly underlined its indebtedness to the world of Debussy and Ravel. Typical of the way Vaughan Williams's new-found technique serves his poetic and philosophical agenda, comes in the fifth song, in fact the longest and the heart of the cycle. The opening reverie of the hillside view of the "coloured" counties underlined by distant bells is a timeless vision, and the image of the bells resonates the message of transience and renewal at the heart of the cycle. The bell sonorities created by double-stopping muted strings and piano chords of piled-up thirds (all on white notes), while exhibiting a passing echo of Debussy's *La Cathédrale Engloutie*, demonstrate specific points of technique that Ravel's practical example must have given to Vaughan Williams. In his orchestral version at the words "Come out to church, good people" Vaughan Williams underlines the despairing and haunted climax with evocative falling horn calls, a brilliant individual sound familiar from the orchestral music of Debussy. After the climax, Vaughan Williams's last chosen poem "Clun" has the character of an Epilogue, and the setting of the last verse leads to a gentle fade-out: a wonderful evocation of the inexorable passage of the river, of time, of life, a vision found on a much larger canvas elsewhere, notably in the Epilogue of *A London Symphony* only a few years later. The music looks forward to the *Pastoral Symphony* and Vaughan Williams's work in the 1920s, in what A E F Dickinson has called "a remarkable early link with third-decade workmanship". Vaughan Williams had at last arrived as a mature composer with a throw of genius.

The concerns of *On Wenlock Edge* are curiously paralleled in that work which stands astride the Great War: *The Lark Ascending*. This glorious evocation was completed as a piece for violin and piano before the War but did not appear as an orchestral work until after. With its quiet pastoral surface, it is possible to forget what a revolutionary piece this was in the context of the British music of 1914. Not revolutionary, perhaps, in the same breath as the revolution that the composers of the Diaghilev ballet were disseminating far and wide, but in its time its rhythmic freedom and flow and avoidance of tonic-and-dominant cadencing, together with its vivid imagery, makes it very much of its time. It created an idiom.

In fact the short evocative movement for violin and orchestra became something of a genre piece for British composers between the wars, examples including Julius Harrison's *Bredon Hill*, Robin Milford's *The Darkling Thrush*, and, less successfully, Freda Swain's *The Harp of Aengus*. In his musical autobiography, Vaughan Williams describes how at a Three Choirs festival in the early 1930s he was suddenly "moved to seize W H Reed's violin and play through Raff's *Cavatina* by heart, double stops and all."[15] It is not surprising that he should be so sympathetic in writing for the instrument, and that in a large percentage of his big orchestral works there is a passage for solo violin at a point of personal involvement: it became a fingerprint.

Vaughan Williams established not only a distinctive voice for the British music of his time, but also a climate in which it could be played. In this his achievement is unique. Maud Karpeles wrote in a memorial tribute: "He found in folk-song the affirmation of his musical philosophy: that music is a 'spiritual necessity' and that the making of music is not just the prerogative of the chosen few".[16] Although the folk-song elements are deeply integrated into his music on many levels, he did not set out to imitate folk music, the idiom merely became a point of departure, a fact true for all the great figures of the new music in the first decades of the new century.

15. Ralph Vaughan Williams: "Musical Autobiography" IN Hubert Foss *Ralph Vaughan Williams*. Harrap, 1950, p 19.
16. Maud Karpeles: "Ralph Vaughan Williams, OM" *Journal of the Folk Dance & Song Society*, December 1958, p 12.

In *The Lark Ascending*, the music is enclosed by the melismatic voice of the carolling violin, evoking the flight of the song bird: another metaphor for man's spirit. RVW quotes no folk songs, the themes are his own. But nevertheless the music is coloured by the atmosphere of the folk idiom, though far more integrated than in his earlier folk-song rhapsodies. The modal feel underlines the hazy dreamlike sense of the onomatopoeia of the remembered country scene. We are, perhaps, on the Malvern Hills, the coloured counties of the Worcester plain below softened by a blue haze. The central panel of the piece, characterised as it is by the chiming triangle, reminds us of the faint buzz of human activity below, pointed up by the distant church bells, and is exactly caught by RVW. In this summer landscape the larks soar continually from the hills – invisible to the eye – and with them soar the spirits of the listener. Heard with these associations the piece is as religious a work as his church music with biblical words.

Vaughan Williams development during the inter-war years was signposted by a succession of remarkable works, written between the ages of 50 and 71, that is 1922 and 1943. The remarkable succession of the Third, Fourth and Fifth symphonies, punctuated by big-boned orchestral scores, and five utterly personal choral works – *Sancta Civitas, Flos Campi, Dona Nobis Pacem, Five Tudor Portraits* and the *Serenade to Music* – written for a wide variety of forces, and with a sureness of touch and a heartwarming memorable invention that put them (well, not perhaps *Sancta Civitas*, which was for many a "difficult" modern work for decades) into the repertoire of choirs everywhere, though the virtuosity demanded by *Five Tudor Portraits* made it really a work for professional performers or at least a crack amateur choir. Together with the earlier *Toward the Unknown Region, Five Mystical Songs, A Sea Symphony*, and the late *Hodie* they make a rewarding and involving repertoire.

All this time, too, Vaughan Williams's pre-war opera *Hugh the Drover* saw several productions and a pioneering early recording, and *The Poisoned Kiss* and *Sir John in Love* were written, while Vaughan Williams wrestled with his material to realise his vision of Bunyan's *Pilgrim's Progress* as a stage work.

And again what memorable material – one only has to listen to the succession of glorious tunes in the cantata he generated from *Sir John in Love*, which he called *In Windsor Forest*, to realise this.

Vaughan Williams was thus nearing 70 before he came to grips with writing music for the films, and yet the experience surely provided him with a springboard, a renewal, an opportunity to develop a new appreciation of orchestral sonority which informed his remarkable final sequence of symphonies after the war. Vaughan Williams composed his first film music in 1940–41 – for the film *Forty-Ninth Parallel* – and his last, a group of songs for voice and oboe for the film *A Vision of William Blake*, in 1957, eight months before he died. Over the intervening years he wrote music for no less than eleven films. *Coastal Command* was a fine example of that wartime genre, informed by the experimental work of pre-war film makers, in which dramatised documentaries used real people rather than actors to play the various parts, a cast that did it surprisingly well, only one or two showing momentary stiffness. It is a memorable film, notable for the fine black-and-white photography, and magnificent aerial shots, welded into a unity by Vaughan Williams's remarkable score.

The film opens with the Sunderland flying-boat at its moorings at Port Ferry Bay in the Hebrides. The action falls into two parts: first we follow the Sunderland on convoy patrol in the Atlantic, ending with the sinking of a U-boat by its relieving Catalina. Then the much longer story of the search – now in the North Sea – for the German surface raider *Düsseldorf* and the attack and eventual sinking of the enemy. The film ends as the Sunderland takes off for its next mission, this time in West Africa, the music and the shot suggesting a sense of adventure and optimism. It is only from the perspective of the 1990s that we can appreciate the added pathos that we now know that soon after the film was completed the Sunderland's crew we had become familiar with in the film was, in fact, lost on active service.

Vaughan Williams's music for this story is superb, reflecting his music of the thirties but also looking forward to what would come later. There are resonances of the Fourth

Symphony rubbing shoulders with the Piano Concerto and *Job*. For example, the loading and taxying and general airport business on the ground finds Vaughan Williams in his most rumbustious mood. Later the mountain backcloth of the early part of the flight is underlined by Vaughan Williams's contrasting lyrical invention and the wonderful moment when the engine noise which counterpoints much of the music throughout the soundtrack ceases, leaving a high held violin line and a gentle fragmentary theme on clarinet. This is aural imagination of a high order. Ken Cameron, the recording engineer on the film, was speaking for the whole Crown Unit team when he wrote: "We knew that here was something great, something, indeed, finer and more alive than any music we had ever had before. On the rare occasions when the music was slightly too long or too short to match the existing picture, then it was the visual material which suffered the mutilation. The music for *Coastal Command* is as VW composed it. It is, in fact, the picture."[17]

This is of course the essence of what would become the mind-set in which RVW would give us his *Sinfonia Antartica* from the music for the film *Scott of the Antarctic*. But there was a stepping stone to that film and it is much less well known. This was the film *The Story of a Flemish Farm*. This is a typical wartime production, though it is atypical in that it has not resurfaced on television in quite the way many of the others have. The story is based on a true episode and dates from 1940. Vaughan Williams wrote his music in 1943 and the film was first seen in August that year.

When the Germans invade Belgium during the second week of May 1940, two men escape via France to England. Just before one of them is killed he explains that the squadron's flag – of the Belgian airforce – is buried on his farm. Returning to retrieve it the major gives himself up so that his companions might escape. Without the action of the story and the images of the film, some of RVW's music may not make as much sense and the symbolism of the flag may not, fifty years on, engender as much sympathy as it did at the time. Yet this score has a haunting atmosphere. In a movement such as "Dawn in

---

17. John Huntley: *British Film Music*. Skelton Robinson, nd [1947], p 111.

the Barn" RVW's delicate tendrils of evocative folk-inflected instrumental lines and the soaring violin part is pure RVW as is the throat-catching entry of the full orchestra that follows. The hushed music of the closing passage of this sequence has more than an overtone of the Sixth Symphony, and indeed the composer has told us that discarded themes from this film score were later the germs from which the Sixth Symphony grew. Here, however, it wells to an affirmative climax and fades to an utterly personal quiet texture as haunted quiet horn-calls fade over soft tympani rolls, like the faintest murmur of distant thunder. It is again the Sixth Symphony and even the remote vastness of the *Sinfonia Antartica* which inform the other big movement, "The Dead Man's Kit", with its haunted textures, Sibelian soft drum rolls and *tremolando* strings.

In the *Sinfonia Antartica* the various threads of Vaughan Williams life draw together in a remarkable *coup de théâtre*, indeed *coup d'orchestra*. Although this is an orchestral work Vaughan Williams heads each movement with a literary quotation, assembling another of his diverse and brilliant anthology librettos, though not actually setting it to music. This time he visits Shelley, the Psalms, Coleridge, Donne, and Captain Scott's diary. The manuscript full score of the last movement shows that RVW had at first intended a tag from *Let Us Now Praise Famous Men* (Ecclesiastes) "Their bodies are buried in peace but their name liveth for evermore".

The writing of his Scott film music took Vaughan Williams a few weeks during 1948. The integration and development of the materials of the film into the *Sinfonia Antartica* took three years from 1949 to 1952, and it was first heard in Manchester on 14 January 1953 with the Hallé Orchestra conducted by Sir John Barbirolli. Apart from the unconventional number of movements – five – and the programmatic overtones, possibly the main cause for comment at the first performance was the forces the composer required; the use of a vocalising soprano voice and women's chorus, and the battery of chiming percussion including gong, bells, glockenspiel, xylophone, vibraphone, piano, celesta and, above all, wind machine.

The constant theme in Vaughan Williams's life has been renewal: his ability to hit the musical headlines every time he appeared to have reached a plateau. This was particularly true after the Second World War, when the impact of the Sixth Symphony was truly explosive. It sounded so new a note, had so many seeming resonances with then current political realities, and had such a powerful physical impact in memorable music of strength that it achieved some hundred performances in its first two years.

The desolation Vaughan Williams paints in the final movement of his E minor symphony he explained (in a letter to Michael Kennedy) by reference to *The Tempest*: "We are such stuff as dreams are made on, and our little life is rounded by a sleep". Paradoxically, while Vaughan Williams deprecated the discussion of this symphony in terms of non-musical imagery, his following symphony – the mighty *Sinfonia Antartica* – does not need the prop of its Captain Scott origins to function, indeed it is in a sense belittled by it. For in that great work Vaughan Williams's treatment of his forces is nothing less than inspired – taking great blocks of sound to evoke an elemental world, at once celebrating the human spirit and returning us again to that beach at night alone, that tide's edge from which Man confronts Eternity. Here Vaughan Williams has indeed found a language and a palette with which to paint his vision, and he succeeds in shattering terms, and as the voices fade at the end and the wind machine blows the sky clear we are left with the immensity of the Universe, but man's place in it has shrunk since Vaughan Williams's first vision of this reality nearly fifty years before, on the beach at night alone.

There is no doubt, to this commentator at least, that with the majority of his music available on CD, much of it in multiple readings, the extent of Vaughan Williams' immense achievement is self-evident, and on so many levels. He repays exploration; the satisfactions from knowing his music are manifold, and once discovered he takes a central place in one's musical experience. Yet his appeal is surely not a narrowly nationalist one: the medium of compact disc has made him available to all who can respond to his restless variety. Today Vaughan Williams communicates increasingly to an international audience.

II

Jeremy Dibble

Parry, Stanford and Vaughan Williams the creation of tradition

=>◦◦◦<=

IN HIS ESSAY 'MASS-PRODUCING TRADITIONS: EUROPE, 1870–1914',[1] Eric Hobsbawm draws our attention emphatically to the forty or so years before the First World War when the invention of traditions was at its most assiduous. The enthusiasm with which it was grasped and practised was due to many factors. In the second half of the nineteenth century most of the countries of continental Europe were experiencing major changes in their social structures. In some instances, in the cases of Germany and Italy, the recent creation of nation states had introduced the need for new social devices of cohesion and identity. Growing democratisation, particularly in Britain and France, had begun to forge new structures of social relations in which the state had to re-adjust in order to establish common bonds of loyalty, identity and participation. With an increasingly better educated society, notably in the socially mobile middle-classes, the state, conscious of its administrative intrusion into people's lives, needed to promote a means of defining citizenship. As Hobsbawm has stated: 'The standardisation of administration and law within [the state], and, in particular, state education,

1. See Eric Hobsbawm and Terence Ranger eds: *The Invention of Tradition.* Cambridge, Cambridge University Press, 1983; reprinted 1993, pp 263–307.

transformed people into citizens' in which the 'state, nation and society converged' into an inseparable unit.[2] Indeed, this whole period witnessed the most fertile spawning of nations, national identity and nationalism. Perhaps, most potently it gave rise to the creation and invention of tradition.

In the nineteenth century the issue of expressing national sentiment and identity in music became paramount. Nationalism promised to be a potent medium of originality. It was purportedly a means of '[manifesting] the origins of a [composer's] existence which encouraged a move away from eclecticism towards a greater individuality.[3] There was also the discourse of 'authenticity' espoused by composers such as Glinka who maintained that the true 'national spirit' could only emanate 'from within' and thrive on 'ethnic substance' which was of itself defined by language, myth, folklore and a shared historical past.[4] Together these maxims became imperatives for most European nations. Whether for reasons of a struggle against either political or cultural hegemony, nations or emerging nations sought for literary, dramatic and musical work which, through public consensus, could become forms of public property,[5] and thereby a means of consolidating a sense of identity. This was certainly true of Weber's *Der Freischütz* which emerged at a critical time in the move towards the creation of Germany. Similarly Glinka's *Life of the Tsar* fulfilled a need in Russia. Heritage-gathering also became a common feature of all nations attempting to assert a traditional message. Inherent in the meaning of 'tradition' was a sense of invariance, continuance and the reassurance of cultural security and distinctiveness which found expression in the rediscovery of centuries-old literature, poetry and music, notably folk music.

By the mid-century, and certainly by the 1870s, Britain appears to have been increasingly aware of the European nationalist trends, which consequently gave rise to self-examination. Writing in *St Paul's Magazine* in 1873, Francis

2. Ibid 264–5.
3. C Dahlhaus: *Nineteenth-Century Music.* California, University of California Press, 1989, Eng trans J Bradford Robinson, p 37.
4. *Ibid* p 39.
5. *Ibid* p 38.

Davenport, composer and counterpoint teacher at the Royal Academy of Music, attempted to articulate what is now a commonly received understanding of British music before and after Purcell:

> That the English are musically inclined is proved by the musical history of the nation, which seems to have surpassed all others both in precocity and development up to the time of Purcell and the commencement of the 18th century, when, although we had Handel working in the midst of us, the influence of the house of Hanover and the influx of foreigners, foreign habits and languages, caused a sad depression in musical taste. But from this we are rapidly rising; . . .[6]

Inherent in Davenport's commentary are several major points: first, a sense of history and the desire for continuity; second, the need for the nation, bearing the anxiety of a cultural inferiority complex, principally to Germany, to convince itself of its own musical potential and capacity; third, that, in spite of the value of foreign musicians who had created an extraordinarily cosmopolitan environment in London and the provinces, the task of restoration had to come from 'within', from indigenous talent.

Davenport's article draws attention to the extent of music-making in Britain – to choral societies, orchestral concerts, and to some degree to opera – but beyond the scope of his article is the discussion of the musical values, aesthetic tenets and educational aspirations of the time which together informed a British tradition.

During the course of the nineteenth century, composers in Britain seeking further specialised training looked principally to Germany, to the pedagogical centres of Leipzig or perhaps Dresden; or, at home the only possible 'right of passage' was to supplicate for a degree at one of the ancient universities, Oxford, Cambridge, Dublin and later Durham and London. These degrees, which were non-residential (and thereby implicitly diminishing the status of music as a discipline in university education), encapsulate a great deal of what had become acceptable in British musical life. The exercise, the

---

6. F. Davenport: 'Music in England', St Paul's Magazine, 1873 Part xiii (Sept) p 276.

genres of sacred oratorio and cantata and the stringency of counterpoint reflected on the one hand aesthetic values which found their way back to the lectures of Professor William Crotch – who advocated fugue and the grand oratorio chorus as the most sublime form of musical art[7] – and on the other to the perpetuation of the cathedral organist. Furthermore, it also underlined a strongly ingrained attitude in Britain that the index of genius was technical assurance rather than, as Wagner maintained, inspiration. Erosion of these traditional values was slow, and in fact, rather than disappear completely, they were instead absorbed into a new sense of tradition which emerged in the last three decades or so of the nineteenth century.

In the 1870s Britain saw the emergence of its first important educational experiment in music in the National Training School with Sullivan and later Stainer at its helm. This provided an important prelude to the Royal College of Music which, more than any institution before it, carried significant ideals of opportunity in the form of scholarships. At its helm was Sir George Grove who, as a central figure, was perhaps most responsible for constituting a network of almost political proportions in which few aspects of musical life, be they concerts, academia, libraries, publishing, and composition, were left untouched. Central to Grove's plan for composition, which was essentially Teutonic, rooted in Beethoven, Schubert and Brahms, were the appointments of Parry and Stanford. As is well known, both these men are well accepted as principal pioneers in the regeneration of musical standards in this country. However, it is worth examining more closely what visions they brought and what deeper influences they exerted as part of the legacy, or one might say 'tradition', the first half of the twentieth century inherited.

Although Parry is perhaps best known, in the first period of his employment at the Royal College of Music – that being 1883 until the end of 1894 – his chief responsibility at the RCM was as Professor of Musical History, and even after

7. *See* Peter Le Huray and James Day: 'William Crotch' in *Music and Aesthetics in the Eighteenth and Early-Nineteenth Centuries.* Cambridge, Cambridge University Press, 1981; abridged edition 1988, pp 281–296.

undertaking the Directorship in 1895, he still insisted on continuing his history teaching, work he performed until his death in 1918. Although in this country, Parry is best known as a composer of major influence, his historiographical work is vital in providing crucial pointers in the formation of values that became prevalent towards the turn of the century. Grove had enlisted Parry's assistance as sub-editor of *Grove's Dictionary of Music and Musicians* in 1875. This work of itself, mobilising large numbers of indigenous writers and academics, stood self-consciously as a seminal document of British musicology. Parry contributed over one hundred articles on matters technical, formalistic and generic. His articles on such topics as 'Harmony', 'Symphony', 'Sonata', 'Variations' and 'Form' are notable milestones in British historiography, not only through their breadth of view and analytical insight, but also in what they communicate in terms of ideas, aesthetics and philosophy. Furthermore, only four years after beginning his work at the RCM he published *Studies of Great Composers*, a compilation of articles written for *Every Girl's Annual*. Both these publications proved immensely popular and influential, not least on Elgar and Vaughan Williams.

Parry attended Ruskin's lectures which attempted to confront the issues of art and its relationship to religion and ethics. After graduating from Oxford, Parry read Ruskin's lectures on Greek mythology published as *The Queen of Air*. In these writings Ruskin made it clear that music was the most directly ethical of the arts:

Exactly in proportion to the degree in which we become narrow in the cause and conception of our passions, incontinent in the utterance of them, feeble or perseverance in them, sullied or shameful in the indulgence of them, their expression by musical sound becomes broken, mean, fatuitous, and at last impossible; the measured waves of the air of heaven will not lend themselves to expression of ultimate vice, it must be for ever sunk into discordance of silence. And since, as before stated, every work of art has a tendency to reproduce the ethical state which first developed it, this, which of all the arts is most directly ethical in origin, is also the most direct in power of discipline; the first, the simplest, the most effective of all instruments of moral instruction; while in the failure and betrayal of its functions, it becomes the subtlest aid of moral degradation.[8]

8. John Ruskin: *The Queen of the Air*. Smith, Elder & Co., 1869, pp 58–9.

Parry remained firmly allied to Ruskin's moral aesthetic throughout his life. Indeed, it is potently evident in his later articles such as 'The meaning of ugliness in art' delivered at the International Musical Congress in London in May 1911 and 'Things that matter' written for Oscar Sonneck's new *Musical Quarterly* in 1915. In *Studies of Great Composers* (1887) Parry needed no prompting in idolising Beethoven as the embodiment of Ruskin's ideal:

One of the most interesting things about the history of music is the way in which it invariably illustrates in some way or other the state of society, and the condition of thought of the people among whom it is produced. Second-rate composers illustrate the tone of mind among second-rate people, and the greatest masters of their art express things which are characteristic of the best and foremost of men of their time; and, yet further, when some exceptionally splendid genius appears, who is fully in sympathy with the best tendencies of his day, and capable of realising in thought the conditions and feelings which men are most prone to in their best and truest moments, he becomes as it were a prophet, and raises those who understand him above themselves, and ennobles and purifies at least some of those traits and sympathies which combine to make the so-called spiritual element in man; and so comes to be a leader, instead of a mere illustrator, of contemporary emotion.[9]

Words and phrases such as 'sincerity', 'genuineness of expression', 'earnestness', 'nobility of character and thought', 'exalted emotions' are prominent components of Parry's Ruskinian vocabulary. Class consciousness, a recurrent feature of Parry's writings, is also invoked in his denunciation of the aristocracy's 'external culture', to use Matthew Arnold's phrase from *Culture and Anarchy*. The conclusion to *Studies of Great Composers* underlines this artistic quest for the high and noble as represented by the then unfinished work of Brahms.

Parry's preoccupation with the moral element of musical criticism resulted in major prejudices elsewhere. Florid song, colaratura and a large proportion of opera was frequently the subject of vehement denunciation. In *The Art of Music*, Parry early on described ornament as 'the part of anything which makes for superficial effect'[10] and went even further in 'Things that Matter' by saying that:

9. C Hubert H Parry: 'Beethoven', *Studies of Great Composers*. Routledge, 1887, p 156.
10. C Hubert H Parry: *The Evolution of the Art of Music*. Kegan Paul, 1893; revised ed. 1896, p 59.

The worst kind of such decoration is afforded in the horrible inanity of what is called 'coloratura' in Italian operas from almost the earliest days till the first half of the nineteenth century. Such decorative adjuncts have generally no meaning at all, and were introduced for no other purpose than to show off the vocal vanity of the singers. Some of the worst and most aggressive are in Meyerbeer's operas.[11]

Indeed, Parry had personal problems with opera generally. It is quite possible that this resulted from failure with his only unfinished work in the genre, *Guenever*, in 1886. Certainly, however, Parry remained uncomfortable about the role of opera in Britain's musical development as a nation as is evident from an interview he gave to the press in 1892. 'Dr Parry evidently does not think the great growth of what may be termed the operatic school has a healthy tone, or is calculated to advance our musical future as a nation. Operatic treatment was, he said, often vulgar, frequently vicarious, and the least pure of all music.[12]

Parry believed that the true inner life of man's emotions could be equated with notions of organic coherence, the fusing of older methods with new and formal involution through intellectual application. This naturally led towards J S Bach, Beethoven and especially Brahms, though it should also be noted that he admired Wagner, less so for his contribution to drama, but rather for the predominantly instrumental polyphonic dimension of the orchestra and its concomitant harmonic results. It is also certain that Parry's high regard for Wagner derived substantially from the close association with his teacher and mentor Edward Dannreuther, whose pioneering efforts to promote Wagner's work in England during the 1870s resulted in the establishment of the London Wagner Society as well as the production of numerous articles and two books, *Richard Wagner: His Tendencies and Theories* and *Richard Wagner and the Reform of the Opera*, both published in 1873. Dannreuther's close involvement in the production of the first performances of the complete *Ring* cycle at Bayreuth in 1876 led to the procurement of free tickets for Parry (who attended the second cycle of performances). Parry and

11. C Hubert H Parry: 'Things that Matter', *Musical Quarterly*, I no 3 (1915), p 318.
12. Interview in *The Sheffield and Rotherham Independent*, September 1892.

Dannreuther also attended the first performances of *Parsifal* at Bayreuth in 1882.

Ruskin's influence on Parry was, therefore, far-reaching. Not only was it projected in his historical writings but also in his choral and instrumental works. Early on it is present in the somewhat controversial dramatic cantata *Prometheus Unbound* of 1880, but also in the philosophical allegory of the oratorio *Job* (1892), and, most conspicuously, in the series of ethical oratorios such as *A Song of Darkness and Light* (1898), *War and Peace* (1903), *The Love that casteth out Fear* (1904), *The Soul's Ransom* (1906), *Beyond these Voices there is Peace* (1908) and the setting of his own poem, *The Vision of Life* (1907). The sentiment of these works was later to find resonances in Walford Davies, Holst, Bliss and Howells, but perhaps most of all in Vaughan Williams.

The other major influence on Parry's perception of history was social-Darwinism, and more specifically, the *Synthetic Philosophy* of Herbert Spencer. Spencer's influence on Parry's view of musical history can be felt in various ways. As a main and guiding principle it was claimed that the evolution of man's biological past found a parallel in human social and intellectual history, and that music as part of that history could not be excluded. Evolution also strengthened the notion that the development of music was dependent on changing environmental conditions. It was vital to consider the circumstances under which composers lived, the historical position in relations to the musical genres in which composers chose to work and the importance of individual and national character. Writing about Wagner in *Studies of Great Composers*, such thinking loomed large:

People commonly speak and write as if they thought that works of art and imagination, and all products of what they call genius, sprang by inspiration from nowhere, and were the independent creations of their originators. They can understand how natural laws work elsewhere; that a plant will not grow unless the seed is put where it can germinate, and that it requires light and heat and moisture and nourishment to bring it to mature to perfection. But they seem to think it is quite different with art and things which grow in the human mind.[13]

13. p 322.

But perhaps most telling of all, the adoption of evolutionary and hence scientific theories within the province of music history bolstered the notion that music historians had a scientific earnestness which was different from the more arbitrary journalistic musings of the past. It is significant that *The Art of Music* of 1893, published in a revised edition three years later as *The Evolution of the Art of Music* (to clarify its 'scientific' aspiration) formed, as Volume No 80, part of Kegan Paul's strongly Darwinian *Scientific Series*, rubbing shoulders with works by Bain, Huxley, Tylor, Spencer, Oscar Schmidt and Walter Bagehot. Huxley's book *Science and Culture*, published in 1886, and which Parry read in 1886, was almost certainly significant in that it argued for scientific methods of enquiry to be applied to areas other than the physical sciences.

The Art of Music is most representative of Parry's philosophy of musical history. The views expressed in it were to recur again and again in his lectures for the Royal College of Music and during his tenure as Professor at Oxford. In acknowledging the influence of Spencer and the work of the famed explorer, Harry Johnston, Parry included a chapter entitled 'Preliminaries' on the music of savages, folk music and medieval music. This chapter, intended to demonstrate man's 'instinctive desire to convey impressions and enjoyments to others, and to represent in the most attractive and permanent forms the ideas, thought, and circumstances, scenes or emotions which have powerfully stirred the artists' own natures', was designed to chime with the debate over Spencer's essay 'The Origin and Function of Music', a debate which both Darwin and Gurney had joined. It also very likely that Parry was influenced too by the work of Edward Burnett Tylor, Oxford reader in Anthropology, whose *Primitive Culture* of 1871 Parry had read in 1885. Tylor's work and theories were to be particularly conspicuous in *Style in Musical Art*.

From the expressive cries and gestures of savages, Parry moved on to a discussion of scales and folk music in which he must have drawn on the work of Carl Engel as well as that of Hipkins whom he acknowledged. From chapter IV, 'Incipient Harmony' and the music of the early Christian Church, Parry embarked fully on his conception of musical history as a

continuous progression. Most common to his description
are words like 'instinct', 'character', 'phase', 'stage', 'step'
and the two watchwords of Spencer: 'homogeneity' and
'heterogeneity'. Here is an extract from Chapter V 'The Era of
Pure Choral Music' – an era regarded by Parry as the
'babyhood of modern music':

The manner in which the inevitable homogeneity of an early stage of art
presents itself is still discernible from every point of view. The most
comprehensive fact is that almost all the music of these two centuries [i.e. the
fifteenth and sixteenth centuries] is purely choral – that is, either written for
several voices in combination without independent accompaniment, or
devised upon methods which were invented solely for that kind of
performance. It followed from this general fact that the methods of art were
also homogeneous; for the processes which are fit to be used by voices alone
are more limited in range and variety than those which can be employed by
instruments.[14]

Other watchwords such as 'expression' and 'design' are
ubiquitous to Parry's critical vocabulary. The relationship and
equilibrium between these two elements, between form and
content, becomes fundamental to Parry's thesis as his book
develops. In consequence, we find that generative processes of
form, notably instrumental form, and the expansion and
increasing sophistication of structure, are venerated and seen
as culminating in the sonata works of Beethoven.

One of the most conspicuous of Parry's critical criteria,
stemming again directly from Spencer's suggestions about race
and culture, is the attempt to connect artistic attributes to racial
types. Though this stance has now been categorically rejected
by the scientific community, Parry believed in the connection
between race, style and national character. This belief gave rise
to a cultural hierarchy in which Teutonic art held sway. The
idea is introduced in his discussion of 'Folk Music' and further
polarisations are evident in his deliberations on the music of
the seventeenth century in which northern composers are seen
as superior to their southern counterparts. This was an
objection voiced later by Dent in his criticism of Parry's
contribution to the Oxford History of Music – *The Music of the
Seventeenth Century* – in which he saw that century primarily as

14. *Art of Music* p 103.

a preparation for J S Bach. In *The Music of the Seventeenth Century* this polarisation is clearly made as follows:

The Northern composers, dwelling with intense and loving concentration on every detail of their work, brooding on its deeper spiritual meaning, and glorifying it by the full exercise of intellectual as well as emotional qualities; where the Southern composers, taking things more lightly and with little exercise of self-criticism, fall into trivialities, conventionalities and purely mechanical artifices, and in a branch of art which requires any copious exercise of intellect, are speedily left in the lurch.[15]

Parry confessed himself an out-and-out pro-Teuton in one of his RCM addresses, though ironically it was delivered within the context of the First World War when he felt himself betrayed by German militarism.

The reason for labouring these aspects of Parry's understanding of history and artistic value, and the consequences of those values in his own music, is that they were considerably influential on Vaughan Williams from his schooldays. Many of the events described in Vaughan Williams's own essays, particularly 'A Musical Autobiography', bear this out.[16] While at Charterhouse he was introduced to *Studies of Great Composers* by his friend Stephen Massingberd with the Ruskinian maxim: 'This man Parry declares that a composer must write music as his musical conscience demands'.[17] The same Spencer-derived vocabulary – words such as sincerity, character and instinct – re-echoes through the recollections of his lessons. Though repelled by the Beethoven idiom, he nevertheless absorbed Parry's admiration, and passed on his master's *dicta* of organicism to his pupils. Parry's reverence for Bach is also evident in Vaughan Williams's essay 'Bach, the great bourgeois', not just in the technical aspects but because, to both men, Bach respresented a higher democratic purpose: one of appeal, accessibility and education. These two values remained the touchstones of Parry's belief in musical citizenship and

15. C Hubert H Parry: *Music of the Seventeenth Century*, (*Oxford History of Music* vol III). Oxford, Clarendon Press, 1902, 118–9.
16 R Vaughan Williams: 'A Musical Autobiography' (1950), *National Music and Other Essays*, Oxford, Oxford University Press, 1963; 2nd Edn. 1986 ed. Kennedy, pp 177–194.
17. *Ibid* p 180.

democracy, values that were propagated by Vaughan Williams in his own choral works. In quoting Parry's now famous statement in 1950 – 'Write choral music as befits an Englishman and a democrat'[18] – RVW was at once stressing the core of an agnostic, humanitarian tradition of which he had become a part with *Toward the Unknown Region, A Sea Symphony, Dona Nobis Pacem* (a work exhibiting a distinct affinity with Parry's *War and Peace*), *Sancta Civitas, The Pilgrim's Progress* and *The Oxford Elegy*.

Parry took a considerable interest in folk-song as part of his evolutionary development of music, and his inaugural address at the opening of the Folk-song Society in 1898 is testimony to his encouragement of the movement. On several occasions he did attempt to note down local songs and melodies, but was not moved to incorporate folk-tunes in any of his own music. The study of folk-music, as Parry saw it, played an important role in the evolutionary and ethnocentric dimensions of his writings and these undoubtedly chimed with Vaughan Williams's views in his book *National Music*, a compilation of the Mary Flexner lectures given in October and November of 1932 at Bryn Mawr College, Pennsylvania.[19] In the first of his lectures, 'Should Music be National?', Vaughan Williams paraphrased what had become an ingrained tradition in the minds of many British composers and writers:

Hubert Parry, in his book, *The Evolution of the Art of Music*, has shown how music like everything else in the world is subject to the laws of evolution, that there is no difference in kind but only in degree between Beethoven and the humblest singer of a folk-song. The principles of artistic beauty, of the relationships of design and expression, are neither trade secrets nor esoteric mysteries revealed to the few; indeed if these principles are to have any meaning to us they must be founded on what is natural to the human being. Perfection of form is equally possible in the most primitive music and in the most elaborate.[20]

18. *Ibid* p 182.
19. This is also evident in Vaughan Williams' four lectures given in the Autumn of 1902 at Pokesdown Technical School, Bournemouth (and in Gloucester in January and February 1903), notably the final lecture 'The importance of folk-song', which ethnocentrically linked national music with national temperament. See M. Kennedy: *The Works of Ralph Vaughan Williams*, Oxford, Oxford University Press, 1964, p 35.
20. See R Vaughan Williams: 'Should Music be National?', *National Music and Other Essays*. Oxford, Oxford University Press, 1963: 2nd Edn. 1986 ed. Kennedy, p 6.

This same view was again paraphrased years later in a lecture on 'The Folk-song Movement' at Cornell University in 1954. Much has been made of Vaughan Williams' disenchantment with Britain's musical scene at the turn of the century, and of his need to find salvation in native resources – the folk-song being the prime raw material. That he forged new directions is undeniable in his assimilation of modality, both melodically and harmonically. His outspoken essay 'Who wants the English composer?', published in the *RCM Magazine* in 1912,[21] upset a number of his seniors including Stanford, largely because it made reference to the imitation of European models which he took as a personal insult both to his music and teaching. Parry's letter to Colles, the editor of the magazine makes informative reading:

I had not heard that Vaughan Williams's jokey article had raised a lot of discussion and opposition here. I only heard of Stanford's taking offence and taking his name and Lady Stanford's out of the list of the [Graduate] Union. I thought everybody was agreed that it was a very silly thing to do, including Sir Walter [Parratt] and Stanford's own very special friend and sympathizer Harry Greene. I think it will be much better to leave it alone. To take serious notice of it must call attention to Stanford's touchiness, and make him ridiculous in the eyes of many who otherwise would not think much of it. Moreover Vaughan Williams's article was mainly chaff, and to answer it is to take it too seriously. It would certainly arouse feelings which had much better be left quiescent. Stanford couldn't stand quite out of it himself – and if he came in there would be broken heads and caps on the green and various other things which are most undesirable. I have constantly maintained that there was nothing personal in the article, or anything any sensible person could take offence at – and that if there had been it was not sufficiently emphasised to justify your declining the article at the last moment. And that neither you nor the Committee were answerable for heresies which irritable brains read into it. But all this would be brought into discussion if any further notice was taken. So I am sure it will be much better to leave it alone now.[22]

Parry's counsel was wise. Vaughan Williams's article, perhaps over-pugnacious in tone, did make a case for folk-song as an alternative to the Teutonically-derived material of his

21. See R Vaughan Williams: 'Who wants the English composer?', *RCM Magazine*, vol 9 no 1 (1912), pp 11–15.
22 Letter from Parry to H C Colles, 14 Feb 1913, Colles Collection, McMaster University, Hamilton, Ontario.

forebears, but he did not and could not deny the tradition he had inherited. The high, 'evolved' ideal of organicism, of intellectualism, continued to be germane to his technique. Central to Vaughan Williams's entire output are his symphonic instrumental works which essay a generative technique gleaned and developed from his teachers. Moreover, it should be stressed that Vaughan Williams, Parry, and Stanford for that matter, were actually conscious of an unfolding national musical history. Parry believed implicitly in the importance of tradition, of inherited values and techniques as part of his evolutionary philosophy (a stance which incidentally tended to underestimate experimentation and empiricism) so that to err from this path of gradual change was anathema to him. In the seventh of his lectures, 'Tradition', Vaughan Williams paid heed to this philosophy, making passing reference to Colles whose own book, *The Growth of Music* (1912), continued to develop Parry's Darwinist outlook: 'Most of the best things in modern music come from composers who have kept close to their several native traditions and whose individual genius has enabled them to extend it in directions undreamt of by their predecessors.'[23]

When recollecting about Parry in his 'Musical Autobiography', Vaughan Williams affirmed his indebtedness to Parry in numerous ways, but perhaps the most telling reference in the context of national tradition, was the creation of a spiritual ancestral consciousness. 'We pupils of Parry,' he wrote, 'have, if we have been wise, inherited from Parry the great English choral tradition which Tallis passed onto Byrd, Byrd to Gibbons, Gibbons to Purcell, Purcell to Battishill and Greene, and they in their turn through the Wesleys to Parry. He has passed on the torch to us and it is our duty to keep it alight.'[24]

Stanford's role in the creation of a British tradition needs to be perceived in a rather different form from that of Parry. He is of course well-known, perhaps best known, as the teacher of

23. R. Vaughan Williams: 'Tradition', *National Music and Other Essays*. Oxford, Oxford University Press, 1963; 2nd Edn. 1986 ed. Kennedy, p 60.
24 R. Vaughan Williams: 'A Musical Autobiography' (1950), *National Music and Other Essays*. Oxford, Oxford University Press, 1963; 2nd Edn. 1986 ed. Kennedy, p 182.

a lengthy catalogue of British composers, many of whom (including Vaughan Williams) expressed their admiration and gratitude after his death in 1924. According to George Dyson, Stanford 'had aspired to be the acknowledged fount of a school of composers'.[25] Like Parry, he believed implicitly in the superiority of German models and these he was determined to pass on to his pupils. Diverse and eclectic as many of them have proved to be, it is hard to deny that the essence and imperatives of Stanford's principles, enshrined in *Musical Composition* (1911), is to be found in all of them. Strongly conservative in his views whether musical or political, Stanford had largely hoped that his pupils would stand back from the brink in the their pursuit of modernities. In the end, it was only figures such as the brief-lived Coleridge-Taylor and Hurlstone who remained 'sane'.[26] In this sense Stanford believed he had failed. And yet, the generations that followed Stanford upheld his conservatism in their cleaving to largely traditional means of tonality, forms and critical criteria in the light of continental developments. The symphony remained a predominant form of large-scale intellectual expression, as in its different way did the string quartet. Moreover, the paradigm of Stanford's symphonic canticle settings has never been superseded in the repertoire of the Anglican church, as is attested by Dyson, Ireland, Noble, Wood and Howells.

In many ways the effectiveness of Stanford's teaching stemmed from his instincts as a practical musician. As a student in Germany he became increasingly aware of the emphasis in composition teaching on study but with no practical opportunities of learning from performance. As a composition teacher at the RCM Stanford's confessed aim was to allow his students the chance of hearing their works played, either by the RCM orchestra or, better still within the framework of the Patron's Fund. This was also reflected in his work as Professor of Music at Cambridge University in the way he transformed the whole nature of the degree system so as to emphasise importance on the practical application of

25. *See* 'Charles Villiers Standford by some of his pupils', *Music and Letters*, July 1924, V no 3, p 197.
26 *Ibid* p 201.

technical assurance in creativity. A freer manner of
composition replaced the BMus exercise, a new degree of
MMus embraced the old technical skills of the DMus, while a
new doctoral degree, to match those in science and letters, was
instituted based purely on the submission of a portfolio of
compositions. It was controversial, not least amongst those at
Oxford, Dublin, London and Durham who stood out against
his reforms. But Stanford was insistent that 'some distinction
ought to be drawn between the artist and the skilled workman,
and that to the former alone should the highest degree in
Music which the University confers be restricted. The works
which the Referees pronounced worthy of acceptance would
not merely exist on the shelves of the University Library, but
be able to bear the test of performance and publicity. ... The
Doctor of Music under the New Regulations would thus carry
credentials entitling him to be considered a composer of
acknowledged merit and practical usefulness.'[27] This tradition
of university music, of the study of history, composition and its
illumination through practice still informs the Anglo-Saxon
system of musical education today. Stanford, who authored
these changes in 1893, was the key figure in their
implementation (though he was almost certainly assisted by
Parry). Vaughan Williams was himself a fervent advocate of
Stanford's musical pragmatism and was forever grateful to him
for providing him with the opportunity for first performances
at Leeds of *Toward the Unknown Region* in 1907 and particularly
A Sea Symphony in 1910. As an indication perhaps of his
spiritual affinity with Vaughan Williams's symphony, he never
believed that any other of his works he heard before his death
exceeded it. Parry too was affected by its nobility, even though
he admitted privately in his diary that there were 'some
aggressive perversities, obtrusive consecutives [and] rough
progressions.'[28]

Many of the innovations with which we credit or centrally
associate Vaughan Williams – the folk-song and Tudor
revivals, the symphonic tradition, the aspirations for a national

27. C V Stanford, [Memorandum] 'To the Members of the Senate', 30 May
    1893
28 Diary of Sir Hubert Parry, 4 February 1913.

opera – find Stanford at their roots. Recent recordings of Parry's five symphonies and Stanford's seven have already demonstrated that Britain enjoyed a symphonic tradition well before the turn of the century, and that Elgar and Vaughan Williams were not the prime-movers but participants within it. Stanford's work as an editor and arranger of folk-song and his belief in its educational value was well known before the English Folk-song Society was born and his use of folk melodies in symphony or, more successfully, in the more rigorously argued Irish Rhapsodies has more than a prophetic ring. (See Ex 1 on following page.)

It is perhaps no accident that Vaughan Williams played through this work with his friend Richard Walthew as students at the RCM.

Similarly, Stanford was keenly aware of Britain's musical heritage. He was the first to revive Purcell's *Dido and Aeneas* in 1895 at the RCM (Vaughan Williams sang in the chorus) and was deeply frustrated in his own exploits as an organist at Cambridge when he was prevented from promoting the works of Tallis, Byrd and Gibbons. Last but not least, and in a more negative sense, Stanford must be seen as the first in a line of aspiring composers, including Vaughan Williams, to have failed in their bid to establish a national opera in spite of the enormous success of *Shamus O'Brien* in 1896 and the relative renown of *Hugh the Drover* after the First World War. Unlike its central role in the continental national movements, opera, as Parry had hinted, failed to establish a place in the creation of tradition in Britain.

Vaughan Williams's own perception of Britain's musical heritage, from Byrd to Parry and onwards, has much to say about tradition and style and about Vaughan Williams's need to belong. On more than one occasion he drew the connection between S S Wesley and Parry,[29] though tantalisingly no further explanation was forthcoming. What Vaughan Williams most likely observed, but did not articulate, was the common predilection shared by Wesley and Parry for an essentially

29. *See* R Vaughan Williams; 'What have we learnt from Elgar' (1935) and 'A Musical Autobiography' (1950), *National Music and Other Essays. op cit*, pp 182 and 253.

Ex 1: Stanford *Irish Symphony*

diatonic voice, in which a language of higher diatonic dissonance was developed. This stylistic avenue became consolidated into a tradition bolstered and imparted by both Parry and Stanford. Hearkening back to traditional Ruskinian sentiments, Stanford eschewed the 'crushing chromaticism' of

Tristan und Isolde, preferring instead the 'healthy' diatonicism of the *Siegfried Idyll, Die Meistersinger* and *Parsifal*, while Parry's musical parallel of Milton's 'harsh din' in *Blest Pair of Sirens* is an allusion to the *Tristan* chord. Vaughan Williams declared that *Blest Pair of Sirens* was his 'favourite piece of music written by an Englishman';[30] for Elgar too it was amongst the 'noblest works of man.'[31] *Blest Pair of Sirens*, with its tight, organically driven musical structure, rich diatonic language of dissonance and multiple appoggiaturas, counterpoint redolent of Bach (which prompted Hanslick to dub Parry the 'English Bach'), not to mention a heightened sense of choral pragmatism and accessibility, symbolised an English aesthetic. It is not difficult to understand the appeal of such gestures as the attitudinising secondary seventh of 'O may we soon again renew that song' with its yearning aspiration,

Ex 2: Parry *Blest Pair of Sirens*

30. *See* R Vaughan Williams, 'A Musical Autobiography' (1950), *National Music and Other Essays. op cit*, pp 180.
31. Jeremy Dibble, *C Hubert H Parry: His Life and Music*. Oxford, Clarendon Press, 1992, p 390.

or the epigrammatic final gesture of the final chorus with its
triumphant appoggiatura

Ex 3: Parry *Best Pair of Sirens*

In Vaughan Williams's first major setting of Whitman,
Toward the Unknown Region (1905-6), a text which incidentally

Stanford set shortly afterwards,[32] these elements recur with striking resemblance. Note (a) the progression of the opening bars, the polyphonic treatment of 'nor touch of human hand' and (b) the resolute final paragraph 'Then we burst forth':

(a)

(b)

Ex 4: *Toward the Unknown Region*

A less cohesive but not dissimilar model can be observed in Parry's earlier ode *The Glories of our Blood and State* which

32 *See* Stanford's *Songs of Faith* (Set II) op 97 no 4 'To the Soul'. This song was later orchestrated, probably for Stanford's visit to Norfolk, Connecticut, in 1915, but which he never made owing to the sinking of the *Luisitania* on which he was booked to travel.

Vaughan Williams also greatly admired.[33] Parry likewise was impressed when *Toward the Unknown Region* was given at the RCM on 10 December 1907; 'imposing and fine in intention' was his characteristic description.[34]

This legacy of diatonicism, passed on by Parry and Stanford, can be felt in other works by Vaughan Williams. *Linden Lea* has all the economy and simplicity of Stanford's strophic settings; *Whither must I wander*, with its characteristic suspensions, bears the deep imprint of Parry. Outwardly, the primary stimulus of *In the Fen Country* would appear to be folk-song, and certainly the modal inflection of the melodic material reinforces this impression, but the climactic accumulation of diatonic dissonance and the prominent use of appoggiatura, reveals its true source, as does the stirring passage of the first movement of *A Sea Symphony*, 'And on its limitless, heaving breast'. Even in mature works the presence of this diatonic inclination can be profoundly felt. The opening of the *Serenade to Music* is one such instance, or there is the even later Fifth Symphony of 1943 whose radiant white-note polyphony at the close of the last movement symbolises the extraordinary longevity of this stylistic tradition. Furthermore, it is impossible to ignore the unashamed diatonicism of Walton (eg *Belshazzar's Feast*), Ireland (*These Things Shall Be*), Bliss (*Morning Heroes*) or, most of all Finzi (*Dies Natalis* and *Intimations of Immortality*).

In discussing the creation of tradition in Britain, Vaughan Williams stands as a major force not least in that his long life encompasses sixty years of our musical history. More than any other composer he provides a tangible link with the progenitors of the so-called British musical renaissance as well as being a mentor for composers such as Finzi, Howells, Gurney, Walton and Moeran. Indeed, Vaughan Williams's association with nationalism, the folk-song and the English pastoral idyll of the *Fantasia on a Theme of Thomas Tallis* and *The Lark Ascending* have in some ways tended to make him the focus of a created tradition rather than his more Teutonic forebears. This was certainly true after the First World War

33. *See* M Kennedy: *The Works of Ralph Vaughan Williams.* op cit, p 385.
34. Diary of Sir Hubert Parry, 10 December 1910.

when, firstly, the Victorian and Edwardian values of Parry, Stanford and Elgar were rejected wholesale and, secondly, anti-German sentiments inevitably advanced the cause of nationalism and identity at a time when it was required by the public. And yet, with shifting values, it is perhaps significant that, during the anti-Establishment years of the 1960s, Vaughan Williams himself should have been rejected. With the luxury of almost a century's hindsight, and with the reassessment of our late nineteenth-century heritage, it has become easier to estimate and chart the nature of this country's musical history. As our judgmental criteria have changed, we no longer glibly dismiss Parry and Stanford for imbibing continental stimuli with such enthusiasm. Similarly, it is necessary to reassess and re-examine the popular nationalist image of Vaughan Williams if only to recognise that his 'discovery' of folk-song has frequently obscured our view of his indcbtcdncss to his forefathers both ethically and stylistically. As a composer of symphonies, ethical choral works, hymn tunes and *Gebrauchsmusik*, he lived up to the role of Parry's composer-democrat, upheld the craftsmanly principles of Stanford and thereby participated in a much broader, deep-seated tradition, confident of Parry's belief in Spencerian evolutionism.

III

Tony Kendall

Through Bushes and Through Briars . . . Vaughan Williams's earliest folk-song collecting

VAUGHAN WILLIAMS'S DISCOVERY OF FOLK SONG AND the development of his collecting activities signalled a turning point in his music and was a major milestone in the emergence of his mature style. To follow his earliest folk-song collecting excursions in the villages around Brentwood in Essex, while not allowing us fully to appreciate the rural circumstances in which he found himself, nor to relate those folk songs to their contemporary rural setting, nevertheless gives us some appreciation of the impact of his discoveries on Vaughan Williams.

Yet we need to remember that Vaughan Williams had already written songs which audiences would later equate with folk song, including his setting of William Barnes' *Linden Lea* and *Blackmore by the Stour*. We know from Ursula Vaughan Williams's biography of her husband[1] that he was already familiar with John Broadwood's *Sussex Songs* published in 1889[2] and Lucy Broadwood and J A Fuller Maitland's *English County Songs.*[3] Vaughan Williams was thus already lecturing on the

1. Ursula Vaughan Williams: *RVW – a biography of Ralph Vaughan Williams.* Oxford University Press, 1964.
2. *Sussex Songs. Popular Songs of Sussex etc* [Collected by J Broadwood]. Arranged by H F Birch Reynardson. S Lucas, Weber & Co., nd [1890].

subject of "The Characteristics of National Songs in the British Isles", and it was to lecture on this very subject that took him to Brentwood in Essex in the early Spring of 1903. It was later that year, while accepting an invitation to tea from the vicar of Ingrave, that he decided to embark on collecting folk songs from the old people of the village. The next day Vaughan Williams collected his first folk song, *Bushes and Briars*, and as Ursula Vaughan Williams has written "when Ralph heard it he felt it was something he had known all his life".[4]

Through bushes and through briars   I lately took   my way

Ex 1: *Bushes and Briars*

This song collected by Ralph Vaughan Williams in December 1903 from Charles Potiphar, a land worker from Ingrave, stimulated great changes in the composer's style and brought about a quintessential Englishness (via England's traditional folk songs!) to his future compositions. How RVW came to arrive in Ingrave to start a monumental collection of around 140 songs was a veritable sequence of coincidence – much like my own more recent retracing of his footsteps.

Some colleagues of mine[5] had carried out some research into the "Ingrave canon" in 1980, and a small book entitled "Bushes and Briars – an anthology of Essex folk songs"[6] was published. Even so it was not until the late 1980s, when a chance meeting with Ursula Vaughan Williams finally set me on the road.

I had been at a reception at the English Folk Dance and Song Society, Cecil Sharp House, and was introduced to RVW's widow by a friend knowing of my abiding love of all things Essex particularly its folk music. "Well you know" she

3. Lucy E Broadwood and J A Fuller-Maitland: *English County Songs.* Leadenhall Press, 1893. [Publication taken over by J B Cramer & Co Ltd.]
4. Ursula Vaughan Williams *ibid* p 66.
5. David Occomore and Philip Heath-Coleman: *Folk Songs Collected in Essex by Dr Ralph Vaughan Williams.* Unpublished, 1980.
6. David Occomore and Philip Sprately: *Bushes and Briars – an anthology of Essex folk songs.* Monkswood Press, 1979.

began, "Ralph's folk song collecting really started in Essex. He was invited to an old people's tea party at a rectory in Ingrave and an old shepherd sang a song for him." At that stage this was all I knew – RVW collected his first folk song in Ingrave, but many questions remained with me – who was the singer? what was the song? how did RVW come to arrive in Ingrave, in Essex of all places? how many other songs did he collect? what happened to the songs? can we revive and perform them anew?

So, how did the story begin for RVW? As we have noted, some years before setting foot in Essex he had seen in the music in the book *English County Songs* by Lucy Broadwood (a near neighbour of RVW's family) and J A Fuller Maitland, in which appeared the song *Dives and Lazarus*.

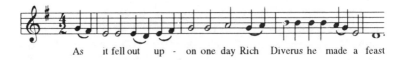

As it fell out up - on one day Rich Diverus he made a feast

Ex 2: *Dives and Lazarus*

He went on in later life to write the orchestral work *Five Variants of Dives and Lazarus,* a piece which permeated his whole life and was performed at his funeral service in Westminster Abbey in 1958. From these earliest beginnings came a deep love, interest and respect for the folk song of England, and an understanding that unless something was done to notate these songs that they would die out along with the ageing singers.

It would appear that the new generation shaken out of an agricultural economy into the industrialised Britain of the late Victorian times, wanted professional entertainment and was not inclined to learn these rustic songs of their forefathers. They went more for the music hall songs, the wax cylinders and the phonograph. Family singing started to become marginalised – even though in my own family, singing at family get-togethers has survived into this decade.

RVW threw himself into a comprehensive technical and historical study of folk song. After his father died in 1875, his mother returned to the family home at Leith Hill Place in

Surrey, close to the home of the Broadwoods at Lyne. Lucy Broadwood was co-editor of *English County Songs* mentioned above and was well-known to RVW. Ralph's knowledge of these collections, including John Broadwood's volume of songs collected from singers in his native Surrey as well as Sussex[7] gave Ralph the necessary building blocks to assemble his "Six Lectures on the History of Folk Song". These lectures under the auspices of the Oxford University Extension Delegacy, were to play a key role in starting the Vaughan Williams folk song collection. The lectures were also to include the occasional use of Lucy Broadwood to sing illustrations of the songs. The Lecture Series comprised:

1. Introductory. The Foundations of National Song.
2. Design and Expression in National Song.
3. The Characteristics of National Songs on the Continent.
4. The Characteristics of National Songs in the British Isles.
5. The Characteristics of National Songs: Religious Songs.
6. The Importance of National Songs.

The syllabus stated that "it is particularly hoped that students will freely consult the Lecturer as to the choice of the best books upon the subject of the course", even though it might well have been a challenge for RVW to do so in 1902 when the lecture tours began; there being so few source books available on the subject of English folk song. The lectures were intended as an extra-mural activity for schools intent on raising cultural standards and impressing the Government Departmental Boards of Inspectors, inaugurated under the Education Act 1871.

So it was that on 29th May 1902, Mr J A Marriott, the secretary to the Extension Delegacy wrote this letter to RVW:

Dear Sir,

I have much pleasure in forwarding to you an invitation from Pokesdown, Bournemouth to give a course of six fortnightly lectures on Monday afternoons beginning on October 6th at 3 pm. I hope we may accept this for you.

---

7. *Old English Songs, as now sung by the Peasantry of the Weald of Surrey and Sussex, and harmonised by one who has learnt them by hearing them sung every Christmas.* Harmonized for the Collector [John Broadwood] in 1843 by G A Dusart. Balls & Co., for the Collector nd [1847].

Pokesdown is a sub-centre of Bournemouth centre which is one of the most important we have and is now extending its work in the outlying portions of the town. Pokesdown has at present only had two courses. The secretary says that there would be no difficulty in procuring vocalists and instrumental performers to illustrate your lectures. If you are able to accept as I hope you will I will put you into communication with her.

Yours very truly,

J A Marriott[8]

For the third lecture at Pokesdown, which was "Continental Songs", Magyar and German music was included alongside some Hungarian dances arranged by Francis Korbay. Then for the fourth lecture ("Songs of the British Isles") the illustrations were sung by Lucy Broadwood, who was later presented with a bouquet "comprised chiefly of chrysanthemums, maidenhair fern, etc., with orange coloured streamers attached" – according to a local newspaper report.

The lectures at Pokesdown which took place between October 6th and December 14th 1902, were a qualified success. Ursula Vaughan Williams in her biography refers to one hundred and twelve students, of which two were examined and one passed with distinction. RVW wrote in his lecturer's report:

I hope that the lectures were interesting to those that attended, but it would have been very helpful to me if there had been more discussion and more questions asked. As musical lectures are comparatively rare it is difficult to know whether the points discussed have been made clear or not

The local education committee's report refers to the lack of text books on the subject; a point on which RVW would be well aware. The committee report also refers to three candidates having been examined; two passed, one with distinction, and that average attendances were 89 students. "I must say that the best paper showed an intelligent study of the subject and some real musicianship."

RVW began another course of lectures on 19th January 1903, this time in Gloucester, and these ran through until 30th April 1903. This seems to have been a more successful course with higher average attendances (120), and Ralph commented:

8. Quoted by Occomore and Coleman, *op cit*, from an original in the British Library, as are the succeeding quotations.

The audience seemed very ready to take a keen and intelligent interest in an subject. Those who stayed for the class helped the lecturer much with their suggestive questions. The lecturer particularly wished to thank those ladies and gentlemen who so kindly sang the illustrations

This was, then, RVW's journey so far, two courses of lectures had been undertaken but he had apparently not collected a single folk song himself. The visit to Brentwood was to change all this.

Miss Kate Bryan had established a girls' school at Montpelier House (corner of Queens Road and Rose Valley now 39 Queens Road) Brentwood in Essex, in 1879. Miss Bryan was then 32 years of age. The popularity of the school was such that in 1886 a dining room was added, then in 1898 a new classroom was built. By the turn of the century the school had a staff of four resident teachers and in 1905 it was recorded there were 37 day students and 8 boarders. In July, in order to ensure Board of Education recognition, the school was inspected and a report published in 1906:

The Inspector of the Board of Education reported that the discipline and organisation of the school were good. They further reported that the Headmistress has the welfare of the school very much at heart, has regularly devoted all the annual profits to its improvement and exercises a very thorough supervision over the whole school.

Eventually this became a county school under the Education Act 1944 (Brentwood County High School for Girls); the school is now a co-educational comprehensive school in separate buildings and Montpelier House itself has been demolished and replaced on site by a block of flats named Montpelier Court.

Miss Bryan was the Hon. Secretary of the local Oxford University Extension lecture committee, and the lectures appear to have taken place at Montpelier House. Between 1st October and 10th December 1902, a series of literature lectures were give on the subject of Tennyson, as a result of which the lecturer reported: "The secretarial work needs strengthening, something has been done by the calling this term of a committee, which had fallen into abeyance, hence my recommendation."

The Extension Committee which was formed in the Autumn of 1902 comprised: Miss Bryan (Secretary); Miss Biggs, Westbury Lodge; Miss Dowson, Earmont; Miss Steinmedz, Queens Road; Mrs Taylor, Shenfield House; – all of Brentwood, and Miss Heatley, Ingrave Rectory. The involvement of Georgiana (also known as Georgina) Heatley in this Committee was to prove instrumental in there being an Ingrave folk-song collection – she was most certainly a key player.

Miss Bryan had written to Mr Marriott to complain about the literature lecturer, and as a result, on 13th December 1902, he wrote back:

Dear Madam,

Thank you for your letter. I am sorry that you have not found Mr Dale very effective as a lecturer. We have most excellent accounts of him from some centres but of course no one is always at his best.

As to next term he could come to you on alternate Tuesdays beginning January 13th or 27th, or he could come to you on six Wednesdays in continuous weeks beginning March 4th but I am sorry to say that he is continuously engaged on Wednesday from January 21st to February 25th. I hope that you may be able to take Tuesdays, but if not may I suggest to you the names of one or two other lecturers. How would you like a course on Folksong from Dr Vaughan Williams? They have been given this term at Bournemouth with immense success and he could give these on the Wednesdays you name and a change of subject of this kind might serve to arouse the interest in other quarters especially as I see that you have a shining choral society to illustrate the lectures. Dr Vaughan Williams is still class B. If you prefer to go on with literature we shall have I expect one or two new lecturers.

Yours truly,

J A Marriott

Miss Bryan sent a telegram accepting the change of course subject to Folk song and of lecturer to Dr Vaughan Williams. It is still quite amazing to me that one of the world's greatest collections of folk songs should begin so indirectly and so subtly – from Miss Bryan's willingness to accept a change in course subject and to engage Vaughan Williams – all because she was unhappy with the performance of another lecturer. Ursula Vaughan Williams refers to the lecture series having started in the Autumn of 1903, but in fact the lectures in

Brentwood ran from Wednesday January 21st till April 1st 1903, and went concurrently with the Monday course in Gloucester. In his report on the course RVW wrote:

The lecturer found the audience very ready to be interested in all the aspects of music referred to in the lectures. The lecturer wishes to thank those ladies who kindly sang the illustrations. The illustrations are a very important part of a musical lecture and in this case the lecturer was very fortunate in finding competent musicians to help him in this part of the task

There was a thriving music department at the school under the supervision of Miss Hulm, LRAM, who taught pianoforte and class singing. There were sessional teachers for pianoforte, solo singing and violin. It is likely that musicians for the course would be drawn at least in part from the school. The average attendance at the course was 50 and included 3 school pupils. Miss Bryan reported on the course as follows:

The course was very successful. More tickets were sold chiefly owing to the energy of the committee. The lectures were much liked and the illustrations (sung by different members of the audience) proved bright and attractive. Dr Vaughan Williams is a very good lecturer and an enthusiast on the subject of folksong.

It is important to note the role of Georgina Heatley (daughter of the Rector of Ingrave) in these proceedings. She and her sister Florence attended the lectures and gave RVW a series of handwritten notes during the course. These are examples:

March 13th 1903

Fragment of a song sung by an old woman living at Stambourne in Essex about 36 years ago. She was then about 60 or 70 years of age.

Title –   Cold Blows the Wind

Chorus – Blow the winds High O
          A-roving we will go
          To part no more on England's shore
          So let the music play.

              GJH   (Georgina Jean Heatley)

April 1st 1903

Mrs Humphreys, Ingrave

Songs she *sang* to me
    I   Young Napoleon or The Bonny Bunch of Roses
    II   The Green Mossy Banks of the Lea
    III   The Little Town Boy
    IV   The Undaunted Female or The Banks of Sweet Dundee
    V   Adieu My Lovely Nancy
    VI   Female Cabin Boy
    VII   The Isle of France.

Tunes I think she *could* sing
1. The Farmer's Daughter
2. The Pretty Ploughboy
3. Susan's Adventures
4. Undaunted Mary
5. The Merchant's Daughter and the Farmer's Son
6. The Foggy Dew.

This latter note continued with details of *Come buy me a hawk* which was sung by Mrs Humphreys' grandfather at Blackmore in Essex in 1758. Georgina Heatley says "Mrs Humphreys recollects a song called *The Milkmaid* in which the milkmaid killed the squire down by the sheepfold, but not the words properly." Miss Heatley details the repertoires of Emma Turner (housemaid at Ingrave Rectory); Mrs Turner at Navestock; Alice Horsenell of Ingrave; and Ingrave children's singing games. In addition there are details of how to find local singers. This account appears on the back of this note:

Also I hear that at Navestock (about 6 miles from here) all the cottage people meet and sing to each other. Also at Mundon out on the marsh country beyond Maldon there is any quantity of singing of old songs at the public houses by men, and the boys pick them up and go with them. I am told one of these is a song of 24 verses and they say the men will go on ...

Sadly the rest of the message is lost as the page is damaged. Note that the dates of these notes were quite near to the end of the lecture course. RVW was surprised that local people living among folk singers were oblivious to their existence. He wrote some time later on this subject in a letter to the *Morning Post* on 4th October 1904:

I was grateful to the Misses Heatley of Ingrave Rectory for arranging for singers to meet me so that I could note down the songs ... it is interesting to notice that although these ladies have lived in Ingrave for several years and are intimate with the village people, they had no idea that the folk song still survived there until I suggested the possibility to them some time ago ... If the Miss Headeys had not realised that songs existed in their parish until I suggested it to them, they certainly did their homework thoroughly.

I would venture that Georgina and Florence Heatley had been well aware that songs were sung locally, they even referred to songs sung at harvest suppers in connection with RVW visiting the Rectory. Perhaps it took the catalyst of RVW to make them realise that these were proper English traditional songs and should be valued as much as any other classical music source; he would also have made them realise the frailty of the oral tradition and of the apparent danger that these fine tunes would be lost forever on the death of this generation of singers. The sisters had effectively taken these songs and singers for granted; one wonders whether the art form was subjected to ridicule in much the same way as other vanishing traditions – like Morris Dancing is today!

It remains for me a mystery as to why, following these enticing notes from Georgina Heatley in March and April 1903, that RVW did not get to collect his first folk song in Ingrave until 4th December 1903. Had he set to immediately on completion of the course, he would have preceded Cecil Sharp's first collected song by four months.

There is also a mystery around the meeting with Charles Potiphar (not Pottipher, as popularly recorded). RVW in his lecture in 1912 states:

I was at that time entirely without first hand evidence on the subject. I knew and loved the few English folksongs which were available in printed collections but I only believed in them vaguely, just as the layman believes in the facts of astronomy, my faith was not yet active. I was invited to a tea party given to the old people of a village in Essex only twenty miles from London. After tea we asked if any of them knew any of the old songs whereupon an old man, a shepherd, began to sing a song which set all my thoughts about folksong at rest.

This is at odds with the account in Ursula Vaughan Williams's biography:

Yet another of his courses of lectures on folk song took Ralph to Brentwood in Essex during the Autumn. After one talk two middle-aged ladies told him that their father, the vicar of Ingrave, was giving a tea-party for the old people of the village and some of them possibly might know country songs;

he would be very welcome, they said, if he would care to come. Though
Ralph was rather shy of a Parish Tea, and though he felt it was most unlikely
that anyone there would know any folk songs, he accepted the invitation.
The vicar's daughters introduced him to an elderly labourer, Mr Pottipher,
who said of course he could not sing at this sort of party, but if Ralph would
visit him next day he would be pleased to sing to him then. The next day, 4
December, Mr Pottipher sang *Bushes and Briars.*[9]

Critics of the "English" influence of folk song in the early
1900s would claim these songs were corrupted, and this
argument had some justification in regard to the words. As to
the tunes, RVW was to comment: "If Bushes and Briars is a
corruption, what must the original have been like." Indeed it is
difficult to exclude the impact of this song in any discussion of
his Symphonic Impression *In the Fen Country* written in 1904.
The rustic voice of Charles Potiphar seems to be intermingled
with the orchestra – "an old man began to sing a song which
set all my doubts about folk song at rest."[10]
But what of the circumstances of the collection of this first
song. I am inclined to believe that Ursula Vaughan Williams's
version is most likely to be correct. RVW's lengthy delay in
returning to Ingrave could have been due to the prospect of
arriving at a Rectory – he was more inclined to humanism
than the Anglican fold even though he did not entirely reject
it, and the fact that two middle-aged ladies appeared to be
pursuing him might well have dampened his enthusiasm.
Charles Potiphar's reluctance to sing at the rectory could have
been due to the presence of the rector, Rev Henry Davis
Heatley, a man of Victorian values, and the content of the
songs themselves – after all *Bushes and Briars* deals graphically
with young love and suicide! It was likely that the songs sung
in these surroundings would give offence. Besides I am finally
swayed by the romantic notion that RVW heard his first folk
song on a crisp December morning on the front porch of an
Essex farm labourer's cottage.
Charles Potiphar was born on 29th November 1829[11] and

9. Ursula Vaughan Williams, *op cit*, p 66.
10. Michael Kennedy: *The Works of Ralph Vaughan Williams.* Oxford
    University Press, 1964, p 29.
11. All genealogical material cited henceforth is from Ingrave Parish Records
    now in the Essex Record Office, Chelmsford.

would have been 74 years of age when he sang for RVW. He was originally employed in South Weald, Essex by local landowner Colonel Lawrie, who also owned land at Ingrave. The census of 1851 shows Charles Potiphar was by then a train labourer and lived in Warley. He then married Mary Ann Wood on 26th September 1852 at St Nicholas's Church, Ingrave, and is described in the register as a bricklayer. Neither he nor his wife could read or write and both signed the register with a cross. This could be the cause of the perpetuated misspelling of his name which RVW wrote down as it sounded. The 1861 Census showed Potiphar as living in Ingrave and working as a labourer – he could have been working on Colonel Lawrie's land again. Regretably no photograph of Charles Potiphar survives.

When RVW first visited Potiphar his cottage stood in Rectory Lane but since that time a road scheme has realigned the main street and Potiphar's cottage is no longer on the highway but is renamed as 43 Middle Road and accessed via "Kissing Gate Alley". RVW only noted down the first verse of *Bushes and Briars* and completed the text from a broadside version printed by Fortey. He also collected *Willy and the Wagon Train* (same tune as "Bushes and Briars), *The Storm* and an interesting version of *The Bold Princess Royal*, whose tune has a similarity to that of the song *Flash Company* (collected in Blaxall, Suffolk by Peter Kennedy). It is interesting to note that at the start of folk-song collecting, RVW troubled to collect the full lyric on occasions but made few margin notes about the singers.

Although RVW tended to place references on manuscripts to available ballad sheets where he did not collect the full lyric, there is no evidence amongst the Essex songs of his bowlderizing any song words. Roy Palmer[12] refers to just one instance where RVW bowed to prevailing taste. This was a song called *The Cobbler*; he published just the tune and one verse, commenting "The rest of the words are not suitable for publication." Among the lyrics collected by RVW in Essex there are still many interesting variations as between collected

12. Roy Palmer, ed: *Folk Songs Collected by Ralph Vaughan Williams*. Dent, 1983 p xv.

song words and published ballad sheets – unfortunately there is not space here for the further development of this topic, another time perhaps!

It was only when RVW revisited Potiphar in February 1904 that he asked him whether he made up his own songs – something he must have suspected on hearing *Willy and the Wagon Train*. Also collected from Potiphar on 4th December 1903 were *Here comes little David, The Cruel Father and the Affectionate Lover*, and *The Sheffield Apprentice*. This last song under its alternative title of *Died for love of you* is a traditional song standard these days.

I   was brought up in Sheffield   a   place   of   high de-gree

Ex 3: *The Sheffield Apprentice (Died for Love of You)*

Also on the first day of collecting he visited Mr Sewell of Ingrave from whom he got *It's of a fair damsel* – RVW notes that Sewell was aged about 40 years.

He next visited Mrs Horsnell of Ingrave and her daughter. RVW noted "she learned them (the songs) from her husband, his mother and her mother. She originally came from Willingale Doe in Essex (RVW would later visit this village to take down songs in The Bell public house). Mrs Horsnell's mother also knew a song called *The Red Barn* about a young man and woman who were murdered. Her mother knew the man and woman and the barn; but she would not teach this song to Mrs Horsnell but said she would keep it to herself till she died. Mrs Horsnell was of the opinion that in modern songs there were no rhymes and that you could not fit in the words no how."

I am tempted to wonder what Mrs Horsnell would have made of today's pop songs. The first of Mrs Horsnell's songs was *Fair Phebe*, better known as *The Dark Eyed Sailor*, this is a classic of the traditional repertoire. It is interesting to note that although the music notation is correct, RVW omits part of the second line words – "for to take the air" is missing. This could have been because Mrs Horsnell just could not remember them on what must have been quite a stressful experience for these old singers He notes against the title "I will get the words of these songs". The next song *The Tarry Sailor* has no words at all and the manuscript notes state "I cannot be certain that the rhythm of the first two bars is not common time but there is no doubt about the last 4 bars being in 3 time". RVW also collected *There was a Fearless Highwayman, With Her Cheeks as Red as Roses* and *The Streams of Lovely Nancy* – Mrs Horsnell could not remember the words of these.

The next stop on the first day of collecting was Ingrave Rectory. Here Emma Turner, the house maid, sang *In Jesse's City* (this turns out to be a variant of *Died for Love* – not the same song as *The Sheffield Apprentice*). The other song he collected from her was *The Farmer's Daughter*. The handwriting of the lyrics gives away the fact that Georgina Heatley sat in on this session and acted as RVW's secretary. The bold and highly legible writing makes this humble researcher sorry that she did not accompany RVW more often. In the notes to *Jessie's City* RVW explains "she learnt this at home (Chigwell, Essex) where they often used to have the neighbours come in and sing in the evenings. Her mother also knew a song called *The Spotted Cow* but she could not remember it" RVW was able to obtain *The Spotted Cow* from Mr Harris at Little Burstead on 16th April 1904 – a lovely cheeky song which I get great enjoyment from singing. Georgina Heatley's notes referred to the singing games sung by local children, and it would appear that she had arranged for RVW to hear one such song at the Rectory; this was *Boots of Spanish Leather*.

The final port of call on this first day of folk song collecting was to James Broomfield, a woodcutter of West Horndon. Both RVW and the Misses Heatley referred to him as Broomfield but further research indicates that his name was Bloomfield. I spoke to his grandson Mack Bloomfield of Ingrave and he remembered his grandfather singing at "The Old Dog" public house at East Horndon. RVW notes "Mr Broomfield (Bloomfield), woodcutter of West Horndon is well known as a singer and has been known to go on for hours when well provided. I think he sang these songs in the traditional manner shutting his eyes tight and speaking the last

line of the song". On this occasion RVW would take down
Bloomfield's versions of *Ingatestone Hall*, *Died for Love*, *Ever So
Poor*, *Young Jimmy* or *Into the Deep* (which is a shortened version
of *The Constant Lover's Garland* and works very well)
Bloomfield's variant of *In Sheffield Park* and a "doubtful"
version (RVW's remark) of *On the Banks of Invaree*.

RVW had become anxious about the parlous state of
English folk song and felt that the process of folk-song
collecting should be better organised and got on with at all due
speed. On Wednesday 2nd December 1903, just before his
first visit to Ingrave, this letter from RVW appeared in the
Morning Post:

Dear Sir,

All lovers of music must have been interested in the report of the 2nd of Mr
Cecil Sharp's lecture on folksong. Everyone who has had the opportunity of
hearing the genuine traditional music of England must have come to the
conclusion that it is quite as beautiful as that of any other nation.

In France as Mr Sharp pointed out the work of collecting and preserving
traditional tunes has been undertaken by the Government. Why should the
folksongs of England be left to the casual attention of a few enthusiastic
collectors.

I understand that some of our county councils are undertaking the
preservation of ancient buildings. Our national songs are at least equally
worth preserving and recording not only as interesting relics but as beautiful
works of art. Is it too much to hope that among our county councils there
are one or two song lovers who would endeavour to act on Mr Sharp's
splendid suggestion that county councils should undertake the work of
collecting and committing to writing these fast disappearing traditional
songs. The work need not entail much experience, it only needs
organisation. The priceless treasures which have been unearthed during the
past fifty years by collectors should encourage us to continue the search and
it is the opinion of these collectors that there must be countless rich veins of
folksong still entirely unexplored. Whatever is done must be done quickly.
Every day some old village singer dies and with him there probably die half
a dozen beautiful melodies which are lost to the world forever, if we would
preserve what still remains we must set about it at once.

Ralph Vaughan Williams

So began a correspondence in the *Morning Post* which lead by
October 1904 to the establishment of a national archive of
folksong, under the supervision of Lucy Broadwood and the
Folk Song Society (what was to become the Vaughan Williams
Library of the English Folk Dance and Song Society).

After Christmas 1903 RVW returned to Ingrave to collect more folk songs. The visit took place on 22nd February 1904 and his first port of call was "The Cricketers" public house in Herongate where he took down more of James Bloomfield's songs, as well as definitive versions of songs he had got in December; these included *Never Sail No More, Died for Love, On the Banks of Invaree, Edinburgh's Town* (a lyric which fits to the tune *Banks of Sweet Dundee*), *Ever So Poor, Down in the Valley (Lost Lady Found)* (RVW provides two verses only but on a separate sheet in Georgina Heatley's hand appears the full lyric), *A-Nutting We Will Go* (a fairly sexually explicit song with cheeky use of innuendo!), and *The Green Mossy Banks of the Lea* (a beautiful ballad similar in structure to *When First unto this Country* possibly an Appalachian variant). I have recorded versions of both these last two songs on my album *A Bicycle Ride with Vaughan William.*[13]

RVW then revisited Charles Potiphar in Ingrave. This time the atmosphere between collector and singer seemed more relaxed, as the manuscript notes state: "Mr Pottipher (Potiphar) made the following remarks about the origins of folk song – "Whenever there was a murder or anything some one would be sure to make a ballet[14] on it". Asked who made the tunes he said "If you once get the words it's easy to find a tune" "If you can get the words the Almighty sends you a tune". This is still a maxim, for today's singers and songwriters. "Pottipher (Potiphar) said he had invented tunes himself but would not sing me any". Again here Potiphar was displaying a retiscence he had first shown by not wishing to sing at Ingrave Rectory. The songs RVW collected from him included *Spencer the Rover* (a version which closely follows that of the Copper Family from Rottingdean in Sussex – however the song includes a piece of Essex dialect "prittle prattle" (gossip) which would not have been such common parlance in Sussex, evidence perhaps that this song had travelled south), *The Pretty Ploughboy, In Jessie's City* (same tune as Emma Turner's

13. "A Bicycle Ride with Vaughan Williams" Tony Kendall (1995) Stormforce Arts Compact Disc STFC006CD; Chrome Cassette STFC006MC. Available from: ADA Distribution Tel: 01482 868024
14. Old English usage "ballet" for song/ballad.

version), *The Farmer's Daughter*, *The Tarry Sailor*, *With Her Cheeks as Red as Roses (By the Banks of Lovely Nancy)*, and *The Pride of Kildare*.

On 14th April 1904 RVW ventured a little further afield. The fact that Willingale and Fyfield were visited may have had something to do with Mrs Horsnell's family connections. RVW notes "these are songs sung by Mrs Charles White (Fyfield, Essex), Mr Samuel Chiles (research shows this name should be Childs) (Willingale Doe, Essex), and an unknown singer at 'The Bell' public house, Willingale Doe". The building in which "The Bell" operated is now a private residence but the cellar doors and a lovely pargetted inn sign remain to remind us of its former glories. Mrs White sang *The Farmer's Boy* in a slightly different version to the one RVW was aware of in *English County Songs* to which we are invited to refer for the words. She also gave a version of *Banks of Sweet Primroses*, as did Samuel Childs and two unknown singers at The Bell. Mr Child's version is a classic and again follows a Sussex version (Copper Family).[15]

Oh three long steps I step-ped up to her

Ex 4: *Banks of Sweet Primeroses*

Samuel Childs was the parish clerk at Willingale and was 44 years of age when RVW met him. Edna Veal who was Mr Child's daughter was interviewed in March 1979 and said her father worked at Torrell's Farm and she remembers him singing at Christmas when the family met. She said that when he sang *Sweet Primeroses* he would pronounce "stepp-ed" as a two syllable word. Edna Veal's mother's single name was Horsnell. I recently spoke to Samuel Childs' grandson, Cyril Veal, and he was able to guide me to Pound House in Rouse Lane where his grandfather once lived. Mr Childs also sang a version of "*Twas down in the Valley (Lost Lady Found)*"; RVW also had this song from James Bloomfield. Two unnamed singers at

15. *A Song for Every Season* by Bob Copper. Heinemann, 1971.

The Bell sang *The Poachers Song, On Monday Morn* and *How Old are You.* This last song appears to follow the song *Seventeen come Sunday* – RVW was eventually to collect this song also, in Braithwell, Yorkshire in September 1907. The following day (15th April 1904) RVW was again in Ingrave at the home of Mr and Mrs Ratford from whom he collected *The Irish Girl, The Constant Farmer's Son* and *Green Bushes.*

Then on 16th April he went to Little Burstead where Mr Harris gave him *Down in our Village* and *The Spotted Cow* – another double entendre song which I much enjoy singing. He visited Ted Nevill to collect *Three Weeks before Easter* (a version of *No Roses* again found in Sussex), *The Jolly Harin'* (a list song also found in Scotland) and *I'm a Rover*, then from Mr Peacock of Ingrave he got *John Barleycorn* – possibly at lunch.

Just two days later he was back in Ingrave to note down 15-year-old Rob Johnson's version of *The Farmer's Boy* – Rob said he had learnt the song from George Sewell. Then on 19th April 1904, RVW collected a modern day hit – for the band Steeleye Span. This song was a No 1 hit record in the 1970s. He visited Mr Harris of Little Burstead again, who gave him *All Around My Hat* (or *The Willow Green*). RVW states this song was "heard by Mr Harris sung by a clown at Chelmsford Races about 1840." Quite coincidentally I have recently found a tune called "The Chelmsford Races" which dates from around that time.

RVW returned on 21st April 1904 for James Punt's repertoire – one of the largest of the local singers. Mr Punt lived in a cottage which stood on what is now the car park to The Old Dog public house, East Horndon and was related to both John Peacock and James Bloomfield. The songs collected from him were *The Painful Plough, The Thresher and the Nobleman, Bold Turpin Hero, The Streams of Lovely Nancy, The Three Butchers, The Gallant Hussar, The Lost Lady Found* and *I am a Stranger.* On 22nd April 1904 RVW made his third call on James Bloomfield; this time at the Old Dog public house in East Horndon. Here Bloomfield gave him *Silvery Silvery, Van Dieman's Land, The Factory Girl* and *Garden Fields.* James Bloomfield was an accomplished singer and much in demand locally. Also at the Old Dog that day were John Peacock, from whom he got *The Nobleman's Daughter*, and James Punt, *New*

Garden Fields (a version of mine appears on my album[16]), *Newport Street, Courtship, The Fisherman, Admiral Benbow, Long Life to young Jimmy, Jacky Robinson, The Cobbler* (this is precisely the same song as that mentioned in the example of bowlderizing of lyrics but for this earliest collected version RVW refers to the Cecil Sharp Collection of English Folksong Volume 2 for the words), *Died for Love* and *The Sprig of Thyme*, then Tomas Ellis for *The Angel Inn at Manchester*.

A two-day break and the RVW ventured back to Ingrave yet again. Here he met Mrs Humphreys. She originally came from Laindon in Essex but now lived in Ingrave in a house which must has been quite close to that of the Potiphars. As one of Georgina Heatley's notes points out – "I think Mr Pottipher (Potiphar) would ask Mrs Humphreys to come in and then she would sing with the other's aid. After her cold is better perhaps she would ask her sister to come over from Harold Wood and join in." Mrs Humphreys sang *The Golden Clove, Tarry Trousers, The Poacher's Song, Cone Buy Me a Hawk and Hound, I'm a Stranger, Silvery Silvery,* and *Cambric Shirt* (a version of *Scarborough Fair* later a sizeable hit record for Simon and Garfunkel). Mrs Humphreys' repertoire and that of Charles Potiphar overlap in some respects. This became important later on when RVW wanted to commit his singers to wax cylinder. Although the date of the cylinder recordings is not noted down, it is thought to be around 1910 – following Percy Grainger's experience with cylinder recordings in Lincolnshire, especially the sessions with Joseph Taylor who sang *Brigg Fair* for him. It is likely that when RVW returned to Ingrave that he found Mr Potiphar had either passed on or was too ill to sing – Potiphar died in the Summer of 1909. Mrs Humphreys was alive and well and it is believed that it is her voice we hear on the Vaughan Williams cylinder recordings of *Bushes and Briars* and *Tarry Trousers* – these cylinder recordings both appear on my own CD recording along with the singing of an unidentified old man who renders a version of *Banks of the Nile* (the lyrics follow a version of the same song which my grandmother Edith Loomes of Walthamstow would sing at the piano but the tunes are quite different and it is rumoured in the

16. See footnote 13.

family that she may have got the song from a soldier from the Essex Regiment).

On the 25th April 1904 RVW ventured to the Billericay Union (The Workhouse) to note down the songs of John Denny. These songs included *The Indian Lass, Robin Wood (Robin Hood) and Little John, The Smuggler's Boy, The Bonny Blue Handkerchief, The Old Fashioned Farmer, The Farmer's Boy, Lord Bateman, The Shady Green Tree, The Bold Young Farmer*, and the delightful *Little Oyster Girl*. I get great pleasure in singing this last song to my own fiddle accompaniment.

O   I was a-walking   up   a   fair   London   street

Ex 5: *The Oyster Girl*

There were to be further visits to East Horndon and Herongate in October 1904 and February 1906 when 16 more songs were collected. Even so, the rich vein of English traditional song discovered in these Essex villages so close to London was beginning to be worked out. RVW's own prediction that the songs would die with this fragile generation was tellingly true. His own efforts in this short period of a little over two years had saved these marvellous songs for us to enjoy anew and a new national archive could be enhanced by the inclusion of 140 Essex songs.

This was not to be the absolute end to the *Bushes and Briars* story. Georgina Heatley's diary shows in an entry for 14th April 1914, "Good Friday. Mr(Dr) Vaughan Williams came with Mr Morris (his brother-in-law) – tea, on an excursion to hear folk songs"[17] There do not appear to have been any new songs collected on this occasion as no manuscripts survive, but it is just possible that this visit was the one on which the cylinder recordings were made. Ursula Vaughan Williams makes reference to RVW's lack of expertise in dealing with mechanical things and the inclusion of R O Morris (who married Adeline, RVW's wife's sister) in this excursion could

17. Georgina Heatley's diary, Essex Record Office, Chelmsford.

have been to help operate the wax cylinder machine. I have also spoken to Ursula Vaughan Williams about any photographs of RVW with the Essex singers and unfortunately there are none. Unlike Cecil Sharp, RVW was not machine-orientated

That these beautiful rustic songs affected Vaughan Williams's work so deeply is a matter of history, but the fact that this last visit to Essex took place so close to the start of the Great War, is an event of some poignancy given the lasting effect that the brutality of war would have on him.

In the year 2003 it will be the centenary of RVW's first bicycle ride into Ingrave to collect songs from the old people, an occasion which deserves a fitting celebration.

As   I   walked out one   fine summer's morning

Ex 6: *Tarry Trousers*

". . . The collector of folk songs gives them back again to the world . . . will they not once more make their way back to the mouths of the people?"

Ralph Vaughan Williams[18]

18. Kennedy, op cit p 74

IV

Andrew Herbert

Unfinished Business:
the evolution of the "Solent" theme

I N THE FIRST YEARS OF THE CENTURY VAUGHAN WILLIAMS
embarked upon an orchestral piece entitled *The Solent*.[1] It
was performed, probably privately, in June 1903. The
composer showed it no great fondness and it was neither
played again nor published. Nevertheless, it provided material
for three major works. Michael Kennedy wrote: "It contains a
theme which haunted Vaughan Williams all his life, appearing
in various guises in *A Sea Symphony*, the Ninth Symphony and
in some late film music ... What special spiritual significance,
one wonders, did this melodic phrase have for its creator?"[2]
This paper, following a musical trail spanning more than fifty
years, is an attempt to address Kennedy's query.

The Solent opens with the theme in question (the "Solent"
theme), first stated by a solo clarinet.

[clarinet solo]

ppp *molto legato*

Ex. 1: *The Solent*

1. British Library Add Ms 57278.
2. M Kennedy: *The Works of Ralph Vaughan Williams*. Oxford University
    Press, pp 83 & 367.

This is the piece's basic building block. The predominant pitch is E, the other pitches being F sharp, G, A, B, D; the sixth scale degree, C, is omitted. This allows the theme tonal ambiguity and provides added potential for subsequent harmonic reinterpretation. After the first announcement the theme is repeated by divided strings. It is harmonised in the aeolian mode but with a distinct E minor flavour; the cadential *tierce de picardie* further emphasises this:

Ex 2

A second phrase is treated in an identical manner, stated first by solo clarinet and then harmonised by muted strings:

Ex 3

However, unlike its counterpart, it has no part to play in the main body of the piece and only reappears in the closing bars.

The meditative atmosphere is interrupted by a second, somewhat more active, theme. Stated tutti, it uses aggressive double-dotted rhythms and emphatically diatonic harmonies:

Ex 4

A third theme follows, comprising two elements in aeolian

mode. At some point after the piece's completion (possibly during rehearsals) four bars were crossed out in blue pencil, effectively joining the two phrases into one:

Ex 5

Vaughan Williams then uses these, together with the "Solent" theme, as the basis for a developmental passage. For the most part each phrase is treated as a separate and unvaried entity; they do not inspire further melodic invention. Instead, the music is subject to a continually shifting harmonic backdrop, which swings without ceremony between modal, diatonic and chromatic idioms. The effect is one of ever-swirling currents as the music rises and falls, one moment on the crest of a wave, the next deep in a trough. However, this method of construction is problematic. Its short, choppy nature, whilst analogous with the movement of the sea, does not make for a cohesive whole. The music builds gradually to a climax but then falls away very suddenly:

Ex 6

This is immediately succeeded by the "Solent" theme stated by solo horn. It is accompanied by muted violins *divisi à 3*. Each part descends chromatically at a different pace, obscuring any real sense of a tonal centre:

Ex 7

As the passage continues the chromatic descent is abruptly anchored by diatonic harmony previously associated with the second theme:

Ex 8

The final section, fifty-two bars in length, is the longest homogeneous passage in the piece. It is based upon contrapuntal working both of the "Solent" theme and its complementary phrase, not heard since the opening. The harmony hovers, almost humorously, between G major and C major. The 'Solent' theme is harmonised in mixolydian inflected G major (F sharp altered to F natural), whilst the second phrase is harmonised by lydian inflected C major (F natural altered to F sharp):

Ex 9a

Ex 9b

The music fades away gradually until only the solo clarinet remains. The piece ends inconclusively with dyads in the lower strings:

Ex 10

Without orchestral performance the overall impression of *The Solent* is difficult to gauge: so much of Vaughan Williams's output looks dubious on the page but sounds convincing. The opening and closing passages bring to mind music written for later works, particularly the Fifth Symphony. Yet the diatonically driven second subject belongs to a markedly different, more Brahmsian, sound-world. It seems unlikely that these differing moods could gel within the slight framework of the piece.

The relationship between the music and its title is also difficult to gauge. There is, however, an inscription in the composer's handwriting at the top of the score:

> Passion and sorrow in the deep sea's voice,
> A mighty mystery saddening all the wind.

At first glance this seems to be an unproblematic reference to the sea; it is depicted in human terms, compassionate but darkly ominous. There is something of these words in the music, particularly in the modal first theme, which seems to evoke the mystical powers and age of the sea. However, as one

of the calmest stretches of ocean, The Solent does not seem
particularly pertinent.

The lines are by a little-known nineteenth-century poet,
Philip Marston. They are from a long poem, "To Cicely
Narney Marston", in which Marston remembers childhood
with his sister.[3] Vaughan Williams's epigraph was extracted
from a somewhat unexpected context:

> Ah, precious days we knew not how to prize!
> If they were slighted then, 't is now their turn
> To slight, and look with sad, reproachful eyes,
> And whisper with white lips: 'In vain you yearn;
> You longed for other days, and they are come.
> Now you look back ...
> Did we not share our sorrows and our joys
> In later years, when we awoke, to find
> Passion and sorrow in the deep sea's voice,
> A mighty mystery saddening all the wind'?

This rather changes the import of the epigraph. The
apparently uncomplicated reference to the sea becomes part of
a much more complex reminiscence. Whether or not Vaughan
Williams was thinking of such things when he composed the
music, it is difficult to believe that the implications of the poem
were not the subject of unconscious reference.

It is worth remembering that Vaughan Williams was dealing
with a subject of some pyschological significance. The Solent is
close to Leith Hill, the house in which he was brought up.
Traditionally, these quiet waters provided ideal riding-grounds
for ships, and both the Royal Navy and commercial ocean
liners made heavy use. Vaughan Williams, looking for
substance upon which to base his musical exploration, seized
on subject matter associated with home-coming, security but
also imperial expansion. When coupled with the sense of
regret which permeates the unused verses of Marston's poem,
this presents a potent pyschological mix.

In any case, technically *The Solent* represents a microcosm of
the composer's most pressing dilemma: how to create and
employ a satisfactorily individual harmonic language.

3. L C Moulton: *The Collected Poems of Philip Bourke Marston.* Ward & Locke,
    1892, pp 191–196.

Although drawn towards modal harmonies, he appears uncertain how, or perhaps whether, to incorporate them within diatonic musical language. Whilst at times such indecision inhibits this music, he must have recognised a degree of potential because he returned to it when sketching *A Sea Symphony*.

In 1903, the year in which *The Solent* was performed, Vaughan Williams began work on a setting of Walt Whitman's poetry. It began modestly enough as 'Notes for choral work Songs of the Sea.' For six years he sketched and re-sketched the work, slowly forging the composition which was to become *A Sea Symphony*. During this process huge chunks of music and text were discarded, most notably an entire movement complete in vocal score. Vaughan Williams retained a large number of manuscript books which bear witness to a prolonged and frustrating battle with his musical material.[4]

Naturally enough, Whitman's charged poetry was the primary stimulus. The long and metrically irregular lines, the demanding but evocative vocabulary, and above all, the sheer unrestrained exhilaration clearly acted as a liberatory force. However, the seeds of at least some of this music are found elsewhere.

By 1906 Vaughan Williams had drafted five movements for the symphony. Four of these were to be used in the final version. The additional movement, entitled *The Steersman*, was interpolated between the last two movements. It was completed in vocal score on the 17th August 1906 but subsequently rejected. Red pencil markings on the manuscript British Library Add. Ms. 50362G imply at least one trial run-through'. Essentially a song for baritone soloist, it can be performed in under ten minutes, but nevertheless would have brought *A Sea Symphony* to approximately seventy-five minutes in total.

The Steersman uses text from *Aboard at a Ship's Helm*. Although predominantly descriptive, the poem ends with lines of affirmation which, according to Michael Kennedy, 'must have been those which attracted Vaughan Williams's attention.'[5]

4. British Library Add. Ms. 50361–50366.
5. M Kennedy: *The Works of Ralph Vaughan Williams*. Oxford University Press, 1964, p 445.

Aboard at a ship's helm,
A young steersman steering with care.

Through fog on a sea-coast dolefully ringing,
An ocean-bell – O a warning bell, rock'd by the waves.

O you give good notice indeed, the bell by the sea-reefs
ringing,
Ringing, ringing, to warn the ship from its wreck-place.

But as on the alert O steersman, you mind the loud
admonition,
The bows turn, the freighted ship tacking speeds away
under her gray sails,
The beautiful noble ship with all her precious wealth
speeds away gayly and safe.

But O the ship, the immortal ship! O ship aboard the ship!
Ship of the body, ship of the soul, voyaging, voyaging, voyaging.

Vaughan Williams adheres to Whitman's verse structure, articulating each verse with an instrumental bridge passage:

introduction	1–19	(piano)
verse 1	20–30	(baritone)
bridge 1	31–35	
verse 2	36–49	
bridge 2	47–52	(overlapping)
verse 3	53–64	
bridge 3	65–69	
verse 4	70–96	
bridge 4	97–126	
verse 5	127–164	(baritone plus female chorus)

The principal theme (6–19) is now familiar. Once again beginning as a solo line, the "Solent" theme bobs up. Although not used in the vocal part, variants recur in each bridge passage, glueing the movement together. Yet the surrounding harmonic landscape is markedly different to that of *The Solent*. This is immediately demonstrated by the opening chord progression. By using diatonic triads in a non-diatonic context Vaughan Williams opens up a sound world more akin to Debussy than Parry or Stanford. The theme's basic four-bar unit (6–10) is used as the basis for a continuation (10–20). This is accompanied by chords derived from the opening, but the F sharp major triad has already been corrupted: the C sharp is raised to D sharp. The technique of altering or adding pitches to diatonic triads and then treating them in a non-functional manner becomes the principal method of harmonic construction. In order to counter potential tonal insecurity Vaughan Williams makes copious use of pedals: witness the held B which underpins the first three verses.

Of the verses, the first is recitative-like and unassuming. The baritone assumes the pose of narrator, whilst an atmospheric accompaniment sets the scene. Building on the harmonic technique of the introduction, the second verse is characterised by repeated corrupted chords. The all-enveloping fog is depicted by the disjointed rhythm of these chords, whilst the baritone part is now rather more mournfully lyrical. The third verse is set in quasi modal B minor which bears strong resemblance to the language of *The Solent*. However, it is the fourth verse which stands out. With the ship's escape from danger the music soars into diatonic rhapsody, using a decidedly Ravellian tune. As the jubilation gradually recedes, the harmony returns to its initial state and the ship, recovering equilibrium, disappears toward the horizon much as it arrived. This final verse is augmented by the introduction of female chorus, hymning the ship on its way.

The orchestral bridges develop the principal theme as indicated:

Ex 11

In bridge 1 the theme is harmonised by chromatically descending triads moving from A flat minor to E major. The theme itself is altered, allowing the triplet rhythm increased prominence. In bridge 2 this triplet, used in inversion, becomes the primary melodic element. It is the shortest bridge, and the least obviously related to the principal theme. The harmony oscillates between two chords: G sharp minor and diminished G sharp minor. The syncopated rhythm of this accompaniment serves further to emphasise the melodic triplet figure. Bridge 3 is lifted directly from *The Solent* (see Ex 7). The theme remains constant, but chromatic movement completely destabilizes any sense of diatonic security. Consequently, the theme and its harmony now seem to inhabit different tonal worlds.

In contrast, bridge 4 begins in unclouded C major. However, this diatonicism is gradually supplanted and when the warning bell peals (116–125) the harmony has reverted to the original non-functional idiom. A portion of this was re-used in *The Explorers (L⁻⁹)*:

Ex 12: *A Sea Symphony* – fourth movement

The Steersman is something of a departure from the style of previous Whitman settings by English composers. Vaughan Williams's contemporaries were little more adventurous than their teachers: men from both generations (Stanford, Charles Wood, Coleridge-Taylor and Holst) all rooted their settings in diatonicism. The only exception is Cyril Scott, whose song, *Lilac-time* bears some resemblance to *The Steersman*. He uses a similar technique of anchoring non-functional chord progressions with pedals, witness the opening:

Ex 13 Cyril Scott: *Lilac-time*

However this was written in 1914, well after *The Steersman*. Even Scott when setting *My Captain* in 1904 kept to a more traditional harmonic idiom.

The harmonic language of *The Steersman* is more progressive than that of the other movements of *A Sea Symphony*. Probably this was the main reason that it was dropped. However, there are other problems. Although in many ways a substantial advance on *The Solent*, it still suffers from a similar harmonic dilemma. Having replaced modal inflections with a more pungent mix of non-functional triads, the climax of *The Steersman* then retreats into diatonic language. This may indicate that the composer, at the crucial point, was unable to sustain the harmonic world he had set up; unlike his ship, he was not yet free from prevailing danger.

Nevertheless, the "Solent" theme is invigorated by the fresh environment. It is now explicitly programmatic and deals with the passage of the ship. The symbolism behind this is revealed in the final line, "Ship of the body, ship of the *soul* voyaging, voyaging, voyaging." This is the real preoccupation of Whitman's poem: the exploration of the human self, the voyage toward self-discovery. These transcendental trappings reach a safer port of call in *The Explorers* where the 'Solent' theme once again occurs, not only at the point already noted (see Ex 12) but also immediately preceding the first movement's second subject. The significance is rather disturbing. In *The Explorers* the "Solent" theme appears at the culmination of Whitman's eulogy to the artist:

> After the seas are all crossed,
> After the great captains have accomplished their work,
> After the noble inventors,

> Finally shall come the poet worthy that name,
> The true son of God shall come singing his songs.

In *The Solent* it is connected with ideas of safety and childhood. In *The Steersman* it is connected with journeys of self-exploration. In *The Explorers* Vaughan Williams went one step further and explicitly connected the theme with a declaration of the artist as saviour. By using the "Solent" theme at this point, the composer makes Whitman's eulogy potentially self-referential. Whilst perhaps closer to a Freudian slip than any conscious declaration, the drawing together of Whitman's singer and Vaughan Williams's singing is thought-provoking.

The story of the voyage of the 'Solent' theme then skips almost half a century. In 1950 the historian A L Rowse wrote, 'The Elizabethan Age is not something dead and apart from us; it is alive and all round us and within us.' His book, *The England of Elizabeth*, was designed not only as a historical text but as a political statement. History was pressed into the service of the present, acting both as reassurance and an inspiration. To this end, the recently concluded Second World War was compared directly with the threat posed by the Spanish Armada:

The English people in our time have been through a crisis of their fate to which the nearest parallel is that they passed through in the Elizabethan Age. Only ours was a nearer thing and even more depended on it.[6]

Five years later the British Transport Commission, acting on rather different motives, produced a film, also entitled *The England of Elizabeth*. Rowse acted as the historical advisor, but the war was ten years past and now the aim was to encourage visitors to England's shores. Vaughan Williams provided the music for the film, and chose to include material which had long lain dormant: the 'Solent' theme.[7] It is used most prominently to highlight the bustle of the River Thames, London's artery, as the narrator solemnly intones:

London streets and the Thames highway were a seething hotchpotch in which the beautiful and the barbaric bubbled together: perfumes from the east and the stench of sewage, old St Paul's and the singing of boys sweet voices and the plague each summer, the tower with its headsman and his

6. A L Rowse: *The England of Elizabeth*. Macmillan, 1950, 1962, p 1
7. British Library Add Ms 60392.

sharp axe, high up on London tower the heads of the traitors, the gulls flying round them, the bear-pit, the bawdy house and the theatre with its poetry. What a time to be born.

The theme is carried by low brass and accompanied only by a G pedal.

Ex 14 *England of Elizabeth*

The manuscript score indicates that the theme was also originally intended to accompany footage of Tintern Abbey and King's College, Cambridge, but the confusion of the film studio's cutting-room floor ensured otherwise. The 'Tintern' extract is similar to the opening of *The Steersman*, except the harmonic progression is modified. The shift of a major third is retained but the move from F major to D minor is replaced by D minor to B flat minor.

Ex 15 *England of Elizabeth*

Although the triplet motive developed in *The Steersman* is again used here, the "King's College" extract bears more resemblance to the closing sections of *The Solent* (see ex 9).

Ex 16 *England of Elizabeth*

Three years later the "Solent" theme was finally included in a published score. It opens the second movement of the Ninth Symphony, once more as a solo line.

Ex 17 *Ninth Symphony*

Yet now the theme is coupled with an unexpected programme. Alain Frogley's work on the sketch material indicates that Vaughan Williams was greatly influenced by Thomas Hardy's *Tess of the D'Urbervilles* when writing the symphony. In some passages the plot of the novel and the atmosphere of the music seem to correspond event by event. Although these programmatic associations were later deliberately obscured, the sketches imply that the 'Solent' theme was initially associated with Stonehenge.

There are a number of possible reasons for this connection. Firstly, Stonehenge is surely one of England's best known mysteries. The elemental, magical atmosphere of the site itself is complimented by the apparent impossibility of its construction. The 'Solent' theme previously suggested various forms of incomprehensible mystical power – the sea in *The Solent* and *A Sea Symphony*, the River Thames in *The England of Elizabeth* – and here it suggests another.

Secondly, Thomas Hardy seems to have brought forth in Vaughan Williams a response derived from the past, from his years of learning. Perhaps with Tess's naiveté, lay Vaughan Williams's own. The "innocent" 'Solent' theme is juxtaposed first with a barbaric march and then with a romantic tune. At times it develops the characteristics of the other themes, and seems in danger of losing its identity. However, the storm is weathered and the movement closes with an uncorrupted version of the "Solent" theme. Is it possible that this symbolises life's dangers during formative years, remembered by the composer in the twilight of his life? The striving to fulfil the potential offered by the theme was an important element in his development of compositional technique. Could the use of the theme in the Ninth Symphony have been a symbol of gratitude, or perhaps even of conquest?

Although tempting, probably it is foolish to try and convert music into personal narrative quite so readily; in order to construe any serious reading of this type, it would be necessary to examine the movement in greater depth than is possible here. Yet the fact remains: the "Solent" theme was used as a springboard for experimentation in this early work, and in one of his final and most mature compositions. Vaughan Williams frequently thought in terms of symbolic musical motifs and the issues raised are not simple. Having worked through some of the pyschological possibilities in the re-use of the "Solent" theme, it has become apparent that a great deal more untangling is necessary. The composer's feelings regarding his childhood and social relationships, as well as many other issues, are either left undiscussed or, at best, broached tentatively. However, for now it is enough to conclude that in the 'Solent' theme Vaughan Williams found a fundamental resonance.

The Steersman music score

An exact transcript of Vaughan Williams's manuscript.

The Steersman is reproduced by kind permission of Ursula Vaughan Williams. It is not for performance or further reproduction without permission, © Ursula Vaughan Williams, 1998.

V

Stephen Lloyd

Vaughan Williams's A London Symphony
the original version
and early performances and recordings [1]

———◦◦◦◦———

IT IS PERHAPS RATHER STRANGE THAT THE ONE SYMPHONY out of Vaughan Williams's canon of nine which has generally proved to be the most popular, *A London Symphony*, (which is also said to have been Vaughan Williams's own favourite) is the one to have caused him the most trouble in revisions and rewritings.

To begin at the beginning, we need to go to the immediate years before the First World War when there were two notable series of concerts in London that owed their existence to private patronage. The first of these was the *Balfour Gardiner Concerts* in 1912 and 1913, chiefly of British works, that introduced four Vaughan Williams works to London: the Second and Third *Norfolk Rhapsodies*, the *Tallis Fantasia*, and the *Fantasia on Christmas Carols* (the first two of these works being conducted by Balfour Gardiner and the last two by VW himself). The other notable series of concerts was *Bevis Ellis's Concerts of Modern Orchestral Music*, at which on 27 March 1914 the premiere of *A London Symphony* was the high spot. Geoffrey

---

1. An expansion of an article written for the Spring 1996 edition of *International Classical Record Collector*, 'Vaughan Williams: A London Symphony – the first recordings'.

Toye, who was making his first appearance as a symphony conductor, conducted the Queen's Hall Orchestra in what George Butterworth described as a 'magnificent performance ..., perhaps as good a first performance as it would be possible to obtain'. The work was later dedicated 'To the memory of George Butterworth' who had in part been responsible for its genesis. As Vaughan Williams wrote in *A Musical Autobiography*[2]:

We were talking together one day when he said in his gruff, abrupt manner: 'You know, you ought to write a symphony.' I answered, if I remember aright, that I had never written a symphony and never intended to. This was not strictly true, for I had in earlier years sketched three movements of one symphony and the first movement of another, all now happily lost.[3] I suppose that Butterworth's words stung me and, anyhow, I looked out some sketches I had made for what I believe was going to have been a symphonic poem about London and decided to throw it into symphonic form.

In a letter to George Butterworth's father, he also wrote:

From that moment, the idea of a symphony dominated my mind. I showed the sketches to George bit by bit as they were finished, and it was then that I realised that he possessed in common with very few composers a wonderful power of criticism of other men's work and insight into their ideas and motives. I can never feel too grateful to him for all he did for me over this work and his help didn't stop short at criticism.

The work was completed towards the end of 1913, but it seems that even before its premiere RVW was not entirely satisfied with its final shape and length. His doubts may have been fuelled by friends' comments. As he wrote in the George Butterworth memorial volume[4]:

When Ellis suggested that my Symphony should be produced at one of his concerts, I was away from home and unable to revise the score myself, and George, together with Ellis and Francis Toye [brother of Geoffrey], undertook to revise it and make a 'short score'[5] from the original – George

---

2. In R Vaughan Williams, *National Music and other Essays*, OUP 1963, p 193.
3. There was, of course, also the *Sea Symphony*, but RVW had written to the critic Herbert Thompson that he used the word 'Symphony' because the treatment of the words was symphonic rather than dramatic.
4. *George Butterworth 1885–1916*, privately printed 1918, p 93.
5. In the British Library.

himself undertook the last movement. There was a passage which troubled him very much, but I could never get him to say exactly what was wrong with it; all he would say was 'It won't do at all'. After the performance he at once wrote to tell me he had changed his mind.

Butterworth's much valued advice was 'not to alter a note of the symphony until after its second performance'. Elsewhere, in an article in the *Royal College of Music Magazine*,[6] he had written of the last and longest of the four movements as being the least satisfactory:

not that there is any falling off in the interest, but, as in the last movement of the "Sea" Symphony, there is a feeling that the composer is straining himself to express just a little too much; in this case, however, the flaw is a much slighter one, and may easily prove to be illusory when the work is heard a second time.

There was, of course, much encouragement from friends, particularly from Gustav Holst who wrote characteristically to VW after that first performance:

You have really done it this time. Not only have you reached the heights but you have taken your audience with you. Also you have proved the musical superiority of England to France. I wonder if you realised how futile and tawdry Ravel sounded after your Epilogue. [The *Valses Nobles et Sentimentales* was the last-but-one item in the programme.] As a consequence of last Friday I am starting an anti-Gallic League the motto of which shall be 'Poetry not Pedantry'. More when we meet!

Probably the most favourable review was that in *The Daily Telegraph*[7] whose critic, Robin Legge, was a strong supporter of British music. He called the symphony

not only the most masterly, but also the most beautiful work, musically or psychologically considered, from the pen of any musician of his generation. True, it is very long; it occupies some fifty-five minutes in performance, and there are spots on the sun here and there, as if the 'thought' were becoming a little involved and getting a trifle out of hand. But nevertheless, we should be loth to suggest where, if anywhere, cuts should be made. If they are possible, the composer will know what to do. In any case, spots or no spots, the symphony is of quite extraordinary beauty.

This mention of cuts may have sown further doubts in VW's

6. *The RCM Magazine*, Vol 10 No 2 Easter Term 1914, p 144–6.
7. *Daily Telegraph*, 30 March 1914.

mind. But in fact three further performances and a misfortune occurred before any revisions were made.

The second performance of *A London Symphony* was in Harrogate, with Julian Clifford conducting the Harrogate Municipal Orchestra on 12 August 1914[8], just over a week after the outbreak of war and shortly before Vaughan Williams had volunteered his services, initially in the Special Constabulary. The critic Herbert Thompson who attended the performance, besides noting the timings of the movements, wrote in his diary: 'Sym. has poetic charm, but wants relief, too uniformly dark and strenuous.'[9]

This performance has not, to my knowledge, been identified before, and it was unfortunate for me that when my book on Dan Godfrey[10] was published last year I took, as many others have done, Dan Godfrey's later Bournemouth performance to be the work's second. With the help of two friends I was able to pin down this Harrogate performance. Although some of the advertisements suggested that VW was going to conduct the Symphony, and even after the event *The Musical Times* incorrectly stated that he conducted it, other reviews make it perfectly clear that Clifford conducted the Symphony while VW was present to conduct the *Wasps* Suite.[11] All that the critic for the *Harrogate Visitor* could write was that 'an artistic reading of the symphony inspired the orchestra to a very fine rendering' and showed 'the composer [to be] in the vanguard of the modern school of musical illustrators'.

Now, this performance raises an interesting question. The score is said to have been sent at some stage to Fritz Busch in Germany, probably in hope of another performance (other versions have it that it was sent to Germany for engraving), but then it was lost. As there was only one full score, one may fairly assume that Clifford used it for the Harrogate performance. But with England one week into war with

8. *Harrogate Advertiser and List of Visitors,* 15 August 1914, p .7
9. The diaries are in the Brotherton Library, University of Leeds.
10. *Sir Dan Godfrey: Champion of British Composers,* Thames Publishing 1995.
11. *The Musical Times,* October 1914, 626, incorrectly states that Vaughan Williams conducted the symphony, although in the same concert he did conduct his Aristophanic Suite, *The Wasps.* The author is indebted to Tony Benson, Lewis Foreman and Elizabeth Kershaw for their help in identifying this performance.

Germany, it would surely not have been sent there either for a performance or for engraving. Some writers say it was sent in July. If so, what score did Clifford use? This is a mystery yet to be solved.

Nevertheless, the score *was*, it seems, *lost*. So some friends set about reconstructing the full score[12] from the surviving band parts. These friends have generally been named as Geoffrey Toye, George Butterworth and Edward Dent, but the catalogue for the British Museum's VW Centenary Exhibition in 1972 stated that Butterworth's hand has not been traced in the reconstructed full score, so it may have been just Toye and Dent.[13] Anyway, the first performance of this reconstructed score was another provincial one, given at Bournemouth on 11 February 1915 by the enterprising Dan Godfrey and his Municipal Orchestra. Dan Godfrey was a great champion of British composers, especially young ones at the outset of their careers. He had given Holst a first (and to date its only complete) performance of his *Cotswold Symphony* – which VW attended, and Godfrey had already given over ten years earlier the premieres of Vaughan Williams's early *Serenade*, his *Symphony Rhapsody* and his *Bucolic Suite*.

By the time of the Bournemouth performance, of course, Butterworth had enlisted. In fact, by September 1914 he, Bevis Ellis, Geoffrey Toye and Reginald Morris (soon to be Vaughan Williams's brother-in-law) had all enlisted in the Duke of Cornwall's Light Infantry[14,] transferring in November to the 13th Durham Light Infantry. In the first half of 1915 they moved to France, and in August 1916 Butterworth was killed, followed in September by the death of Ellis. After Butterworth's death, the published score of the *London Symphony* was inscribed to his memory. But publication was

12. The reconstructed full score was given by Vaughan Williams to Sir Adrian Boult who has written in his autobiography, *My Own Trumpet*, that it was 'bound in such a way that one can see the processes of revision very clearly'. It is now in the British Library.
13. During my four visits to the British Library manuscript department while researching for this talk, I was not able to check the handwriting. However, armed with suitable samples of handwriting, it should not be difficult to verify who was responsible for which movement.
14. At this early stage of the war, it was permissible for friends to enlist in the same regiment.

four years ahead, and that only came about through the intervention once again of private patronage.

In 1916, under the auspices of the Carnegie United Kingdom Trust, set up in 1913 through the generosity of the Scottish philanthropist Andrew Carnegie (1835–1919), a scheme for the publication of British music was announced, and works were invited for consideration. 136 scores were received and early in 1917 *A London Symphony* was among the first batch of works to be selected for publication. It shared honours with Edgar Bainton's choral symphony *Before Sunrise*, Granville Bantock's *Hebridean Symphony*, Rutland Boughton's opera *The Immortal Hour*, Frank Bridge's *The Sea*, Sir Charles Stanford's opera *The Travelling Companion*, and Herbert Howells' Piano Quartet. RVW's symphony was judged to be 'a work which made a great impression at its first performance in 1914, and which in itself would be sufficient to stamp as memorable the standard of awards for this year'.

At the time of the Trust's announcement, RVW was on wartime service with the Royal Armoured Military Corps in Salonika (oddly enough the same region where over a year later his friend Holst was to be sent). On 9 April 1917, in her husband's absence, Adeline Vaughan Williams acknowledged receipt of the award, adding: 'I am sure that he will feel much gratified at the honour which the Carnegie United Kingdom Trustees have done him in deciding to publish his work.' But on his return home RVW was quick to write to the Trust, on 25 July:

I have just returned from abroad and have received your kind letter with regards to my 'London Symphony'. Owing to absence from home I was unable to revise the score before I sent it in. It is absolutely essential that it should be thoroughly revised before printing and, owing to my military duties I see no chance of being able to do this during the war. In these circumstances would you still wish me to send the score to Messrs Stainer and Bell and to sign the agreement?

Publication was delayed and it was three years before the score appeared in print with substantial revisions. There was also a gap following the 1915 Bournemouth performance.

In October 1916 Arthur Bliss, writing to the *Pall Mall Gazette*, was concerned at the programming of German works by such orchestras as the London Symphony, and, urging that national feelings should prevail over orchestras' financial security, he recommended a performance in London of VW's symphony as not being 'altogether unfitting at this time'. But his suggestion was not taken up, at least for a while.

The next development was that on 18 February 1918 the up-and-coming Adrian Boult put *A London Symphony*, still uncut, in the second of four Queen's Hall concerts he gave with the London Symphony Orchestra. When, because of an air-raid (not actually a Zeppelin raid, as has been stated in one or two places), the audience at that second concert hardly out-numbered the orchestra, the symphony was repeated 'by desire' exactly a month later at the last concert. (Much later, Boult told how, because on the night of that air-raid they were not allowed to go home straight away, they had a 'jolly party in the Queen's Hall cellar'. One has visions of mugs of Horlicks!)

A week after the first of those two performances, VW wrote to Boult from the Hampshire barracks where he was then posted:

Dear Boult,

In all the hurry of Monday I never had an opportunity of thanking you

(1) for doing my symph.

(2) for giving such a fine performance – it really was splendid[.] you had got the score right into you & through you into your orch.

May I say how much I admired your conducting – it is real conducting – you get just what you want & know what you want – & your players trust you because they know it also – I heard many expressions of admiration from both audience and performers (Von Holst & A Hobday [Alfred Hobday, LSO violist] among others) – of course you are an experienced conductor by now & your power is well known to many – but to we who have been out of music for 3 years it was new – Good luck to you – I look for great things in the future when such musical ability & such public spirit go hand in hand.

When it came to the repeat performance a month later, VW wrote to Boult, this time from Leith Hill:

Dear Boult,

Thank you very much for your letter. I shd. be proud for any part of the L[ondon].S[ymphony]. to be done again by you – but you certainly mustn't

cut about your programme for it – especially not the 'Shropshire Lad' which
ought to be heard everywhere as often as possible. I agree with you that the
last movement & possibly the scherzo of my symph. are too long – but it is
re-writing they want – I do not think that mechanical cutting – however
skilfully done wd. be satisfactory.

Why not do the 1st movement only? It stands fairly well by itself. I fear I
shall be far away on March 18th – as I am down for overseas – may leave
any day now.

> Ys vy sincerely
> R Vaughan Williams

In fact the *London Symphony* replaced Brahms' Second
Symphony, and Butterworth's *A Shropshire Lad* appropriately
stayed in the programme.

Of the earlier of Boult's two performances, *The Musical Times*
critic wrote that 'in places it broods too much and seems over
long – it took about an hour to perform.' (At its premiere both
The Musical Times and *Musical Opinion* stated that it took about
fifty minutes to play, compared with Robin Legge's estimate of
55 minutes, showing how unreliable such timings can be.) For
Boult's repeat performance *The Musical Times* reported that
'some cuts were made, and the performance was a very fine
one.' Boult was then working for the War Office, promoting a
'war-time standard boot to suit all pockets',[15] and he took the
reconstructed full score of the symphony and eighteen sample
boots with him as he toured the West Country. In a memorial
tribute[16] he remembered how RVW 'came to my room in a
distant outcrop of the War Office and sat among the samples
of boots, which then occupied most of my time, and made
some cuts in the score of the *London Symphony*, ready for its
third [London] performance. Many of us regretted the cuts at
that time, but we now see that he was right.'

The symphony was well received by the musical press,
although many baulked at an apparent piece of programme
music without a clearly defined programme. But it interested
another conductor who had not been able to attend those two
performances. Henry Wood wrote to Boult about the score on
29 July 1918 'to see how much rehearsal it will require in

15. Adrian Cedric Boult: *My Own Trumpet*, Hamish Hamilton 1973, p 35.
16. *The Musical Times*, October 1958, p 536.

London & the provinces ...', adding: 'P.S. Do let me have the cuts.'[17]

Making cuts seems to have been an ongoing process as on 11 August 1919 VW was writing to Boult again, this time from Sheringham:

Dear Boult,
Can you tell me who has the parts of the L. Symph –
Are they at Cheyne Walk – or have you got them?
I have now revised the score and I want to put the corrections into the parts.If you have the parts wd. you mind sending me I copy each of the string parts (preferably 1st desk) & the wind etc. parts to above address. I [felt] sure Stainer & Bell had the parts but I find they have not.

Answering an enquiry about the changes, Boult very much later wrote:

... He slashed the work at least three times to my knowledge.

There are a number of cuts in the Slow Movement which could be seen because the original Carnegie publication of the Score and the Miniature were subjected to these cuts which necessitated altered plates and a fresh edition.

My memory of the first slashing between my two concerts in 1918 was of a third subject which he cut clean out as well as any references to it in the subsequent Movement because he said it was like a bad hymn tune. There was also a cut in the epilogue.

Finally the First Score of the work, which is not in his handwriting, but was pieced together by several of his friends from the Parts after the Score was lost in Germany in 1914, was given to me and subsequently photographed by Mrs Vaughan Williams. I have passed it on to the British Museum, where it can be seen, and my copy is in the Royal College of Music Parry Library. He told me when he had the Score rebound to give to me that he had left the original pages as they stood, in 1918 so that any students could see all the cuts. This is not as easy as it sounds when his writing is concerned ...

As we shall see, that 'bad hymn tune' that Boult mentioned actually occurred in the last movement, not the second. Boult seems oddly inaccurate at times as in a 1965 talk he described the slow movement as 'nowhere rising above forte'. More interestingly, in that same BBC interval talk in 1965 Boult remarked that 'we always hear the *London Symphony* in its

17. Letter dated 29 July 1918, in Arthur Jacobs: *Henry J Wood, Maker of the Proms*, Methuen 1994, p 162.

revised version today, although some day I hope the BBC will allow me to do a performance of it in its original form, which takes about seven or eight minutes longer – perhaps a little too long for modern taste.' Sadly, his hope was never granted.

But it was the performance under Albert Coates on 4 May 1920 at Queen's Hall that really established the symphony, by which time RVW had made further cuts and in this form it was eventually published, in same year, by Stainer & Bell as part of the Carnegie Collection of British Music. As we shall shortly see, since its premiere the original score had undergone major surgery by 'Dr' Vaughan Williams in all movements except the first which had remained unchanged. Boult continued to champion the symphony and further revisions were made before a Royal Philharmonic Society performance under Beecham on 22 February 1934. The work had by then taken its final form, and this '1933 version', the one used today, was published by Stainer & Bell, probably in 1936, and marked 'Revised Edition'.

In the meantime the symphony had found another champion. Not long after giving its third performance, Sir Dan Godfrey at Bournemouth was programming it every season with his Municipal Orchestra, in some seasons more than once, so that by the time of his retirement in 1934 he could justifiably claim that it had been performed by them 'more frequently than by any other orchestra'. After hearing it at the 1923 Bournemouth Easter Musical Festival *The Times* critic remarked that he had enjoyed Godfrey's performance 'very much more than the one which the composer conducted lately at the Queen's Hall'. At the 1924 Bournemouth Easter Festival Sir Dan conducted the first and third movements only, and it was these two movements that he had recorded for Columbia the previous July with the London Symphony Orchestra on two 78s, the work's first recording.

This acoustic pair, or at least the first movement, was the subject of a detailed analysis by Percy Scholes in the November 1924 issue of *The Gramophone*, reprinted in *The Second Book of the Gramophone Record* (OUP 1925). The first movement had been heavily abridged to fit on to two sides of a 78 rpm record. Despite these cuts – a common practice in many early (and some not so early) 78s – and the restricted sound, the recording gave a fair representation of the first movement while the scherzo was played complete, including the opening repeat section. But it was a piecemeal offering, and in a letter in the July 1925 *Gramophone* a Mr F V Schuster was asking for the work to be recorded complete, adding that 'this should be conducted by Dr Adrian Boult or Dr Malcolm Sargent'. And indeed very soon a complete recording did appear. Again it was conducted by Sir Dan Godfrey whose interpretation of the symphony, according to *The Times*, was 'the outstanding musical triumph' of the 1926 Bournemouth Easter Festival. This new Columbia recording, made in April and May 1925, again with the LSO, also used the acoustic process although electrical recording had by then begun. 'The newest method of recording is apparently not employed in this work', wrote the reviewer in the April 1926 *Gramophone*. But this reviewer was not in sympathy with the symphony, finding 'this curious and powerful, unequal work ... the half-loaf of a "London" symphony without a programme a little disappointing'. As regards the repetitions of the so-called 'popular tune' in the first movement, he concluded: 'Frankly, I do not think Vaughan Williams has the staying power for a would-be powerful movement of this kind.' Even Compton Mackenzie was somewhat dismissive of the symphony when he wrote in *The Gramophone* two months later:

It is a work I enjoy less with every repetition. In all Vaughan Williams's work I am repelled by the self-consciousness. Many people do not object to this in an author or composer. They find other qualities which more than make up for it. I become obsessed by it, and blind or deaf to everything else. These are a fine set of records, and I hope they will have the appreciation they deserve.

For both recordings Godfrey had used what was then the current score, the 1920 version that included two extensive passages that were later cut – in the slow movement and the finale. It was to six particular bars in the slow movement that the composer-conductor Bernard Herrmann later referred in a letter written from California and published in *The Musical Times* of January 1958.[18] His love for the symphony had grown

18. January 1958, p 24.

from his first acquaintance with it – albeit the first two
movements only in a concert performance conducted by
Walter Damrosch. Hearing the whole work two years later
only deepened his excitement and fervour and implanted the
resolve to conduct the work himself, which he did much later
on numerous occasions. He continued:

When I first began to perform the work, the only set of parts and score
available in New York was that of the first version [in fact the 1920 version].
The slow movement at that time possessed six remarkable bars at the letter
K, which later the composer omitted, and I wish to say a few words about
those bars. It has always been my intense reaction, and of course a subjective
one, that these bars were one of the most original poetic moments in the
entire Symphony. It is at this moment as though, when the hush and
quietness have settled over Bloomsbury of a November twilight, that a damp
drizzle of rain slowly falls, and it is this descending chromatic *ponticello* of the
violins that so graphically depicts it … I, for one, shall always regret this
deletion, for it remains in my memory as one of the miraculous moments in
music, and its absence in the present version is felt like the absence of a dear,
departed friend. It will always be an enigma to me why these bars were
removed, for in their magic and beauty they had caught something of
London which Whistler captured in his Nocturnes.

The whole of that section can be heard in Godfrey's
recording (as well as in the later recording by Eugene
Goossens), from just before Letter K on page 92 of the
miniature score.

In the finale, in order to accommodate the movement onto
three 78 sides, Godfrey made a substantial cut in the Epilogue
to the 1920 version. This 1920 Epilogue can be heard
complete in the Goossens recording.

The *Musical Opinion* reviewer in May 1926 called Godfrey's
recording 'an achievement of no mean order'. But this acoustic
set was quickly eclipsed by the arrival of electrical recordings
and soon forgotten. Neither of Godfrey's recordings was
mentioned in *The Gramophone Shop Encyclopaedia of Recorded Music*
(New York 1936) and neither has subsequently been reissued,
either on LP or CD. Yet the later set is an important historical
document as the only recording of that great champion of
British music conducting a major British symphonic work.

However, it was ten years before another recording
appeared, this time from Decca, recorded in April 1936 with

Henry Wood conducting the Queen's Hall Orchestra.[19] Even though Wood used the now familiar 1933 'revised edition', besides omitting the scherzo repeat he also made a six-bar cut of his own in the slow movement.

The only other recording in those pre-LP days was that with Eugene Goossens conducting the Cincinnati Symphony Orchestra, recorded in February 1941 and issued by American Victor. Here Goossens found himself in a situation similar to Bernard Herrmann, for the score and parts at his disposal were those of the 1920 version, the same version as that recorded by Godfrey. Although Goossens omitted the scherzo repeat, his recording is otherwise complete, giving us those extra bars in the slow movement (including the passage referred to by Herrmann) and the full extended Epilogue. Both the Wood and the Goossens recordings were transferred to LP and are currently available on CD[20].

Concert performances of the 1920 version in recent times have been extremely rare, but on 29 January 1972 the wonderfully enterprising Leslie Head gave one with the Kensington Symphony Orchestra at St John's, Smith Square, London. His timings, alongside Julian Clifford's, are tabulated on page 117, together with those of the recordings already discussed, as well as those of the work's first LP recording[21], in the Kingsway Hall, London in January 1952 with Sir Adrian Boult conducting the LPO in the presence of the composer.

* * *

I would like now to take a brief look at the sketches and the original version of the score. The best way to appreciate the changes is diagrammatically (see pages 113–5). This shows the original (ic the reconstructed) score with the later cuts and changes (marked in black and with arrows) showing how the original score approximated to the 1920 version.

In the British Library there are four manuscripts to consider. The first two are Vaughan Williams's sketches. Additional

19. *The Times*'s harsh review of this set and Wood's reply can be read in Arthur Jacobs, *op cit* pp 285–288.
20. Wood's recording was reissued on Decca ACL255 and Dutton CDAX8004; Goossens' on Camden CAL186 and Biddulph WHL016.
21. Decca LXT2693. Reissued on CD, Belart 461 008-2.

Manuscript 50367A is a small music notebook inscribed at the front as

London Symphony sketches (early) symph. finale

At the back of the notebook are some brief sketches for Incidental Music to Greek Plays: *Bacchae* and *Elektra*. These are some of the choruses that were sung by a group calling themselves the Palestrina Society which VW conducted and of which George Butterworth was a member. They do not help to date the sketches with any accuracy, except to suggest 1911 or 1912. The bulk of the sketches otherwise seem to be for the last movement of the Symphony. Anyone who has read (or tried to read) either VW's handwriting or – worse – his music script will know the problems. But there is this sketch marked 'Symphony Finale' in 3/2 time:

Ex 1

This might possibly be a germ for the very beginning of the finale:

Ex 2

or for the 3/2 section just before letter H in the original
version, a section which, as you can see from the diagram, was
later cut:

Ex 3: *4th movement (8 before H)*

There is also this telling sketch for the end of the finale,
recognisable as what one may presume to be the River theme
with which the work opens and closes:

Ex 4

Next we turn to Additional Manuscript 50367B. In larger
format, this is essentially the complete symphony in short
score sketches, with no letter cues, much cut about with
alterations and bits of paper stuck on. To the front of this
volume is affixed a piece of paper marked:

Notes for Orchestral Impression 'London'

It has this opening:

Ex 5

and this, with the River theme and its two fourths:

Ex 6

At the end of each movement is a timing in pencil, and the last page has a sum of the four movements' timings, 54 minutes, with the extra note:

Epilogue takes 5 mins proposed cut 1 m. 15 sec.

Additional Manuscripts 50368A–D consist of four volumes, each a movement of the symphony, in short score, as I quoted earlier, the one that VW said that friends undertook to do in his absence by revising the very first score and making a short score. This was *before* the first performance, and you may remember Butterworth is said to have taken the last movement and been troubled by a passage in it. We need to compare each of these movements with either VW's piano sketches for the whole work or with the reconstructed orchestral score.

It is, in fact, the reconstructed score, Additional Manuscripts 51317 A–D, that focusses our attention. These are full scores of the four movements, each in a separate volume, and each by a different hand, although reading the second and third movements it is difficult to determine where one ends. Conceivably both may have been in the same hand. These scores are very much mutilated – and when Boult used the word slashed to describe how VW altered his score he was not exaggerating.

What I have done on the tabulation is to show as accurately as I can the number of bars in each section, and in black to indicate where there were cuts, and with arrows to show the additions. It is not easy to know when these changes were made. They would seem to represent all changes to the original score up to the first printed 1920 version. Many of the cuts are in blue crayon; others are in pencil. In some cases new pages have been stitched in; in one or two cases pages are clearly in the wrong place. Working conditions and regulations in the Manuscript Department of the British Library do not always make for the easiest working. So you must accept my results with a degree of open-mindedness.

What were these changes between 1914 and 1920, and what have we lost?

The first movement need not detain us as, except for one bar, no alterations were made at all to that movement.

In the second movement the first cut of 18 bars was in the exposition. The familiar themes of this section were played with at greater length, and similarly much later on in that movement after letter H. What VW had essentially done was to tighten the structure with less interplay of the principal themes and taking out another *fortissimo* passage. He rewrote this section for the 1920 version, reducing the section of 45 bars to 27 bars. For the 1933 version he made a further cut, taking out (as we have heard) the bars that Bernard Herrmann particularly liked.

	NO. OF BARS			
	ORIG.	**REVS.**	**1920**	**1933**
1st. Mvt.	408	408	407	407
2nd. Mvt.	202	162	162	150
3rd. Mvt.	386	398	398	398
4th. Mvt.	227	173	173	162
Epilogue	109	85	85	60
TOTAL:	1332	1226	1225	1177

The changes to the last two movements were more substantial. The Scherzo originally ended at the end of the cut section as marked on page 114, where the new letter 'V' begins. There was a solo violin cadenza descending in triplets

from a high D, leading into the bassoon's phrase above
sustained string chords, rather like the familiar version except
that the bassoon's phrase did not gradually slow down in the
original.

The main change in this movement was that a whole section
of 70 bars was cut and replaced by a new section of 82 bars.
This removed what was essentially a second trio and which
included what Arnold Bax in his autobiography *Farewell My
Youth* called a 'mysterious passage of strange and fascinating
cacophony'. Marked *andantino*, over muted tremolando divided
strings with harp and glockenspiel, we hear this figure on the
horns:

Ex7

followed by a violin solo:

Ex 8

and then horns again with their figure almost turned upside
down:

Ex 9

and then, I think the passage Bax liked, marked *poco animato*,
with the violins and violas in the middle stave, repeated
answering horn calls in the long stave, and above this a typical
solo violin changing to flute [Ex 10]:

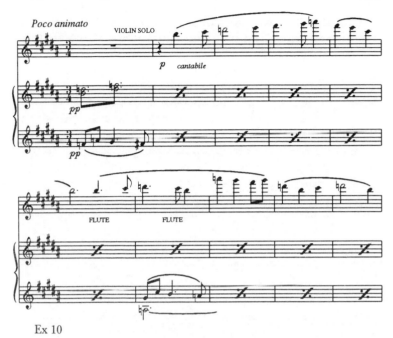

Ex 10

The last movement cuts, as can be seen from the diagram, were quite extensive. More use was made in the original version of the movement's opening theme which at about letter H was heard as in Ex 3 (p 105), followed by much use of these two figures in conjunction with the march theme:

Ex 11

The next big cut, soon after letter L, contains that 'bad hymn tune' introduced on violas and cellos and repeated on woodwind:

Andante ma sostenuto

Ex 12

This led back into the march.

The hymn tune was hinted at on muted brass in the Lento section immediately before the Epilogue, followed by the chimes of Big Ben on harp, but that whole section was rewritten so as to erase any suggestion of a hymn tune.

As you can see, the Epilogue itself was substantially rewritten. Much of the cut part made play with the rising River theme on various instruments against sustained strings. The 1920 Epilogue can be heard complete in the Goossens recording, 25 bars longer than the familiar 1933 version.

We need to note one important aspect of the *London Symphony* which I cannot help bearing in mind whenever I hear the work – its historic setting and the time when it was written. The London that VW had in mind was of course a very different one from the London of today, but it was also quite different from the London of Elgar's *Cockaigne* of 1901. By 1910 motorised transport had largely replaced horse-drawn vehicles, and I wonder how many of the street sellers' cries that VW alludes to were to be heard in 1914. Hansom cabs with their quiet rubber tyres and their jingles (heard in the slow movement) were outmoded. What was it that provoked the stress and anxiety of the last movement? Was it the pace of fast modern development? Was it the unrest of, for example, the suffragettes' marches so prominent in 1912? This is something one could develop from the sociological point-of-view. What we have is a view of the changed London of 1914 into which are interspersed memories of London's past.

One last point. Let's not forget how *modern* this work must have sounded in 1914: that terrifying outburst near the beginning as London comes to life, and the climax of the last movement. The nearest to it in British music was probably the nightmare sequence in the scherzo of Elgar's Second Symphony which was only three years old when *A London Symphony* was first performed. Incidentally, for my money the finest recording is Barbirolli's *first* LP recording made for Pye Nixa and reissued on CD by EMI.

* * *

To conclude. On 21 February 1949 the celebrated documentary film director Humphrey Jennings attended the rehearsal (in the London Welsh Hall) and performance (in the Royal Albert Hall) of a Walton/Vaughan Williams programme with the composers conducting. VW was conducting the *London Symphony*. Jennings' 'working sketches' were printed in Hubert Foss' and Noel Goodwin's *London Symphony – Portrait of an Orchestra* (Naldrett Press 1954)[22]. The following extracts come from his account of the concert.

The tension in the orchestra as they took their places after the interval was something like stage fright. After all, Vaughan Williams was 77, was ill, had lost his voice: possibly this was the last time he would conduct them?

Then the *London Symphony* is not just a piece of great music in the abstract – it is of us, written for us, written about us ... And here he is – a great silver-haired figure, slowly appearing from the artists' room. Silver hair (as I say),

22. pp 240-244.

the most splendid countryman's head and shoulders, huge arms and hand that in past generations held the axe and the plough. The orchestra sweeps to its feet. Here is their god: yes, a god! ... He hesitates, bows to the audience, bows to the orchestra, and slowly (how slowly!) climbs the rostrum to open the huge score (for his sight is not good) like a Bible; spreads his arms like a tree, and with the first four bars we know that we are in the Presence.

... For the rest I cannot emulate the writers of programme notes or the notices of the next morning. I can say that what the music says, we as Londoners had all been through: I remember our worry as the conductor's hand occasionally stole back to the rail to steady himself, that his fingers fumbled in turning the pages, that once the orchestra carried on as he was lost, that there were tears in our eyes, that [the critic] Richard Capell said to Gordon Walker [flautist and LSO Chairman]: 'I say, you chaps backed him up splendidly,' that George Stratton [LSO leader] came off the platform really crying and said: 'You can't help playing well – he doesn't show off! – that of all the minutes of one's life, we can say that those spent this evening *were well spent.*

1. Ralph Vaughan Williams by Herbert Lambert (1923).

2. Ingrave Rectory today.
Plates 2 to 6 are 1990s photographs by Tony Kendall.

3. Charles Potiphar's cottage, Ingrave.

4. "The Bell", Willingale Doe.

5. Samuel Childs' Cottage, Willingale.

6. "The Olde [Old] Dog" Inn, East Horndon.

BBC Internal Circulating Memo

Subject: Dr. Vaughan Williams - Anniversary Programmes

From:
Sir Adrian Boult

To: D.M.
(London)

September 15th 1942

I know it is too late to do anything about it, but I venture to think that something a little more suitable might have been done for my Concert of October 13th in the Vaughan Williams' Week.

It is surely common knowledge that Harriet Cohen's perform-ance of the Vaughan Williams' Pianoforte Concerto caused it to be completely dropped since it was first performed. The work (very stupidly though it was written for Harriet Cohen) was laid out for a pianist of the Busoni calibre, and though she made a very valiant effort, she could get nowhere near the spirit of it or even the notes in many passages.

Frederick Grinke played "The Lark Ascending" quite recently with us in the Studio, and we all agreed that the poor lark never left solid earth. Marie Wilson plays it infinitely better.

It is easy to be wise after the event, and I am continually saying that things must not be held up in an effort to consult me here in Bedford when I am out of reach, but in the one case the matter has been common property for 8 or 10 years, and in the other the performance was so recent that the reports must surely be fresh in the minds of a good many people - I know I myself wrote one to such an effect.

I am indeed sorry that the only contribution that I am making to the Vaughan Williams' Week with our own Orchestra should consist of these two works.

ACB/GB

[handwritten note] But I have really dictated this ... wish to repeat, what A.D.M. ... mind, my request to be allowed to do a number of the other big works during the autumn ... the Studio.

[signature]

BBC/A/20

---

7. Sir Adrian Boult minutes his successor as BBC Director of Music, Sir Arthur Bliss, complaining about the allocation of repertoire and artists for his contribution to the Vaughan Williams's 70th Birthday celebrations. *(courtesy BBC Written Archives)*

8. Vaughan Williams presents a book of tributes to Sir Henry Wood at the Royal College of Music on the occasion of Wood's 75th birthday, 2 March 1944.

9. Vaughan Williams conducts massed local choirs at the Leith Hill Festival.

10. Elizabeth Maconchy.

11. Patrick Hadley, Kendall Taylor and Vaughan Williams at Heacham, 1952.

12. Ina Boyle.

13. Grace Williams.

14. Gerald Finzi by Herbert Lambert.

15. Ursula Wood and Vaughan Williams on the steps of Epsom Parish Church.

16. Mary Habberfield (Music Editor), Ernest Irving and Vaughan Williams recording the music for Michael Balcon's Production *The Loves of Joanna Godden. (courtesy Huntley Film Archives)*

17. Muir Mathieson, Vaughan Williams and Michael Powell at the music recording session for the film *49th Parallel*. *(courtesy Huntley Film Archives)*

A DIAGRAMMATIC REPRESENTATION OF THE RECONSTRUCTED FULL SCORE OF
A LONDON SYMPHONY

The sections in black are those that were later cut by crossing out either in blue crayon or in pencil.
Arrows indicate those sections that were later added. (No changes were made to the First Movement.)

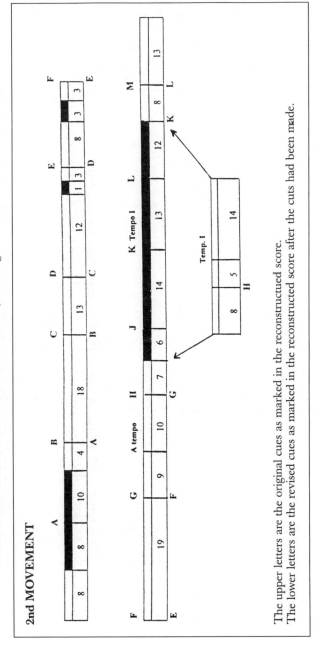

The upper letters are the original cues as marked in the reconstructued score.
The lower letters are the revised cues as marked in the reconstructed score after the cuts had been made.

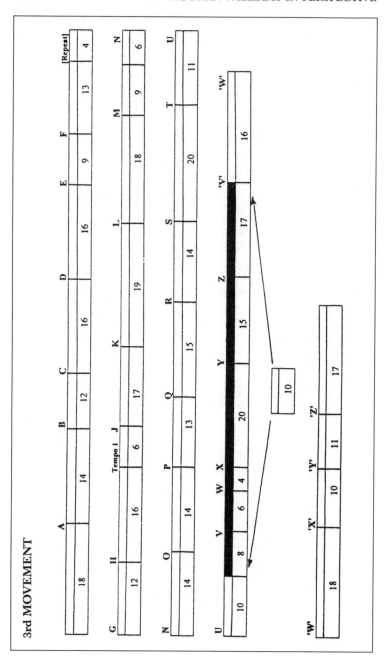

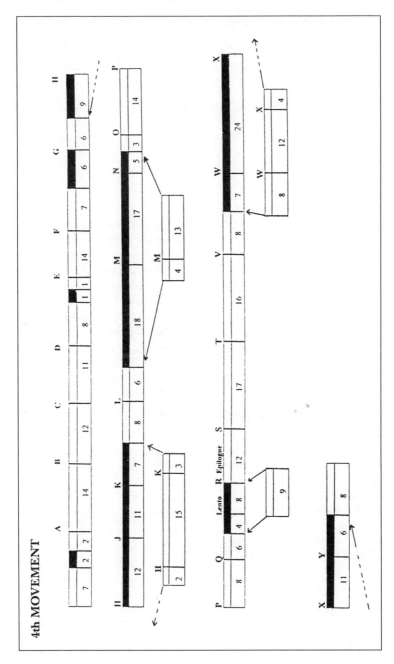

VAUGAN WILLIAMS'S *A LONDON SYMPHONY*

THE ORIGINAL VERSION AND EARLY REVISIONS, PERFORMANCES AND RECORDINGS

SOURCES:

Sketches BL Add. MSS 50367A–B and Piano Score Add. MSS 50368A–D (movements in different hands)

Full Score (reconstructed version) BL Add. MSS 51317 A–D (movements in different hands)

Full Score (1920 version) Stainer & Bell 2230; Piano Reduction by Vally Lasker S&B 339 1922

PERFORMANCES:

1914	27 March	Queen's Hall, London	Queen's Hall Orchestra, Geoffrey Toye
1914	12 August	Harrogate	Harrogate Municipal Orchestra, Julian Clifford
1915	11 February	Bournemouth	Bournemouth Municipal Orchestra, Dan Godfrey
1918	18 February	Queen's Hall, London	London Symphony Orchestra, Adrian Boult
1918	18 March	Queen's Hall, London	London Symphony Orchestra, Adrian Boult
1920	4 May	Queen's Hall, London	London Symphony Orchestra, Albert Coates

RECORDINGS UP TO FIRST LP ISSUE:

1923   24 July:
Columbia L1507–8 (acoustic 78s) [1st Mvt. abridged and 3rd Mvt. only]
London Symphony Orchestra, Sir Dan Godfrey

1925   24 April & 1 May:
Columbia L1717–22 (acoustic 78s)
London Symphony Orchestra, Sir Dan Godfrey

1936   21 & 22 April:
Decca X114–8 (78s, with LP and CD reissue)
Queen's Hall Orchestra, Sir Henry Wood

1941   19 & 20 February:
Victor 11.8253–7 (78s, with LP and CD reissue)
Cincinnati Symphony Orchestra, Eugene Goossens

1952   8–11 January:
Decca LXT 2693 LP, with CD reissue)
London Philharmonic Orchestra, Sir Adrian Boult

SOME COMPARATIVE TIMINGS

	[RVW]	Clifford	Godfrey	Godfrey	Goossens	Head	Wood	Boult
DATE	**	1914*	1923	1925	1941	1972*	1936	1952
VERSION	Sketches	Orig.	1920	1920	1920	1920	1933	1933
1st Mvt.	12'	12'	8'32"+	13'37"	11'06"	14'10"	11'40"	13'25"
2nd. Mvt.	12'	15'	–	12'17"	9'22"	12'05"	8'39"+	11'02"
3rd. Mvt.	10'	9'	7'07"	7'20"	5'09"+	8'07"	5'21"+	7'04"
4th. Mvt.	⎤	⎤	–	8'00"	7'35"	8'30"	7'11"	8'13"
Epilogue	⎦ 20'	⎦ 15'	–	3'45"+	5'40"	5'50"	3'38"	4'09"
TOTAL	54'	51'	–	45'	39'	49'	36½'	44'

** timings written by RVW on Sketches (Add. MS 50367B), with the extra note:
      'Epilogue takes 5 mins proposed cut 1 m 15 sec'

 *   concert performance, 1914 timings as recorded by Herbert Thompson

 +   cut(s) in that movement

VI

Duncan Hinnells

Vaughan Williams's Piano Concerto
the first seventy years

———◦◦◦———

THE PIANO CONCERTO HAS PROVED DIFFICULT
throughout its career, living in partial obscurity and
creating around itself a rather austere and
unapproachable solitude. The score is out of print, the solo
part is formidably difficult, the style seems quite alien to
Vaughan Williams's canonised manner, and in the light of the
composer's multiple revisions, nobody is ever quite sure which
is 'the authorized version'. Its historical reception markedly
contrasts with the immense popularity which many of the
composer's other large orchestral works have achieved and
today, as it approaches its seventieth birthday, the concerto
does not hold a secure place among Vaughan Williams's
canonised works.

Yet despite being rarely seen or heard, the concerto has not
simply suffered neglect. In its rather dark life it has attracted
significant admirers, including many inter-war composers
ranging in outlook from Bax to Bartok. Most significantly,
however, the concerto excited the musical directors of Oxford
University Press and the BBC during the 1930s, and their
championship established important interpretative
foundations. Consequently the concerto has been kept alive,
albeit almost solely in Anglophile literature, concert-life
and recordings, and it continues to have many influential

admirers within a tightly-knit and dedicated community.

This paper offers a kind of biography of the work, an account which seeks to interpret significant relationships between aspects of the concerto's history and its contemporary profile. Since it was first presented in 1996, the paper has been revised in the context of the important issues raised by Alain Frogley's recent discussion of Vaughan Williams's reception[1], and it seeks to emphasize ways in which the life of the concerto may act as a prism through which we may view wider processes in the history of Vaughan Williams.

I am indebted to a number of people for the generosity with which they have allowed access to material and given their time in discussing it; James Arnold-Baker, Andrew Potter, Simon Wright, and Peter Foden, of Oxford University Press; Hugh Cobbe, Music Librarian of the British Library; Joseph Cooper; Lewis Foreman; Hubert Foss's heirs, Christopher Foss and Diana Sparkes (neé Foss); Jacqueline Kavanagh and Jeff Walden of the BBC Written Archives, Caversham; Phyllis Sellick; Mrs Ursula Vaughan Williams. I am sincerely grateful to them all.

Vaughan Williams claimed to have drafted the first two movements of the Piano Concerto in 1926 and the third movement in 1930, and there seems little reason to doubt this chronology.[2] Having completed and revised various major 'English pastoral' scores in the post-war years, Vaughan Williams's compositions of the mid 1920s are frequently described as evolving a new style, and several important pieces, including the Violin Concerto and *Flos Campi* (both 1925) surprised contemporaries by revealing traits largely new to his work; the concision and stylistic modelling of the concerto, it is claimed, make it a rare essay in European neo-classicism, and the bitonality and voluptuous sonority of *Flos Campi* is frequently said to make it Vaughan Williams's most erotic work, attributes which seem to characterise, respectively, the first two movements of the Piano Concerto. *Sancta Civitas*

1. Frogley, 1996, pp 1–22.
2. Kennedy, 1980, p 146.

(also 1925), apparently the composer's favourite among his own choral works, baffled its natural constituency of performers and audience by its exploration of new idioms in a traditional genre, and Vaughan Williams's period of inter-war experimentation is often perceived as climaxing with the seemingly bitter and modernist Fourth Symphony in 1934.[3] This symphony, dedicated to Arnold Bax, is often held to be deeply connected, through style and genesis, with the Finale of the Piano Concerto, a movement which in its earliest form, ended with an explicit quotation, labelled on the Autograph Full Score 'According to my promise'[4] from Bax's Third Symphony. Bax was widely known to be having an affair with the concerto's dedicatee and first soloist, Harriet Cohen, and the quotation has consistently been interpreted as having a 'personal rather than musical significance'.[5] Cohen's youthful beauty and delicate playing seems to have captivated most of England's leading composers, and Vaughan Williams, so the story goes, promised the concerto to her in exchange for over one thousand kisses.[6]

These are the common themes of influential narratives surrounding the early years of the concerto, a story most authoritatively written by Michael Kennedy. The composer-biographical orientation of the account reflects a general tendency of Vaughan Williams scholarship, an inclination which frequently tends to marginalise the potentially crucial relationships between music and its cultural, economic and political contexts. Stradling and Hughes' highly significant

3. Kennedy (1964, Chapter Seven) offers the most authorititive overview of Vaughan Williams' work during the mid 1920s, claiming (p 186) that 'In *Flos Campi* and even more in *Sancta Civitas*, he ploughed a lonely furrow, leaving many of his admirers behind and puzzling even such a sympathetic friend as Holst.'
4. BL, Add Ms 50385, f 73.
5. Foreman (1983, pp 247–248) cites Kennedy (1964 p 237), for this quotation, a statement which I have only been able to find in Howes, (1954, p 109). However, the implication often appears and Foreman's point remains germane.
6. A letter cited by Cohen (1969, pp 260–261) refers to a total of 1065 kisses, a tally which may even appear much reduced from an earlier promise, as revealed by earlier letters which may appear in Hugh Cobbe's forthcoming collection of Vaughan Williams' correspondence.

study of the English Musical Renaissance[7] prioritises these issues, examining the subtleties and power with which inter-war cultural politics appears to have influenced the ambitions and policies of leading musical personalities and institutions. In the case of Vaughan Williams's interwar work, these pressures seem to have been immense; a previous generation of musical leaders had died or fallen silent (Parry, Stanford and Elgar), and even among the talents of the younger generation, many were lost to war (Gurney and Butterworth). Antagonism towards contemporary German music and the difficulty of nurturing significant native composition contributed to a deep anxiety about the future of 'English' music, expressed in a kind of musical nationalism which anxiously sought a new heir, a role of which Vaughan Williams was almost certainly conscious. These pressures seem significant for interpreting his music and writings, particularly in the inter-war years. Frogley[8], alert to the potential separation of music and discourse, summarized an important issue when he observed that Vaughan Williams's inter-war writings may be 'swayed to some degree by the further heightening of nationalistic sentiment' but that his music of same period 'clearly suggest[s] analogies with, if not the actual influence of, continental movements'.

The newly-founded BBC quickly came to dominate contemporary musical life and its characteristics, ambitions and policies appear both to express and influence the pressures and opportunities of the age. The political, economic, and institutional environment, is, I believe, a crucial factor in understanding the creative context and early life of the Piano Concerto. This social, political, and economic context is nevertheless far from fixed or restricted in its significance to the inter-war years; indeed, it is the very dynamism of its changes which appears to have positioned the concerto in new interpretative contexts throughout its history and continues to do so. Observing the instability of its context helps explain the changing relationships between the composer, the score, and its reception and performance, a situation in which each

7. Stradling and Hughes, 1993.
8. 1996, p 18.

constituent element of the work appears mutually reflexive to the others, and yet is also open to 'external' influence. The Model attempts to visualize dynamic relationships between constituent elements of the living work. Given the potential extent of textual, analytical, and historical material which such an account could include, I shall simply highlight certain key moments and issues in its life, referring in footnotes to individual areas to be explored more extensively elsewhere.

A conceptual model of dynamic relationships within a living work

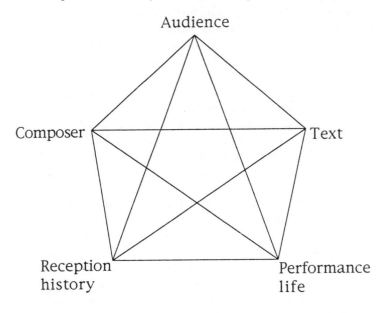

The performance and revisions of the Concerto need to be discussed in the 1930s context. Vaughan Williams's meteoric rise from semi-obscure respectability around the time of the First World War to the revered position of 'Grand Old Man' of English Music within the following decade appears related to his close involvement with two newly-founded and powerful music departments at the BBC and Oxford University Press. Both institutions were sufficiently wealthy, and, at least in public perception, sufficiently philanthropic to support apparently uncommercial 'high art' music.[9] In both cases, the status and philosophy of the relevant institution seems to have given its musical directors the power to exert an important diplomatic leverage on behalf of 'specialist' new English music at a departmental level, under the umbrella of an official corporate aim to educate and entertain 'the general public' in 'the great classics'.[10] Vaughan Williams's familiar style, as witnessed in such works as the the *Lark Ascending*, the *Tallis Fantasia*, *A London Symphony* and *A Pastoral Symphony*, seems to have offered music capable of uniting these ambitions, which is surely significant in understanding the immense success of his career from the 1930s onwards. The BBC actively sought for and requested new works from Vaughan Williams from the earliest years of Boult's appointment (1929/1930), a behaviour in marked contrast to the corporation's dealings with many other significant composers. In the case of the Piano Concerto, it seems that a letter from Boult hoping for a new work may have given Vaughan Williams the impetus to finally complete his 'inchoate' work. By this time, of course, OUP implicitly

9. Scanell and Cardiff (1991, p 198) suggest that at the time when Reith's BBC purchased the Proms in 1927 they were heavily loss-making, but widely regarded as of national cultural significance. In forthcoming doctoral research on the relationship between Vaughan Williams and Oxford University Press, I suggest that its Music Department also reflected an institutional patronage quite new in British music.

10. Scanell and Cardiff (1991, pp 193 & 197) have also written about the widening gulf between central BBC administration under Reith and the policy of the Music Department under Adrian Boult. The BBC, according to the Crawford Committee of 1925, was a 'guardian of cultural values' (in ibid, pp 200–201) and music quickly became its largest department. The relationship of Humphrey Milford, head of OUP and Hubert Foss, its first Head of Music, appears to parallel the Reith-Boult relationship.
    Peacock and Weir (1975 p 95) suggest that contemporary music critics were not clear in their definitions of who constituted their 'general' listener, but, despite its vagueness, the concept nevertheless became crucial in shaping the market place. E M Forster's *Howards End* (1910) seems to illustrate the significance of the music appreciation movement before the First World War, and the novel's character Leonard Bast, may reflect the particular social orientation of pre 1914 self education. Scanell and Cardiff (1991, pp 213–216) articulate the difficulty of defining the post-war social spectrum, but they offer an informal sketch, suggesting that Scholes, Maine and Walford Davies wrote for a general listener who was 'conscience-stricken' about the need to know about art music, and who could not bear Bartók.

guaranteed the publication and wide dissemination of anything Vaughan Williams offered.[11]

The benefits of a BBC performance were, of course, immense. Boult, Vaughan Williams's most loyal and influential interpreter, was famed for his skill in conducting new music. His zealous advocacy of authorial wishes and his command over an orchestra of the highest professional status, ensured what Vaughan Williams described as 'a beautiful performance..[which] made impossible the composer's time-honoured excuse that the work would have sounded all right if it had been properly played – I could not have imagined a better first performance'.[12] BBC patronage not only brought adequate rehearsals, repeat performances (seven out of the nine performances in its first decade were given by the BBC[13]), but also broadcasts, a crucial element in the new economics of inter-war music, shaping and expanding the dissemination of music on an entirely new scale.[14] But perhaps just as important

11. Boult wrote to Vaughan Williams in March 1931 saying how 'delighted' the BBC would be if 'allowed' to take charge of any new work he cared to offer them (BBC Written Archives, Vaughan Williams Composer File 1A). Interestingly, it appears from letters collected by Hugh Cobbe that composition of the concerto may have stagnated until April 1931. when Vaughan Williams began work again in earnest. He completed enough music to arrange a piano run-through in the Summer and he delivered a 'complete' version to Harriet Cohen by October. This chronology is also supported by Harriet Cohen's rather selective account in *Bundle of Time,* (1969, pp 199–200).
Kennedy (1964, p 193), possibly speaking on the composer's verbal authority, asserts that by the late 1920s OUP 'agreed to publish anything that he cared to offer them, and this informal contract held good for thirty-two years'. Naturally such an arrangement appears not to be formally documented in OUP archives, but it concords with the tone of the correspondence files.
12. Vaughan Williams to Adrian Boult in BBC Written Archives at Caversham (WAC), Vaughan Williams Composer File 1A, 7 February, 1933.
13. The Music Department Hire Library Ledger at Oxford University Press records details of British and many continental performances, except those handled by its agencies in Paris, New York, Bonn and Sydney. However, the only contemporary continental performance seems to have been that conducted by Scherchen, with Cohen as soloist (and Bartók as appreciative audience) in Strasbourg in 1933.
14. Peacock and Weir, (1975, p 65) in 'The Music Market 1914-1939', argue that there was 'a growing awareness by composers, publishers and performing musicians that access to the 'air' was as crucial for commercial success as had been access to the concert hall in the

was the BBC's huge publicity machine. Hubert Foss was perhaps the first music publisher in Britain to seize the opportunities of the new age, and he become a frequent and highly-skilled broadcaster. He was regarded as an authority on contemporary music, especially English music, and was frequently scheduled to discuss 'his' composers, most particularly Vaughan Williams and Walton.[15] His introductions to new works established many of the images, terms, and topoi of future interpretations of the music, and, given the prominent times at which pre-concert talks were often broadcast, he probably reached an enormous audience.[16]

The first performance of the Piano Concerto (1 February, 1933) was broadcast live and was preceded by an introductory talk by Hubert Foss, and the transcript offers a classical example of how discourse about music can become established:

As I talk to you tonight I'm in a mood of considerable excitement ... [because of] an event of great importance ... a new work by that most English of composers, Ralph Vaughan Williams, and perhaps the greatest of

nineteenth century.' They also cite evidence from the PR Gazette of 1932, which declared 'Nowadays the majority of our citizens are listeners rather than performers' and that in 1930, 35% Performing Right Society (PRS) income was from Radio whereas in 1945 it was 50% (ibid, p 81), figures similar to those offered by Scanell & Cardiff (1991, p 181).

15. Foss was extremely positive about the potential contribution of broadcast music, taking a distinctive stance in a climate in which 'mechanical' music was widely attacked by composers and the musical establishment. H C Colles, for example, in writing the Preface to the Second Edition of *The Growth of Music* (1939) prioritised the role of wireless and gramophone as the key changes in music education between his first edition in 1912 and the 1939 revision, and he wrote 'The danger to education to-day is lest young people should hear too much music and listen to it too little.' Britten and Vaughan Williams were among other leading composers who on the one hand expressed caution about mechanical music and yet who themselves conducted and supervised recordings and broadcasts of their own music. My dissertation discusses Foss's use of broadcasting far more extensively, but two key texts which encapsulate his views include 'Publicity' (*New Witness*, 26 January, 1922) and *Music in My Time* (1933).

16. Evening broadcasts in an era without multiple channels seem to have attracted large audiences. Scanell and Cardiff (1991, p 362) point out that the huge increase in licences (from 3 million in 1930 to 9 million by 1939) covered approximately three-quarters of British households, ranging across the social spectrum.

them. Here's a chance not only to do homage to a great man but also to enjoy to the full an entirely new phase of his mind ... something as new and as exciting, and yet as solid hasn't come my way for a long time. ...

... It [Schubert's *Unfinished Symphony*, which opened the concert] says simple things we all know in a simple way. Now that, is I believe, true also of Vaughan Williams's Piano Concerto. It's certainly original, and I for one, find it fundamental, and I hope that everyone to whom it may seem unfamiliar in its idiom or language, will remember what I've said about the *Unfinished Symphony* and see the simple truths behind the music which Vaughan Williams is uttering. ...

... the second movement is not only the longest but the most important of the three. Notice that it's called "Romanza" and this indeed is a romantic work, but, if I may coin a phrase, 'new-romantic'. There's something of the spirit of Liszt, that greatest of romantics, in the wild last section of the last movement; but you couldn't imagine anything more different from Liszt and his school than the pianoforte part. The soloist's music indeed, is more like Bartók, uncompromising, with no attempt merely to please you by graceful runs or rapid finger work all over the pianoforte. ... and that is but one of the indications of the way Vaughan Williams has devoted his attention to the percussion side of the instrument. ...

The last movement is called chromatic fugue with finale alla Tedesca. How I dread the word 'fugue'; like the absurd word highbrow it always puts people off. I know there's an idea that fugues are dull, but they aren't really and this one's anything but dull. ... It's not really a text-book affair at all. The dull pedants made it that, not the composers, so don't be put off by the name and listen to the music instead. You won't find it anything but exciting for a moment.

The finale or climax, as it really is, is nothing more or less than a waltz. Some of you may remember the movement marked 'alla Tedesca' in that most glorious of Beethoven's String Quartets, Op 130, the one with that superb cavatina ... the piano has the last word and in a long solo passage sums up the varying moods of the work and presents it, as it were, in a miniature summary.

This broadcast is quoted at length to illustrate the way in which Foss engages in the wider process of constructing Vaughan Williams's reputation. On one level this is done by associating him with the greatest composers of the canon, and on another by invoking already existing images of him (the 'English' composer and 'great' man, whose music is 'solid' and 'expressive of simple truths'); but at the same time Foss prepares listeners for a work whose 'idiom or language' may seem 'unfamiliar'. The care with which Foss situated both the composer and the work in relation to tradition and innovation, and romanticism and modernism, seems to reflect the contemporary ambition of the BBC and OUP to promote new music which appealed to connoisseur and layman alike, an ideal characteristic of the age and which may also have been crucial in the working relationship between Vaughan Williams and his publisher. By positioning the concerto just to the 'right' (ie conservative) side of an imaginary cutting edge, Foss assimilated this music to the existing repertoire and prepared listeners for aspects of its contemporary style, while reassuring them of established values, a balance he also struck in a preview in the *Daily Telegraph*,[17]:

> The piano-writing is like that of an English Bartók. The musical thought has some affinity with that of an English Liszt. I know that to loyalists these comparisons will sound heretical; but to one who admires all these three composers there seems to be nothing but praise to be understood therefrom as nothing but praise is meant. But, to remove misunderstanding, let me say that there is none of Bartók's atonality here; nor a trace of Liszt's keyboard methods. I speak of the thought that lay behind each of the three. ...

One of the only significant differences between the broadcast and the article is that Foss appears more defensive in publishing a written text which invoked Bartók and Liszt; his reference to 'loyalists', 'heretical' and 'misunderstanding' and his qualification of his claims, may suggest that a strong orthodoxy had already entered writings about Vaughan Williams by 1933. It seems that Foss was aware – even before the first performance – of a potential tension between Vaughan Williams's constructed reputation and attributes which he felt characterised this work, a tension which he seems to have attempted to reconcile in this pre-performance publicity. Those who have written about the work since Foss have consistently invoked Bartók and Liszt, a critical handing-down which seems to originate with Foss and whose purpose is apparently to attempt to explain a musical style which seems to conflict with Vaughan Williams's accepted reputation.

Foss had acutely anticipated a major problem; although Harriet Cohen[18] remembered that 'the composer and I had a

17. 28 January, 1933.
18. 1969, p 217.

tremendous reception at the concert, but were not quite sure whether it was for ourselves personally or for the work', reactions to the piece seem to have been very mixed. Vaughan Williams remembered some hissing[19], Colles observed in *The Times*[20] that 'To those who still retain a preconceived notion of what a piano concerto should be, Vaughan Williams's work could not be very acceptable', and Edward Dent, commented of critic's reactions that 'the poor dears were terribly bewildered and anxious not to commit themselves'[21]. Howes, a staunch Vaughan Williams loyalist, heard the work six months later when it was performed at the BBC Proms, and he almost anticipated the Dunkirk spirit when he attempted to construe poor early reception as a virtue[22]: "Vaughan Williams has a way of disconcerting his admirers with almost every new work of any size that he writes. There could be no more reassuring sign of artistic vigour and mental growth. One has only to reflect on the case of Richard Strauss, who has been writing the same music over and over again to different contexts for the last twenty years."

Howes' apparent anxiety to 'defend' VW against the charge of writing a 'modernist' piece was resolved in a stroke of critical inspiration, which may have originated in Foss' reference to Beethoven's Op. 130 Quartet[23] [the concerto] has a 'certain affinity, both spiritual and technical, with third-period Beethoven ... that there must be a struggle to make articulate in music a vision of that ultimate reality which some approach by philosophy, some by poetry, some by religion ...'

By invoking late Beethoven, aesthetic tables are turned; apparent stylistic inaccessibility is not merely justified, but even turned in to a virtue by 'philosophical' and 'mystical' profundity, and responsibility is transferred to audiences, performers, and critics to 'understand' a remote work. The construction of Vaughan Williams's reputation gains a new and powerful rhetoric, and it is precisely during this period

19. Kennedy, 1964, p 236.
20. 2 February, 1933, cited in ibid.
21. Cohen, 1969, p 217.
22. *Musical Times*, October 1933, reproduced in Howes, 1937, pp 29–38.
23. Howes, 1937, pp 30–31.

that Vaughan Williams, in the eyes of critics, is no longer a 'promising' composer, but becomes a 'visionary' master.

Between Foss' 'promotion' and Howes' 'reception' – a duality which at times can appear artificial – Vaughan Williams's own programme-note appeared, and can be seen in two almost identical forms.[24] This note, like many others, seems intended simply as a guide to help listeners follow the principal contours of a new work, and, in its manner of summarising themes and keys, it suggests a contemporary background coloured by the formal models proffered by Tovey, whose programme-notes OUP also published.[25] Howes approaches the form of the work in a similar manner to Vaughan Williams, perhaps partly reflective of a veneration of 'authorial views' which he would surely have known[26] (a prioritisation which typifies the era and also characterises subsequent British musicology), and also because Howes shared significant ideals and a pedagogic heritage with Vaughan Williams.[27] The composer's note, like his other writings concerning his own music, is entirely mute as regards any aspect of the music other than its formal contours. Vaughan Williams's much-professed habit of silence about his music – a stance which appears more complex in relation to the personal views he expressed about a number of major

24. Kennedy, 1964 pp 536-538 & 1980 pp 146–148, and also in BBC WAC, Vaughan Williams Composer File lA.
25. Vaughan Williams himself admired Tovey's musicianship and also seems to have respected his musical commentaries. Tovey was also nurtured and promoted by Foss, and his analytical writings became immensely popular during the inter-war years. Interestingly, like Vaughan Williams, Tovey was subject to critical hostility for a quarter of a century from the later 1960s and has also recently enjoyed a critical revival. The analytical models and manner he adopted are perhaps the high-water-mark of a widespread set of assumptions, whose tenets are articulated by R O Morris, a close family and professional connection of Vaughan Williams, in his instruction book, *The Structure of Music* (OUP, 1935).
26. Vaughan Williams' programme-note was in fact written for the very performance which Howes reviewed, and, on a broader level, Howes was an intimate of the community surrounding Vaughan Williams, Foss, OUP, the BBC, Oxbridge and the Royal College of Music.
27. See Martin Cooper's 'Frank Howes' (*New Grove Dictionary of Music and Musicians*, 1980, Vol. 8, p 747) and also revealed in Howes' writings on Vaughan Williams (1954) and *The English Musical Renaissance* (1966).

works[28] – was largely maintained in relation to this concerto and the lack of any authorial interpretation of its style, origins, or 'meaning' appears to have made the critics hesitant. In the absence of the composer's verbal interpretation of the concerto, the accounts of Foss and Howes, who later became the authors of the first two monographs on Vaughan Williams (1950 and 1954 respectively), gained a surrogate authority.

Despite his apparent silence, Vaughan Williams did, however, explicitly publicise an avenue for 'extra-musical' 'interpretation in his programme-note by highlighting the musical quotation from Bax's Third Symphony which closed the final piano cadenza of the Finale:

Ex 1

In the Autograph score the quotation is indicated by quotation marks (in red ink), in a manner similar to the way in which the theme from Mendelssohn's overture 'Calm Sea and Prosperous Voyage' is marked in the 'Romanza' of the *Enigma Variations*. Vaughan Williams, who admired Elgar's variations and studied its manuscript score in the British Library, must surely have known of the 'extra-musical' speculation which could result by making such a quotation explicit, and his bait has proved attractive from he earliest days; Colles, who would have known of Bax's affair with Cohen, wrote in *The Times*[29], 'Perhaps the composer shared with the pianist some personal secret about it', and it certainly appears possible that Cohen's

28. Among the important apparently 'absolute' (i.e. 'untexted') orchestral music about which Vaughan Williams did talk or offer hints in extra-musical terms, largely in private, are the *London Symphony* (See Frogley, 1993), the *Pastoral Symphony* (Harrington, 1989), and the Sixth and Ninth Symphonies (Kennedy, 1964, p 302, and Frogley, 1986, 1987, & 1989 respectively).

29. Cited Kennedy, 1996, p 9.

role as soloist is involved.[30] Subsequently all commentators have inferred an 'extra-musical' motivation[31], with Kennedy[32], among many others suggesting that it was 'symbol of friendship and a most unusual occurrence in the music of Vaughan Williams, who generally eschewed such personal references.' In late July and early August 1933, in preparing for its second performance, the composer removed the quotation, writing to Cohen that '*we* understand it, but the audience does not. So I will in the next few days think out a new ending'[33]. This phrasing could imply that Vaughan Williams felt the quotation, which may have had a rather specific purpose, failed to mean anything to the audience, and that its removal was in reaction to the first performance. But he was unable to find a satisfactory new ending as he hoped, and instructed

30. A certain amount of confusion surrounds the sequence and chronology of events concerning the involvement of Cohen with Vaughan Williams' concerto and the completion of Bax's Third Symphony, a difficulty recorded by Threlfall (1975, pp 237–238), Foreman (1983, p 248) and Kennedy (1996, p 9).
The problem they identify is that although Vaughan Williams' overt 'quotation' of Bax Third Symphony (apparently composed in 1929) occurs in the concerto's finale (drafted in 1931), the Bax theme is also connected with Vaughan Williams' slow movement which was drafted in 1926.
However, there are numerous possible explanations, including the possibility that either (or both) composers sketched thematic material far earlier than they drafted specific movements and that they exchanged ideas; conversely, aspects of their musical outlook and context which they shared may have prompted them to draft similar material, a relationship which Vaughan Williams may have decided to make explicit by quotation. It certainly appears possible, examining the ink, paper and Vaughan Williams' pagination of the autograph full score (BL Add Ms 50385, f 73) that the Bax quotation was added later than the rest of the movement, which leaves many possibilities open.
Contemplating this chronology may prove fruitful in another respect, however. A letter from Vaughan Williams to Cohen in January 1931 seems to indicate that it was only then that the concerto became 'hers'. This seems to suggest that Vaughan Williams did not necessarily conceive the concerto with her in mind, and conflicts with the assumption of many of those involved. Boult criticised Vaughan Williams for having written a Busonian concerto 'for' Cohen in a letter to Arthur Bliss (15 September, 1942 BBC WAC Vaughan Williams Composer File 2B), and Cohen herself evidently liked to think the concerto was written for her (1969, pp 194–195).
31. Foreman, 1983, p 248.
32. 1996, p 9.
33. Kennedy, 1964, p 237.

Cohen to simply omit the quotation. The work is often presumed to have remained in this form until the two-piano revision of 1946. However, letters between Vaughan Williams and Cohen collected by Hugh Cobbe, and evidence in the autograph score, show that a number of changes were made throughout 1933 and in the first half of 1934, including a minor change in the closing bars, left largely unremarked in commentaries, but which seems to suggest that an original close, perhaps linked to the Bax quotation, shifting from B Flat Major, via B flat minor to a tonicized 'G' was replaced, perhaps at the time the Bax quotation was removed, with an ending which tonicizes 'G' throughout. Examples 2 and 3 respectively

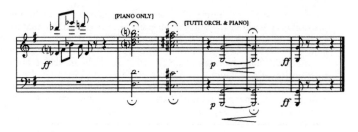

Ex 2

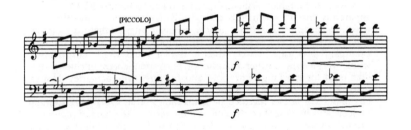

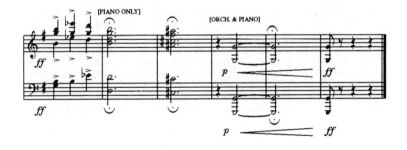

Ex 3

are piano-stave reductions I have reconstructed from the manuscript[34] of how the end of the work, from Figure 52, seems to have been performed before and after this revision.[35]

During the 1930s, the mixed success and comparative infrequency of performances became part of a vicious circle, in which poor critical reception, the cancellation of several potentially influential bookings (including the proposed American premiere mentioned earlier, and dates planned by Ansermet and Mengelberg for 1938), and delays in publication appear interconnected. Cohen not only appears to have been a poor performer of the work, but may even have played a role in delaying publication to preserve her exclusivity, a right which she guarded jealously.[36] Indeed Cyril Smith was the only

34. BL Add Ms 50385, f 74
35. Dickinson (1963, p 420) refers to the passages represented by examples 2 and 3, but seems to suggest that the music of 3 was 'original' and that six bars of example 2 was 'a rejected' possible revision.
    However, the difference between the British Library Pagination of Add. Ms. 50385 (which runs concurrently from ff 70–74, including paste-downs) and Vaughan Williams' pagination (which runs 97, 98, – then apparently inserts a leaf 98B with the Bax quotation – and then 99, which has example 2 in B flat minor), seems to suggest that my example 2 was the earliest link between the Bax quotation and the end, and that example 3 was used between then (c.1933/4?) and 1946. This reading seems verified by further manuscript correspondences (including the inks used for marking figure 52), and by early commentaries. Howes used the early manuscript score when writing for the *Musical Times* of October 1933 (a fact revealed by loans indicated in OUP Hire Library Ledger) and he described the end in these terms: 'Ten bars of orchestral ritornello serve to punctuate the Concerto with its final full stop' (cited Howes, 1937, p 38). Meanwhile, Dickinson, having access to this score many years later, by which time it contained both versions, explicitly placed his trust in the 1936 published solo part (Dickinson 1963, p 420). According to my reading, example 3 would have replaced example 2 by that date, and so it is hardly surprising to find it in the 1936 text.
    Bax's letter to Howells (Foreman, 1987 p 160) written within days of the first performance of the concerto and raising doubts about the form of the end of the concerto, may endorse the possibility, given his intimate involvement with the composer and the work, that Vaughan Williams made this revision very early in the concerto's life.
36. I am grateful to Lewis Foreman for information concerning Cyril Smith's performances.
    There appears to be extensive evidence that Cohen was an inappropriate soloist, including many letters in the BBC files, such as Boult's letter to Bliss cited above (15 September, 1942, BBC WAC Vaughan Williams Composer File 2B). Similarly, Vaughan Williams' letter to Cohen in August 1933, giving her permission to change the solo part, appears to

other major soloist to perform the work in these years and he only appears to have done so twice. What may have been more influential, however, was Vaughan Williams's wish to make revisions, about which Foss would almost certainly have known, and a massive financial retrenchment in OUP's Music Department in the early 1930s, a policy forced by the department's near-bankruptcy which caused the postponement of numerous major projects.[37]

When publication eventually followed in 1936, it involved the printing for sale of 500 copies of the solo part alongside an orchestral reduction, with the full score and orchestral parts made available for hire only. This choice seems to reflect the economics of a new era in music publishing, an age dominated by a 'listening' rather than 'performing' public, and, consequently, one in which financial return occurs through mechanical rights, performing rights and hire library fees, rather than through bulk sales of scores or parts.[38] The consequences of this prioritisation of intellectual property for inter-war music are huge, not least in sociological terms, with distinct communities being established among those who heard or performed the music, the nature of its transmission, and the emergence of multiple canons, variously performed, heard at traditional concerts or familiar through home

reflect her inability to manage it (Kennedy, 1964, p 237), and Hubert Foss (1950, p 142) wrote that 'I have not yet heard one pianist play it as the notes are meant to sound', which appears as only a thinly-veiled attack on Cohen. Cohen's *Music's Handmaid* (1936) and the repertoire for which she was famous suggests that her technique was most suitable for lighter textures, in particular works by Mozart, Bach and Chopin. Foreman (1983) casts a good deal of light on her personality and apparently habitual machinations to retain exclusivity for 'her' works, an impression which seems endorsed by a letter Norman Peterkin wrote to Ethel Bartlett (OUP Vaughan Williams Piano Concerto Files, 30 September, 1946) in which he said 'What *I'm* wondering is how HC [Harriet Cohen] is going to react when she hears all about how 'her' Concerto is being treated. I anticipate some fireworks!'.

37. Doctoral research explores the relationship of Vaughan Williams and the Press during these years, and the consequences which retrenchment during the 1930s had an departmental policy.

38. The enormous cultural change during these years from a sizeable piano-playing market to an enormous potential audience of people who did not read music is relfect in published economics, a central theme in histories of music's economics, including Boosey (1931), Peacock and Weir (1975) and Ehrlich (1989)

listening. In the case of the Piano Concerto, the domination of its early years by BBC performances, only a handful of which were broadcast, means that its early audience may well have been rather small, specialist, and London-based. This pattern is in marked contrast to the audience for other areas of the composer's reception, including the large communities of amateurs devoted to his large-scale choral works, certain orchestral works, and church music. Vaughan Williams's complex relationship and reaction to this changing context has been almost entirely neglected, but preliminary research seems to suggest that he was quite conscious of writing for different communities in appropriate styles and genres. Such an interpretation appears to reconcile the potential tension between his early resistance to the Performing Right Society (PRS) on the one hand[39], apparently from anxiety over the potential damage it could do for amateur music-making, and his appreciation of the benefits and opportunities of increased professionalism and investment in inter-war music, of which he was, as England's leading composer, a major beneficiary[40]. Many of his major orchestral works after the mid-1920s were apparently written for professional musicians, making demands beyond the range of contemporary amateur orchestras, and in the case of the Piano Concerto, he certainly seems not to have been prepared to tolerate any of the practical or technical orchestral constraints which he allowed in other works and genres, music which may have been written for a different community.[41] Ultimately the huge success of the Fifth Symphony and the sensation which surrounded the Sixth crowned him as the first English composer after Elgar to write orchestral music which appealed across a range of society, and Vaughan Williams's works seem to have done so by reaching 'the great listening public' rather than simply by frequent

39. Ehrlich, 1989, pp 60 & 123.
40. I am grateful to Peter Franklin for pointing out the interesting contrast with attitude Richard Strauss expressed towards amateur musicians in *Recollections and Reflections* (1949 & 1953).
41. A letter from Vaughan Williams to Cohen (3 August, 1933) collected by Hugh Cobbe, urges Cohen to refuse to play the work if Scherchen has an 'incomplete or inadequate' orchestra.

amateur performance.[42] Such a broad communal appeal appears central to Vaughan Williams's musical creed, and it seems to have been irksome for him when the Piano Concerto failed to achieve a wide audience, perhaps especially in the context of his huge success in reaching a wide cross-section of British society during the Second World War, and even more particularly as romantic Piano Concertos were in vogue in wartime Britain not least through their prominence in films.[43] In 1942 when the BBC planned its celebration of Vaughan Williams's seventieth birthday, Julian Herbage, then Assistant Director of Music, suggested to the Director, Arthur Bliss, that the F Minor Symphony and the Piano Concerto might not be suitable choices because 'they are inclined to be "inaccessible" and the latter [is] certainly considered as one of his least successful works.'[44] In fact, the concerto was broadcast, apparently thanks to pressure from Bax and Cohen, but the department's wish to broadcast particular works which they believed were characteristic and 'accessible' inevitably engaged in the process of selecting elements from the work of a many-sided artist. Retrospectively, the concerto appears to have remained a specialist preserve by its status on the one hand as a 'non-amateur' work, but on the other by its contemporary position as a 'professionals-only' work which failed to attract frequent broadcasts.

A second consequence of this kind of publication was that, precisely because the score and parts were not printed and widely sold, it was less tempting to regard the work as 'fixed', and Vaughan Williams remained free to make alterations after

42. The late rise to fame of various WW1 works, particularly the *Tallis Fantasia*, might be taken as part of this process, the music having come of age when the composer's reputation was ripe.

43. Myra Hess's role in the musical life of wartime Britain was, of course, immense, and I am grateful to Professor Ehrlich to alerting me to the popularity of piano concertos by Rachmaninov, Beethoven, Grieg, Tchaikovsky and Mozart during the war.
Vaughan Williams' frustration at the poor reception of the concerto is revealed in a number of letters to Cohen which Hugh Cobbe has collected, including one written on 10 June 1934, in which Vaughan Williams claimed she, Arnold Bax and himself were the only people who admired the work.

44. Herbage to Bliss, 19 August, 1942, in BBC WAC, Music General Vaughan Williams File 1,1940–1949.

successive performances. A major revision occurred in 1946 when Vaughan Williams collaborated with Joseph Cooper to make a Two-Piano adaptation of the solo part. The early history and reasons for this adaptation do not appear to be well-documented, although it seems possible that such an arrangement had been canvassed from its earliest years and Vaughan Williams had always refused.[45] Numerous 'musical' explanations were advanced by his contemporaries, including the idea that the original version was 'unpianistic' and that the balance of the solo part and orchestra might be assisted, and antiphonal effects might be created[46]. However, such explanations appear problematic when the two versions are compared; this new version, which Vaughan Williams authorized alongside the single-piano version, amplifies and thickens solo textures, and although antiphonal effects are briefly used, the new solo roles are not characterised significantly in any way different from the earlier text.[47] Interestingly, Joseph Cooper recently recalled that "RVW gave me 'carte blanche' to arrange the concerto as I thought best. But he said that I was to contact him if I needed guidance anywhere. I did need guidance here & there, and he always answered with a good solution."[48]

Vaughan Williams's semi-detachment from the creative aspects of making the arrangement seems problematic in view of his scrupulous attention to detail elsewhere in his compositional work, and it seems strongly to suggest that the arrangement may not have been made in response to ambitions concerning sonority. Conversely, there appears to be a strong possibility that it was an attempt to rekindle – or

45. Vaughan Williams wrote to Cohen in August 1946 that 'At the time of the first performance many people urged me to rearrange it for 2 pftes – they thought it too heavy going for one – But I held on so as to give the 1 pfte a good send off before I did anything' (extract courtesy of Hugh Cobbe) and Foss also recalled that rnany people had advised the change in the early years (1950, p 142).
46. Howes, 1954, pp 110–111.
47. An eight-bar addition (marked 'optional' in the published score) exists in two-piano presentation only, but this exclusivity seems simply to reflect Vaughan Williams never having made or authorised an arrangement of it for single piano.
48. I am grateful to Joseph Cooper for this letter and for permission to quote it.

rather enkindle – its performance life, particularly in a post-war context in which art music generally, and Vaughan Williams in particular, was flourishing.[49] Ethel Bartlett, a distinguished contemporary pianist who worked in a piano-duo team with her husband, Rae Robertson, was closely involved in the BBC–OUP network, and she wrote to Norman Peterkin (who headed the department between Foss and Frank) that, "You remember Hubert [Foss] asking VW years ago, on our recommendation to arrange it for us, & he then refused. I suppose he is tired of waiting for performances in its original form and getting none."[50]

Whether or not Bartlett is reflecting the composer's motivation, her comment certainly casts light on the consequence; following the charity Promenade concert in which the version was premiered, the work was primarily carried in this arrangement for the next forty years. It seemed to fill a small but distinct niche created by a number of piano-duo teams who enjoyed great success in Britain and the United States who were short of repertoire to perform with symphony orchestras.[51] The composer approved both versions of the work, (i.e. with a single or duo-piano soloist(s)) and they have co-existed throughout the subsequent history of the work. Vaughan Williams's preference, if he had one, is not as clear as it might seem from a letter he wrote to Frederick Page in December 1950, because the terms of his recommendation of the two-piano version could suggest that he wished the new revisions to be heard, and they, apparently, did not exist in some older, single-piano material. Those among Vaughan Williams's close circle had slightly different stances; Boult

49. Peacock and Weir (1975 pp 96-97, and p 100) have drawn attention to the effect that the war, and particularly its late days, had on the popularity of a wide spectrum of music, especially orchestral music. In forthcoming doctoral work, Vaughan Williams' wartime contributions and triumphs, and the extensive work of activity of Foss in ENSA and CEMA and via the BBC, will be explored in relation to Vaughan Williams' reception.
50. Oxford University Press Archives, Piano Concerto file, Ethel Bartlett to Norman Peterkin, 22 September, 1946. Interestingly, in the margin, is her autograph comment 'I'm hoping that HC's [Harriet Cohen's] performance with a WPA orchestra & the 'flop' may be forgotten by this time.'
51. The teams included Smith & Sellick, Bartlett & Robertson, Whittemore & Lowe, and Vronsky & Babin.

performed the work in both versions, but apparently preferred the duo-presentation, while Foss seems to have been unequivocal in preferring the solo presentation[52].

Vaughan Williams continued to make revisions, frequently, but not always, in response to a recent performance; in November 1946 he inserted a twenty-seven bar cadenza (at Figure 50 in the score), writing to Alan Frank that 'I think it had better be done in pencil since if the work is ever wanted again with one pfte the extra bar will not be used.'[53] His comment potentially has a dual significance; it seems to imply that he believed single-piano presentation may be less frequent (an implication which could cast light on his motivation for making the dual version), and secondly, it introduces a difference in the text and 'contents' of the two versions, an apparently small difference, but one which would have to be confronted in any systematic musical analysis. Of immense significance for the work, however, was the revision which he made in June 1947, following another BBC performance. Vaughan Williams entirely re-cast the end of the concerto which he had been dissatisfied with after the first performance and which he had already revised several times. Vaughan Williams replaced the quick and exciting *fortissimo tutti* endings which tonicised 'G' and explored the counter-subject of the

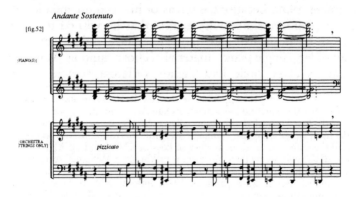

52. Foss, 1950, p 142.
53. OUP Vaughan Williams Piano Concerto File 119B; Vaughan Williams to Alan Frank, 13 November, 1946.

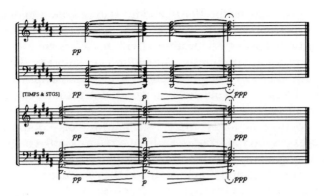

Ex 4

fugue (shown in examples 2 and 3), with a *pianissimo*, lightly-scored and slow-tempo ending in B major (example 4).

The consequences for the work as a whole are immense, and its significance appears to act on several levels; 1946–7 seems to have been a high-water mark of Vaughan Williams's popularity, and his reputation was based on numerous key works which end with quiet, 'visionary' epilogues, a formal innovation which ultimately became a highly characteristic fingerprint of the composer. Perhaps Vaughan Williams's replacement of a densely-motivic and tonally-decisive ending with a more ambiguous, remote close reflects something of a reaction to his own reputation, a re-working of a characteristic pattern, of whose success (in a problematic work) he could be more confident. His choice is usually judged to have been successful, and his self-reflexive response in the revision process may have parallels with Sibelius (see Hepokoski's reading of Sibelius' revisions of the Fifth Symphony).[54]

Over the quarter of a century between Vaughan Williams's last revision (1947) and the publication of the full score (1972), a nexus of influences operated to begin a process of stabilising and fixing the composer's reputation and work, a process which affected texts, performance traditions, reception and discourse. Dr R Vaughan Williams, OM was widely known to

54. Hepokoski, 1993.

be a 'Great Man' by the 1940s, and his stature grew inexorably with increasing age, involvement in public life and continued creativity. Following his death in 1958, his ashes were buried near Purcell's in Westminster Abbey, and in 1960, Mrs. Ursula Vaughan Williams's huge donation of his manuscripts to the British Library became both a wonderful resource and an important symbol of his status. Yet at the same time there were counter-currents; a younger generation of composers, broadcasters, administrators and musicologists was emerging which sought power within the establishments which Vaughan Williams had led and dominated, and they reacted against the older generation. Centre-stage, of course, was Britten, and many of the apparent polarisations between the old and new establishments reflect positioning over such issues as nationalism and internationalism, agnosticism and the established Church, left-wing radicalism and Churchillian 'nationalism', and, to some degree, sexual orientation. Vaughan Williams, perhaps the most 'establishment' composer England has ever had, was identified by the younger men as a principal 'conservative' in cultural, political, and musical outlook, a judgement apparently made in response to his unofficial 'position', but which appears ironic given the radical, leftist, agnostic, pacifist views he adhered to in his private life.[55]

Some of the broader cultural patterns at work during these years have been outlined by Frogley[56] but no small part was played by the gradual supersession of textless orchestral music by opera and song as the most influential forms of new English

55. The letters between Vaughan Williams and Rutland Boughton (cited in Ursula Vaughan Williams, 1964, especially p 322) seem to reveal the way in which Vaughan Williams' less eminent colleagues regarded him as holding an 'unofficial position.'
There has been a number of discussions of Vaughan Williams' political radicalism, most particularly by Harrington (1989) and Frogley (1993). Vaughan Williams' views on a number of subjects often seem surprising, a reflection of how deeply embedded the images and expectations of him have become. For example, Vaughan Williams' reactions to Churchill, who became almost an icon in of established Britain in these years, seem distinctly ambivalent, highly unusual for a man of his generation, as they emerge in documents dating from both before and after the Second World War, illustrated by a memo Vaughan Williams wrote during the 1926 General Strike (collected by Hugh Cobbe) and a letter to Michael Kennedy in January 1957 (Kennedy, 1964, p 388).
56. 1996 pp 20–22.

music, and the concomitant English cultural politics could be stylised as torn between the orchestral 'conservatives' and operatic 'radicals'. The shifting alignment of the BBC appears particularly important, with notable landmarks being Boult's departure in 1950 and the passionate championship of the newest cosmopolitan music by Glock's BBC (1959–1972). Glock's huge upheaval of policy, idolised by some and notorious with others, rapidly replaced one musical establishment with another. Donald Mitchell and Hans Keller also formed a powerful critical axis in British music criticism during these years and 'parochial' music, which was how Vaughan Williams became marginalised, became partially excluded from repertoire and was frequently assailed by critics.[57] This process had profound and complex effects upon the whole corpus of Vaughan Williams's music, apparently not leading to outright rejection (the popularity of key works seems to have made them impervious to the snubs of professional criticism), but rather to complex patterns in performance life, reception and the discourse of musicology, some of which left their mark upon this concerto.

Despite the much-discussed critical hostility of the period, there does not, however, seem to have been a commensurate and universal falling-off in performances of Vaughan Williams's music; indeed initial observations of OUP's hire library ledgers suggest that in many genres, particularly vocal music (except opera) and orchestral music, performances have been maintained at broadly similar levels. More detailed observation, however, seems to suggest an interesting

57. Glock's perception of Vaughan Williams' 'insularity' seems to have begun when his grant application to study with Schnabel in Berlin in the early 1930s was turned down by Vaughan Williams and Howells because "there was no need whatever to look abroad" (Glock, 1991, p 19). Glock's frustration with this kind of parochialism lasted throughout his long and influential career. Alan Frank seems to have been singularly unsuccessful in persuading Glock to arrange a BBC performance of the Piano Concerto during the 1960s, as suggested by a letter from Frank to Glock, 13 January 1961, in OUP Piano Concerto files.

Donald Mitchell's critical hostility to Vaughan Williams during these years has been discussed by others, especially Kennedy (1964, pp 330–331). The relationships between Vaughan Williams and Britten, and their publisher-champions Foss and Mitchell, may offer a fascinating study in the anxiety concerning influence.

sociological shift in his performers and audience; in the case of the Piano Concerto, apparently out of sixteen performances which appear to have been given in Britain between 1950 and 1972, six were given by non-professional orchestras and four by provincial professional orchestras; the London performances were almost exclusively given by Boult with the London Philharmonic. Meanwhile the BBC appear to have played the Piano Concerto only once in the period, a pattern of dissemination in marked contrast to its central role in the concerto's earlier life. These shifting patterns of dissemination will also be seen to characterise recent years of the concerto's life, and in the light of Kramer's *Music as Cultural Practice*[58], it might be proposed that the instability of the communities who hear and perform the concerto is an important element in the changing interpretations of the work. It is perhaps ironic and suggestive that beginnings of this important sociological shift seem to have begun during the very years in which historians, critics, and editors anxiously sought to assert the priority of definitive interpretations.

These tentative observations about social context seem insufficient evidence on their own, and yet the pattern also seems consonant with broader cultural trends. The technical capability of non-professional orchestras and their apparently growing familiarity with early and mid-twentieth century orchestral music, paralleled by the changing institutional pedagogies of pianists, could suggest that the concerto became potentially attractive to a different group of performers and their specific audience. At the same time, Vaughan Williams appears to have still be held in high esteem by influential people who remained outside London's professional musical and musicological circles (in total, twelve of the sixteen British performances from 1950 to 1972 took place in provincial venues in Leeds, Liverpool, Winchester, Scotland, Birmingham, York and Oxford), and other performances were promoted in Australia and the USA. Particularly revealing is that there were numerous performances in continental Europe, (Gothenburg, Oslo, Geneva, Stockholm, Milan, Denmark, and Rotterdam) and these were apparently thanks largely to

58. Kramer 1990.

British Council support, a body with whom Vaughan Williams may have retained high influence. Adrian Boult, who retired from the BBC in 1950, conducted some of the provincial and continental performances cited above (in both single and duo versions), and his recording of the work in 1968 with the LPO and the piano-duo team Vronsky and Babin put the concerto in prominent British record catalogues, and its 'authority' seems to have helped disseminate the work and to have exerted influence over many future performances.

Little documentation of the European reception of these performances appears to have survived, but the extensive promotion files of the New York OUP Music Department suggest that during the mid-century, the work suffered in a critical environment parallel to London's. Lyle Dowling's report, written in 1952 in his capacity as OUP agent in New York, typifies contemporary American critical reaction, and acts as a pertinent example of Treitler's 'politics of reception' (1991):

The most severe of the critical attacks was that of Arthur Berger (New York Herald Tribune). In my opinion, it led to the cancellation of the Frisco performance. Berger is one of the Nadia Boulanger set, a group of composers who are quite clever and write not badly – but who of course feel a sense of personal outrage when confronted by a personality like that of Vaughan Williams. If you are a specialist in turning out little cream puffs – and 'delicious' is the term Thomson, another Boulangerist, used of Berger's recent composition – you cannot bear (stamping the foot in petty indignation) a loaf of solid bread. You must get so mad you could spit! The Whittemore & Lowe performance was not attacked, so far as I noticed – the attack was on the music.[59]

Glock moved in Boulanger's circle, and this letter reveals the clear the politics of the communities involved, and indeed its language seems suggestive of the contemporary polemics of gay-heterosexual hostility.[60] Vaughan Williams's concerto appears not to have established a position with 'conservatives' who supported large-scale orchestral music, and yet neither did it win the approval of the new radical critics and

59. Oxford University Press Music Department, American Promotion Files Lyle Dowling to Alan Frank, 11 March, 1952.
60. I am indebted to Cyril Ehrlich for pointing this out, and particular the resonance of the language with Kurt Weill's *Lady in the Dark* (1940).

composers. The concerto, falling between stools, was largely neglected in the programmes of American orchestras; Ruth Watanabe, writing the programme-note for a 1960 performance by the Rochester Philharmonic was almost accurate when she claimed that the concerto was 'being played for the first time [in America] in well over a decade'.[61] Six years later, in response to an enquiry about performing the single-piano version of the work, John Owen Ward of OUP New York, wrote to Alan Frank that 'I've no idea when this was last done here – not for ages'.[62]

The wider process in which Vaughan Williams's life-work came to be interpreted and polarised can be outlined only briefly here, but the operation of constructing his reputation, against a background of hostility, was intense and immensely influential; seven monographs, for example, appeared in only fourteen years between Foss (1950) and the 'authorized' biographies of Ursula Vaughan Williams and Kennedy (both 1964). Foss was known to have a close professional relationship with the composer, and the impression of authority was apparently endorsed in reader's minds by his inclusion of 'A Musical Autobiography' written by the composer himself as a present to Foss. Not surprisingly, like his broadcasts, Foss's book shaped narratives about individual works, and in this case, they concerned the concerto's problematic status, the shock created by percussive piano-style, and its essentially 'symphonic' nature. Foss's central narrative laid great stress on the English background and heritage, cuisine, landscape and literature as powerful cultural influences on Vaughan Williams,[63] and Percy Young's biography (1953) similarly draws extensively on 'Englishness' and literary images and metaphors. In this context, Foss's identification of

61. Programme in OUP Vaughan Williams Piano Concerto File 119, 17 December, 1960.
62. John Owen Ward to Alan Frank, 12 July, 1966, in OUP Vaughan Williams Piano Concerto File 119B.
63. Frogley (1996, p 20) suggests that Foss's monograph of 1950 could itself make a fascinating object of study. My doctoral research involves examining the role which Foss played in the history and interpretation of Vaughan Williams and I hope to make some observations on Foss's monograph available shortly.

the concerto with Bartók and Liszt, a theme originating in his 1933 broadcast and popularised in his monograph, appeared all the more teasingly to position the work outside the mainstream of Vaughan Williams's music, as did his description of its style as 'experimental'. Frank Howes' biography, published by Oxford University Press (1954), explored the image of Vaughan Williams as a mystic and prophet which has since become a refrain of Vaughan Williams biography, and it also played a major role in prioritising Vaughan Williams's symphonies as his creative pinnacle. In suggesting that the concerto has affinities with Beethoven, Howes repeated his earlier articles (1933 and 1937) and furthered the process of canonisation during Vaughan Williams's later years. Howes' attempt to explain the keyboard idiom by invoking the popular Bach revival – he claimed Vaughan Williams's piano style reflected the 'jangle of the harpsichord' – is perhaps a defensive attempt to salvage a work which he admired but which had not found much success even with Vaughan Williams's enthusiasts, whose general tastes and reactions Pakenham (1957) articulated, in the partial light of some personal contact with the composer.

Day's biography (1961, 1964 rev. 1975), the first to appear after the composer's death, popularised inherited perceptions of Vaughan Williams and established the composer as a 'Master Musician' in Dent's influential series. Perhaps significantly, Day gives very little space to the concerto, and although he touches on two important issues it raises – the apparent conflict between the work and the composer's reputation (the first movement is described as 'Prokofiev-like' and written by a composer 'dismissed as a folky-homespun') and the difficulty of 'reconciling' the styles of its movements – he does not engage in discussion of either. Both he and Dickinson (1963) continue many of the threads concerning Vaughan Williams, although Dickinson brought a closer textual scrutiny, anticipating numerous approaches which have only recently become 'timely', including the importance of the manuscript collection, the subtlety of Vaughan Williams's exploration of mixed scale-types, and the potential relationships between musical style and Vaughan Williams's intended audience. Dickinson put the concerto in a historical context, raising but not answering the problem of its relationship with adjacent works, specifically through drawing contrasts with the richly melodious *Sir John in Love* (1929) and the 'introspective' *Riders to the Sea* (1936) and *Flos Campi* (1925). Like Foss, he stressed the 'symphonic' scope of the work and related it to the Fourth Symphony, identifying the work as belonging to a 'Mephistophelian tradition of Stravinsky and others' (p 308 and a similar observation on p 420). He also emphasizes elements such as 'triumphant bitonality' and mixed scale-types (pp 415 and 416) and the revised ending, which he describes as bring a quiet 'epilogue' with a 'suggestion of remote vistas' (p 420). Dickinson's unique 'musical' focus on works rather than biography – he appears slightly outside the circle and was the first author to historicize the distinctive lineage and patterns of Vaughan Williams history – raises important issues about the score to which we shall return, but his monograph was quickly overshadowed by the appearance in 1964 of two highly influential accounts, by Ursula Vaughan Williams and Kennedy, offering the comprehensive, authoritative and accessible 'Life-and-Works' of Vaughan Williams, studies which cemented and dominated the writing of Vaughan Williams history. Important ingredients were added to the critical recipe; Ursula Vaughan Williams observed that her late husband 'said that he had the Busoni transcriptions of Bach very much in mind' (1964, p 194), and Kennedy (1964 p 263) significantly emphasised the presence of Fauré and Ravel in the slow movement and also gave authority to the interpretation of the Bax quotation as a 'symbol of the friendship between Bax, Miss Cohen and [Vaughan Williams] himself' (p 236). Kennedy, despite his evident respect for the work, shared some of the ambivalence of his colleagues about its status, suggesting that (p 262) that it 'contains some of Vaughan Williams's best music though it is not one of his best works in a complete sense'. Crucially however, it is Kennedy who is widely perceived as the authentic voice, and his account includes extracts from numerous letters between Vaughan Williams and Cohen which revealed aspects of the genesis and revision of the work

(1964 pp 236–238); he also popularised the composer's descriptive programme note by including it in his catalogue of works (1964 pp 536–8 and 1980 pp 146–148). Just as influential, however, on modern Vaughan Williams writings is his almost 'authorial' admonition of writers making claims which the composer might not have wished:

It [the concerto] suffered, perhaps, from the determination of English critics always to cast Vaughan Williams in the role of prophet, or mystic, or metaphysician instead of composer. It is very much to be doubted whether the Piano Concerto, however 'tough' its language, was intended as a sermon in sound. Its successor, the Fourth Symphony, was not, but it soon became so fettered with 'meanings' that it became difficult to hear the notes for the words.

Four years later, Kennedy wrote

Perhaps the percussive treatment of the instrument of the instrument surprised English critics in the 1930s so much that, apparently overlooking how much less ferocious it was than comparable works by Bartók, they decided the concerto was a grim straight-faced affair prophetic of international violence. It even gave rise to a dissertation on mysticism in music.[64]

This resistance to multiple meanings is the negative side of the process of establishing stable, fixed terms for Vaughan Williams criticism. A strong creed had emerged for enthusiasts, embracing a distinct collection of views concerning performance, repertoire, nationalism, judgements of taste and value, and the role of music in society. Such concepts, powerfully articulated in the multiple biographies, became a huge part of a widening gulf and increasing hostility between a huge community of dedicated Vaughan Williams supporters, many of whom are 'outside' music's professions but who contribute to it, and a close circle of music's 'professionals' who are antipathetic to its philosophies. Advocates' constructions of the composer's reputation in a context of increasing critical hostility polarised the terms of the debate, with prevalent images becoming increasingly

64. Kennedy's programme note for a Vaughan Williams memorial concert given by Boult and the London Philharmonic Orchestra at the Royal Albert Hall on 17 November, 1968.

reinforced. Each frequently-recurring adjective contained its equal and opposite connotation, depending upon critical situation: 'traditional' becomes 'old-fashioned', 'honest'/'coarse', 'blunt'/'blatant', 'simple'/'naive', 'national'/ 'parochial', 'accessible'/'amateur', and so forth. It was in the context of this circular but raging debate that professional music historians sympathetic to Vaughan Williams found it hard to position the concerto. Dickinson (1963, p 19) observed 'the piano concerto has not properly arrived' and Kennedy's comment cited above, that it 'contains some of Vaughan Williams's best music though it is not one of his best works in a complete sense' (1964, p 262), reflects uncertainty about how the status and style of the work might be interpreted within the general mid-century impression of the composer. Their comments are, of course, historically situated, and Kennedy later revised his assessment not least in the 1968 programme-note cited above. The history of Vaughan Williams's famous contemporaries as diverse as Mahler and Orwell also reveals complex, shifting patterns of interpretation in which particular works become emblematic while others become neglected[65]. It seems that during the crucial years in which Vaughan Williams's biography was written, the Piano Concerto was cast into the deep shadows of extremely powerful constructions of the composer; and, once marginalised, descriptions of its idiom seemed to fall outside the terms of the Vaughan Williams debate.

The attempts to define an authoritative critical-biographical interpretation of the composer are mirrored in the textual histories of numerous key works during the sarne period, and the Piano Concerto offers a fine example. Vaughan Williams's new ending of 1947, apparently the last major change he initiated, caused a good deal of practical confusion. Some of the scores and sets of parts – amounting to about half a dozen sets of photographs of manuscript copies during the 1950s and 1960s – had been distributed to agencies in the USA, Bonn,

65. See particularly Rodden's *The Politics of Literary Reputation: the Making and Claiming of 'St George' Orwell*, 1989.

Paris, and Sydney. The changes were not consistently transferred into all material; manuscripts were subsequently sent back and forth, and the process of keeping up with revisions was piecemeal. There was a good deal of uncertainty even among Vaughan Williams's publishers and authorised historians as to whether all of the changes applied to both the single and double-piano versions, and even Boult, who had premiered the work and was its most frequent performer, became confused about Vaughan Williams's revisions.[66] In summary, versions explicitly authorised by Vaughan Williams existed as follows:

Single Piano, ending in 'G'	1933–1946
Single or duo presentation, both ending in 'G'	1946–1947
Single or duo presentation ending in 'B'	1947

The situation was slightly more complex, however, because it seems that the use of older, unrevised sets of parts meant that the 'G' ending was also performed during the composer's later years, so in practice all four combinations existed (ie of duo and solo presentation, and closure in 'G' and 'B'). There was

66. Letters between OUP London and OUP New York during December 1949 preserved in the New York Promotion files reveal that there was a good deal of confusion between the various agencies promoting the concerto as to its form, with some staff apparently not realizing that Vaughan Williams had written a Piano Concerto. Letters between Boult, Alan Frank and Christopher Morris between 1959 and the issuing of the full score in 1972 reveal that a number of details of Vaughan Williams's revisions remained obscure, and that Boult had performed cuts which he later regarded as unacceptable.
Howes (1950, p 108) wrote that the work ended in G after the date of the revision to B. The error presumably arose because he re-used the *Musical Pilgrim* article of 1937 and failed to up-date it. Even Kennedy (1964, pp 263–264), Vaughan Williams' most authoritative historian, erroneously believed that the ending remained different in the single and duo versions of the work, when he wrote, '*The ending of the one-piano version* is changed so that instead of the blaze of angry sound there is a quiet and serene disintegration of the fugue subject in the strings, pizzicato, against a chord in the pianos: a beautiful but less convincing finale.' He later revised his critical judgement and swapped his labels around when he wrote (1996, p 9) that VW 'provided the work with a quiet (and more poetic) ending on a chord of B major. Most pianists who have returned to the one-piano version keep the two-piano ending' (the italics are mine). I believe that the simplest way to describe the endings are by key or date, as it now seems evident that both single and duo presentations in each key were authorised by Vaughan Williams at different times.

also uncertainty about the cadenza at 50, and whether or not it was optional.[67]

Alongside the major textual issue concerning versions, a plethora of markings was put in scores and parts, reflecting various levels of 'authority', and causing a good deal of confusion. The piano-duo team Vronsky and Babin helped clear up ambiguities in the solo parts during 1959 and the text remained an 'unstable' mix of versions until Frank and his eventual successor, Christopher Morris, began the process of preparing a 'corrected' edition for publication, timed to appear as part of the celebration of the centenary of the composer's birth. Morris studied various parts and scores, received help from both Roy Douglas and Adrian Boult, and issued a text which presents the single and duo-versions as alternatives (although it implicitly favours the duo version by its position on the page) and prioritises the composer's later ending in 'B'. It also offers an admirable practical solution to the many smaller textual discrepancies. Even in an age of recordings, broadcasts and music hire libraries, the immediacy with which a score is available is surely an important event in the dissemination of music, particularly in an age in which musical scholarship is often based on texts rather than performances. The choices made in the 1972 edition have become crucial, influencing subsequent recordings and discussions, not least in the total absence of the 'G' ending from any performances, and in its marginalisation in discourse as a historical fact, 'an earlier version', rather than a viable musical possibility.

The huge importance of a printed text, however, is also reflected negatively in a tendency to equate 'text' with 'work', a danger which I have tried to address throughout this paper

---

67. In the exchange of letters concerning the text of the concerto between Adrian Boult and Christopher Morris during 1972, Morris explained that the cadenza between 50 and 50A in the score was marked 'optional' because it seemed the most rational interpretation of an early Hire Library solo-part for the two-piano version in which the copyist has marked 'ad lib'. (It seems reasonable to suppose that this was marked in orchestral parts – used for both single and duo-piano performance – to warn players that the cadenza may be omitted as the cadenza has never existed in the single-piano version. In this sense it could only be 'optional' in a two-piano version.)

and in the conceptual model given above. In the case of the Piano Concerto the problem manifests itself in the difficulty that the 1972 score, in having to select between variant readings of details, will permanently 'fix' one solution and destroy another, in instances where Vaughan Williams may have wished to preserve two options. This problem is, of course, far from unique, and it is a dilemma faced by most editors of critical editions, but the problem in the case of Vaughan Williams is particularly acute. On a practical level, we are awkwardly poised between having too much and not enough manuscript evidence; the autograph score in the British Library contains numerous hands, not all of which may be identified, and the older material which survives at OUP also contains significant markings in numerous hands other than those of individuals potentially authorised by Vaughan Williams. There is a superfluity of annotation, affecting orchestration, pitch content, dynamics, accents, tempo and rubato, and I doubt whether it would be possible to find any formal criteria for selection and prioritisation in any self-proclaimed *Urtext* or critical edition.

Secondly, and ironically, casting certain details of a Vaughan Williams score in stone (as the 1972 text effectively does) may run up against the deeply-held (although complex) beliefs of the composer, whose wishes the editor might otherwise seek to fulfil. Perhaps small examples, from the first folio of the British Library autograph full score will illuminate the problems. Such details as those below, although comparatively slight, recur throughout the 77 folios of the autograph score alone, and in each case, editorial choice necessarily changes aspects of the way the music sounds. Bassoons double the trombones and strings at the start of the upward scale which begins in bar 3, and in bar 4 the clarinets join them. It appears that the trombones were at one time cut (in red pencil), and this cut itself appears to be rubbed out. The reprieved trombones do appear in the 1972 score, but the bassoons and clarinets, crossed out in grey pencil in the manuscript, are omitted in the printed text; the strings marked '*poco f*' in the manuscript are marked '*mf*' in the 1972 reading. It is also worth noting that *Allegro* is in the ink of the base layer of the manuscript and 'moderato' is inserted in the blue pencil used for rehearsal letters. The grounds for keeping the trombones and for reading 'moderato' as authorial are strong, although I have not seen anything which clearly reveals Vaughan Williams's wishes as regards the clarinets and bassoons, or 'mf' instead of 'poco f'. Both details probably originate in Vaughan Williams's instruction to Cohen, Boult, and Holst to 'thin' the orchestration if they considered it too thick[68]. This very practical instruction opens a dam: are later thinnings by Boult authorial? Are conductors whom Vaughan Williams may have authorized on other occasions permitted to make similar textual changes? Would the re-instatement of Vaughan Williams's earliest orchestral details be invalid after Boult and Holst had thinned them? Would it be acceptable to perform a hybrid of the base-layer of the manuscript combined with selected cases of Boult's revisions, depending on the soloist, orchestra, and venue? The questions are potentially endless, and the certain answers few; although one might understand the frustration felt by Vaughan Williams's editors and friends when details are changed, it remains, I believe, impossible to assert that any single text ideally represents the composer's 'intentions', although the range of reasonable alternatives is stabilised by the 1972 text.

Even in the twenty-five years since the text of the concerto was stabilised, its meanings and associations have continued to evolve. The cultural changes of recent decades inevitably place the concerto in new contexts, illuminating it from new angles, and also, undoubtedly, casting new shadows over once-visible attributes. A spreading cultural relativism deconstructs the confident hierarchies of inter-war and post-war value-systems and concepts of taste. At the same time, British music has become an attractive field of study in the new institutional climate of English-speaking further and higher education, and the consequent diversity of perspectives and pedagogies inevitably changes the terms and ambitions of discourse. The changing economics of Compact Discs and new recording technology enables rare works to find markets, exploding the

68. Kennedy, 1964, pp 235–236.

powerful role in canonisation played by the older recording oligopoly, a situation potentially paralleled by the impact which cable and satellite broadcasting may have on the BBC's virtual monopoly of broadcast classical music. These, and other factors, appear to be entirely re-structuring music's many canons so comprehensively that the very concept of canonicity seems fragile. The consequences for Vaughan Williams are huge.

Numerous influential conductors in the English-speaking world, including Andre Previn, Leonard Slatkin, Andrew Davis, Richard Hickox, Bryden Thomson, and Vernon Handley, have built a reputation for their performances and recordings of British music, and through their work, neglected scores have been revived. The cumulative effect is to change and perhaps even expand the older selective canons of Vaughan Williams's music, although the process is far from clear; of the four new recordings of the Piano Concerto made in this period, three appear targeted at a rather specialist market, but these recordings, excellent and important as they all are, may be more an indication of cultural or economic change rather than a sign that the Piano Concerto has conclusively 'arrived'. Similarly in his preface, Alain Frogley (1996, pp xii–xiii) urges caution about regarding "positive signs as a fully fledged revival". Indeed, it appears the concerto continues to be an 'exotic' item in concert programmes, 'speciality' performances being promoted by Vaughan Williams's professional champions on the one hand, and by orchestras associated with ambitious education institutions on the other.

Similarly, within the musicological arena, the huge expansion of researchers in the field appears by no means to be conclusive evidence that Vaughan Williams's music is re-emerging from a period of general neglect, as the communities and discourse of studies in the British Musical Renaissance often appear quite independent from recent critical musicology. This rift seems to be reflected in the hostility often shown towards new analytical approaches to the music and works such as Stradling and Hughes' *The English Musical Renaissance* (1993), which challenges assumptions about the independence of music from 'external' forces, including those of a social, economic and political nature. Ironically, resistance to perspectives offered from 'outside' the established traditions of the field seems to run the danger of stifling potentially fruitful arguments about context and perpetuating the marginalisation of the subject within musicology. But even within this arena, Alain Frogley's *Vaughan Williams Studies* (1996), could offer a potentially defining moment in the subject precisely because its distinguished and cosmopolitan writers offer a significant diversity of methodology and situation in a discourse which has perhaps hitherto suffered from its homogeneity and rigidity. Arnold Whittall, one of Frogley's most significant contributors, referred in passing to the attraction exerted by 'problem' pieces, and it is precisely the problematic nature of this concerto which raises important textual, analytical, and historical issues. However, what may be more important, particularly in a wider, post-modernist context, are ways in which the historicizing of interpretations of the Piano Concerto suggest potentially fruitful dialogues and interactions between established discourse about English music and recent musicology.

During the last decade, two of the most influential commentators on Vaughan Williams, Wilfrid Mellers (1989) and Michael Kennedy (1995), have offered fascinating, rather personal reactions to the concerto. Mellers integrates his account into his wider reading of Vaughan Williams as a 'double man', torn between extremes in his psychology and historical situation, an interpretation which Mellers sustains in connection with the concerto by comparing the harsh modernist world of the outer movements with the luxuriant lyrical diatonicism of the middle of the slow movement. His discussion of the style of the concerto embraces the canonised 'influences' (Bach, Busoni, late Beethoven, and Liszt), but also suggests associations with neo-classicism, white-note Stravinsky, Ravel, Britten and Tippett. Kennedy, writing in 1996 reviewed his thirty-year old assessment of the work, now describing the concerto as a 'masterpiece', and in retelling some of the established narratives concerning the work's history, he places a different emphasis than he had in 1964:

Too much was made of the so-called difficulties of balance in the concerto. It is no more problematical in this respect than Bartók's first concerto, with which it has features in common ... In its embrace of neoclassicism, it is not too far away from Stravinsky's Violin Concerto

Revealingly, their readings seem to return to some of the contexts suggested by Foss in 1933 but which largely disappeared from Vaughan Williams criticism after the Second World War. The avenues opened by such readings are immense. Vaughan Williams's contacts with European music, via Foss, Boult, Edward Dent and the ISCM seem far more extensive than has been widely recognised, although Greene's recent account of Holst's *The Planets* (1995) has raised some closely-related material. The interplay in Vaughan Williams's music between 'cosmopolitanism' and 'Englishness' – concepts which themselves are mutable and historically-situated – offers fascinating opportunities for future work in several arenas, not least in the interactions between national identity and tradition opened up by Hobsbawm and Ranger (1983), Boyes (1993) and others. The enduring presence of 'nationalism' in the discourse, and its resistance as a concept to any single fixed definition, makes reception history, now widely practised across the humanities, a crucial ingredient. And conversely, the polemics of the debate concerning national identity in music seem to demand close analytical observation of Vaughan Williams's music in order to interpret its potential relationships with such concepts. Taruskin's monumental and masterly study of Stravinsky – who's career poses extraordinarily complex questions of nationality – explores an interplay of such disciplines, and he offers a rich contextualisation of musical nationalism which could liberate Vaughan Williams's historians from their former anxiety over the pejorative association of nationalism with parochialism.

Similarly, despite problems surrounding formal discussion of tonality in much mid-twentieth century music – of which this concerto offers an interesting example – the recent historicization of analysis does suggest ways in which history and analysis may intertwine. The Toveyesque formal models characteristic of early, semi-authorized descriptions of the concerto are also brought into interplay within recent work on

Vaughan Williams's contemporaries, most notably in Hepokoski's discussion (1993, p 5) of Sibelius's fragmentary and implied 'deformations' of standard-textbook structures. His reading could have wide resonance in Vaughan Williams studies, in ways prefigured in Whittall's reading of Vaughan Williams's Fifth Symphony (Frogley, 1996, pp 187–212), an approach which interweaves history and analysis, and introduces the 'humane' approach heralded by Kerman (1980), while remaining far-removed from the context in which Vaughan Williams studies and structuralist musicology appeared mutually repellent[69].

Hepokoski historicizes the numerous revisions of Sibelius's Fifth Symphony in the context of its composer's changing situation as a 'modern' who became out-moded in the face of an aggressively evolving 'New Music', a reading which, as mentioned above, seems fruitful in Vaughan Williams studies. In the case of the 1947 revision of the Piano Concerto, for example, it appears that the tonal aspect of the revision depended upon the early version being a 'resolution' (in favour of G) of the ambiguity between G and D as tonic at the opening of the Finale (see the Fugue beginning at Figure 30). A reading which embraces the prominence given to D mid-way through the movement (for example, at Figure '39') is suggestive of a 'post-tonal' tonal prolongation, which makes the eventual arrival of 'G' conclusive, a triumphant effect in conjunction with the *Allegro* tempo, rich style and dynamics of the orchestral writing. Conversely, the revised B major end seems to satisfy a tonal pull towards B in the crucial second cadenza, a tendency which existed in the earliest versions of the work (see Figure 51, b. 11 ff.), creating a mediant relationship with the movement's other powerful pitch-centres ('G' and 'D') which mirrors important mediant relationships elsewhere in the concerto.[70]

69. My own analytical work on the concerto's first movement adapts basic techniques from both pitch-class set theory and post-Schenkerian concepts of prolongation to study the ways in which Vaughan Williams sustains the contours and tensions of sontata tradition without referring to many of its standard practices.
70. In his chapter, 'The Wages of War: the Double Man in the Piano Concerto and the Fourth Symphony' 1989, pp 160 ff.

The tonal issues involved in the 1947 revision, however, may also offer important interpretative clues. The second cadenza, which had always tonicized 'B', recalls the music of the central section of the slow movement; primarily, it emphasizes the theme which Kennedy and others have identified as derived from the Bax theme, whose explicit quotation Vaughan Williams had removed after the first performance. By closing the work in the key and atmosphere of the slow movement quotation (the B major revision incorporates a smooth transition from cadenza to orchestral close (see Figure 52)), Vaughan Williams appears to lay the foundation for listeners to prioritise its significance; in the context of the work as a whole, the tonal simplicity of the material, both in the centre of the slow movement (Figure 18, b. 4 to Figure 24) and in its recall in the finale (Figure 51 b. 34, the *Largo Sostenuto*, to Figure 52), acts as a very striking foil to the tonal obscurity and employment of complex scale-types which characterise the concerto. This recollection, which closes with a widely-spaced sustained B major triad, Andante tempo and light orchestration, creates a striking atmosphere, singularly removed from the rest of the work. The effect might be described as a musical image of a tranquil island in a turbulent world, an impression which Mellers likens to the secret garden of Ravel's *L'Enfant et les sortilèges*[70]. Kennedy seems to express this too when he wrote that the music inhabits 'the world of Ravel's enchanted garden in *Ma Mere l'Oye*' (1995, p 9), an atmosphere juxtaposed with an apparently ironic and sarcastic waltz which many, including Kennedy and Mellers (1989, p 161), have suggested is a first-cousin of Ravel's 'savage' *La Valse*.

Both Mellers and Kennedy seem to find in the music the allure of 'other-worldliness', secret, remote, and blissful, and a reading suggestive of musical escapism may offer an interpretative key to the significance of Bax; the 'brazen' romanticism of his music, perhaps mirrored in his escapist identification of his lovers as 'fauns, nymphs, and fairies' (see Foreman 1983 and 1992), may have exerted a strong attraction on Vaughan Williams in a harsh, 'modern' world. Such an interpretation would, of course, be entirely speculative so far as

Vaughan Williams's intentions are concerned, although it seems far from incompatible with Vaughan Williams's instruction to Cohen to play the original passage 'far off, like a dream'. Given the pervasive imagery of successive interpretations of the work, one could even read the succession from an ironised waltz in the 'Finale alla Tedesca' by a French-inspired enchanted garden as embodying an allegory of contemporary politics, a reading which is not incompatible with the possibility raised above, that Vaughan Williams's revision reflects his reaction to his reputation as it had emerged by 1947.

In a post-modernist world, the existence of multiple authorized versions of a work seems far less problematic; a work which provokes questions about inherited interpretations of the composer appears attractive rather than vexing. Yet, despite tracing historical aspects of the shifting interpretative processes and contexts, there remains a sustained cultural tendency which seeks to 'fix' analytical, textual, or interpretative truths permanently, reflecting a deeply-rooted ideology which is often as powerful as it is unspoken. British musicology at times appears resistant to notions of the inevitable 'mutability' and ever-changing meaning of works of art, a stance which appears ill at ease with the concept of a 'living' work. The conceptual model illustrated in figure 1 was introduced to distil visually this concept, and the mutual interactions between the composer, the score, performers, performance and reception history, and ourselves, which lie at the heart of this biography of a living work. Recent French-American post-modernists have tackled this temptation directly, not least by problematising the role which we ourselves play in the work, a power which we exert whether we recognise it or not. The idea that audiences 'construct' meaning, is, of course hardly new or radical. It seems particularly ironic that inter-war British composers should suffer from attempts to 'fix' their work. Lascelles Abercrombie wrote a passionate plea for 'The Liberty of Interpreting' (Abercrombie, 1933), which was published by OUP during the composition of this concerto; Vaughan Williams himself famously and passionately advocated a role for re-interpreting

Bach in way which was meaningful for his own age (Vaughan Williams, 1987, pp 170–177).[71]

In his broadcast before the first performance, Foss described the Piano Concerto as 'new-romantic', apparently in an attempt to situate the work in relation to contemporary styles. Attempting to reconcile the harsh 'modernism' of the outer movements with the pan-diatonic lyricism of the 'Romanza' raises important issues concerning the role of coherence, organicism, and juxtaposition in the creation of form. It also offers striking parallels with some of Vaughan Williams predecessors and contemporaries, relationships which Frogley (1996, p 17) suggests have often been neglected in the emphasis placed on the influence of folk song, Tudor music and Purcell. Whittall's analysis of the Fifth Symphony (1996, pp 187–12) frequently invokes Mellers in his reading of the 'doubleness' and 'ambiguity' of Vaughan Williams's sophisticated compositional technique, and my reading of the concerto similarly emphasizes the constant interplay of traditional forms and procedures with innovation. Hepokoski's observation (1993, p 5) of Sibelius's use of style seems to offer a pertinent approach to discussing the doubleness of this concerto:

within the modern style it was entirely legitimate, and quite normal, to evoke traditional or antiquated gestures in a non-immediate way ... an 'old-world' melody or turn of phrase could be set forth 'as if in quotation marks' or as a retrospective evocation of a not-quite-graspable, naive or pre-modern wholeness remembered or dreamt of, but now fading rapidly or inaccessible in current times. (Although their individual styles and intentions differed markedly, Mahler and Elgar, in particular, would be attracted to this technique.) Even entire structures could receive this quotation-mark treatment ...

Analytical observations of style suggest that Vaughan

71. The very notoriety of the views Vaughan Williams (1950) expressed in 'Bach, the Great Bourgeois' ironically reflects deeply-held British assumptions concerning authenticity. Vaughan Williams' performances of the *St Matthew Passion* and B Minor Mass involved enormous choirs and the adaptation of the orchestral and continuo material in order to span the cultural distance between Eighteenth Century Leipzig and Twentieth Century Dorking. The changed text and context necessarily brings forward new meanings, among others shifting the significance of the event from its context in liturgical divine worship to a secular concert which celebrated the social value of communal music-making.

Williams, in mixing and perhaps 'quoting' musical styles as distinct as Fauré, Ravel, Bartók and Stravinsky, was engaging in a modernist aesthetic practice which Hepokoski identifies as characteristic of Sibelius (ibid, p 5ff.). This observation may help us to interpret Vaughan Williams's relationship with his European contemporaries and to open interpretative windows on the 'other-worldliness' of the concerto's distinctively beautiful 'Romanza'.

The term 'neo-romanticism' itself, however, has also evolved new associations, primarily through Dahlhaus's *Between Romanticism and Modernism* (1980), in which Dahlhaus argued that music gained a special significance in German culture 1850–1890 by its position as a romantic art in a modernist world. Dahlhaus's concept of an emerging new-romantic music, whose power is all the greater because of its abstraction, its 'otherness', its unique romanticism in a positivist, modern culture, may be helpful when considering Vaughan Williams's aesthetic system. The composer's adamant refusal to interpret his music in the terms of the 'real' world around him accorded a special attribute to the remoteness of music's meaning and its unique ability to escape verbal definition. Vaughan Williams, in his late years, wrote to Kennedy that:

I think you are right in suggesting that to attach "meanings" to music is a mistake. Each person may attach their own meaning if they like, but it does not follow that their meaning will have the same meaning to anybody else – music is too universal for that ...[72]

Ironically, however, Vaughan Williams's silence concerning this concerto, and various other important works, left an interpretative space which subsequent generations have zealously claimed and reclaim, as if speaking on the composer's behalf The power of the debate has – in conjunction with other elements kept this work from public view.

But the situation may be changing markedly, not least through the expansion of older, selective canons of Vaughan Williams's music in performance and the opening up of discourse. In relation to this concerto, the recent work of

72. Kennedy, 1964, p 382.

Kennedy, Mellers, and Stradling and Hughes changes the possibilities considerably; the work's stylistic duality may now be taken as an opening – forming connections with other works, and reading it as expressive, for example, of the composer's own personal 'doubleness' or as a political allegory – rather than simply as a stylistic failing. Such an approach opens critical windows, which moves the dialetic process of interpretation forward, in marked contrast to the rather exclusive patterns of its earlier reception. One longs for a major soloist to really take the work up, revitalising it in performance and creating new audiences, a process which in its turn may stimulate fresh critical approaches and enrich perceptions of its composer.

VII

Anthony Payne

Encompassing His Century's Dilemmas the modality of Vaughan Williams

W HEN AS A TEENAGER I FIRST HEARD GEORGE
Butterworth's orchestral rhapsody *A Shropshire Lad*,
it opened a window onto an entirely new and
magical world. Musically I was completely self taught: I
borrowed books from the public library on how to read music
and how to compose, and I was a little shaky on some aspects
of theory. I did not know what it was about Butterworth that
made it sounded so special, but I saved up my pocket money,
plucked up courage and brought a full score at the august old
Novello showrooms. It seemed to me after looking rather
inexpertly at the music as if two keys were being suggested at
the same time. There was A minor in the lower strings, and
strong hints of D major in the melody on top. I didn't know
about modes at the time, but I did know a new and powerful
emotion had been unlocked in me. It was a year or so before
I found out that the Dorian mode was responsible for the
miracle. But with a schoolboy's innocence I had already
perceived what it was about this kind of music which so
attracted generations of English composers – its poignant
ambivalence, producing major chords where traditionally
attuned ears expected minor, and vice versa.

Butterworth, like Vaughan Williams and others, discovered

modes through his folk song collecting, and explored their new harmonic possibilities in providing arrangements for tunes that were originally sung unaccompanied. The new kinds of chords which the modes produced were strongly characterised by the nature of the sixth and seventh notes of their scales. Here's an A minor scale, for instance (Ex 1):

Ex 1

And here's its Dorian mode counterpart (Ex 2):

Ex 2

What about the kind of harmony that stems from these scales? You might think it is only a colouristic detail, but the repercussions were to be momentous.

The effect of this type of harmony is piquant, and it has a poetic immediacy which links it to impressionist harmony. But it took a composer of imaginative genius to recognise there was far more to modality than dressing up folk songs or making picturesque impressions, in other words producing "watercress" or "cowpat music". What Vaughan Williams realised was that modes held the secret to writing a new kind of symphonic music. It would enable him to cast off the yoke of Austro-German practice, and create new sound-worlds. But how did he do it, and what was the vision that compelled it?

The symphonic methods which the young Vaughan Williams imbibed from his Brahmsian teacher Stanford, and indeed through all the music he would have heard and played, were based on the traditional heirarchy of major and minor keys. All such music undertook elaborate tonal journeys. A movement would travel outward from the home key, arrive in a neighbouring key, and then find its way home via a sequence of more or less related ones. The commonest way of establishing each new key was to sound the chord on the fifth note of the new scale, then follow it with the home chord. The most familiar progression in music. The tension and resolution inherent in those chords typifies a kind of music which pursues a dramatic argument, orientated towards achieving a final goal. It builds tension, and then resolves it as it reaches each new stage in the musical argument.

What if, like Vaughan Williams, you were a contemplative visionary, and didn't want to expressive yourself that way? He discovered that by using modes he could achieve two vital things. First, as we've already heard, he could build chords that sound different from traditional tonal ones, and are emotionally ambivalent. Second, and even more importantly, he could move more discreetly between modes than you can between keys. This would make the music less like a journey or an argument, with clearly signposted stages, more like a contemplative experience which floats between areas of feeling. Let's briefly look at the technical reasons for that.

If you play a scale beginning on any of the white notes of the piano, you get a mode. Each scale gives a subtly different pattern of tones and semitones – seven different modes in all, each with its own name, commanding seven subtly different areas of feeling. Yet in traditional tonality the white notes offer only one possibility C major.

Vaughan Williams uses these refinements with consummate skill in one of his most magical transitions. At the beginning of the scherzo in his Fifth Symphony, he gives a unison melody to all the strings in the pentatonic mode. This is not one of the modes I mentioned just now: it's a primitive precursor of them which avoids all semi-tones. Vaughan Williams plays around with it for a while, and then at the top and bottom of the texture he superimposes a tune in the Phrygian mode – that's the one from E to E on the white notes. In spite of the fact that both ideas use only white notes, there's a miraculous change of mood from light to shadowed, (Ex 3, on following page).

It's also worth emphasising one final and very significant difference between almost all of the modes, and the major and minor scales. This is that the modes mainly have flattened leading notes, the seventh note of the scale. The immediate result is to give what's often derided as a folksy sound. The more far-reaching outcome is that the establishment of a modal area does not have the clear focus produced by the sharp

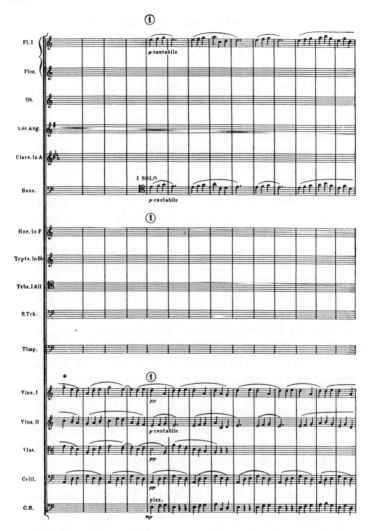

Ex 3: *Fifth Symphony*

leading notes of the tonal system. Those leading notes press
urgently upwards towards resolution, and clearly define key
when they achieve it. With flattened leading notes, resolutions
are less strongly defined and are robbed of their forward
thrust, a further reason for the discreet nature of modal
processes.

I've dwelt on the modal aspect of Vaughan Williams's style because the very word modal has come to be used almost as a term of abuse by critics who haven't understood its true significance. There are still important things to be said about that, and I'll come back to them later. But I don't want to give the impression that there's no more to Vaughan Williams's style than its modality. He was crucially affected by aspects of French impressionism, for instance. Do not forget he went to study orchestration with the younger Ravel – the mark of a truly great man's modesty. Debussy, too, left his mark.

Parallel chords like we find in French impressionists became one of Vaughan Williams's trade marks, but not for the sensuous or evocative qualities they seem to have held for them. To make an involved story short: if you add exactly parallel chords to a simple melody, you get accompanying notes which don't belong to the key of that melody. They gently undermine the tonality, or modality, leading to a general instability or ambivalence. A sequence of such chords appears twice at the beginning of Vaughan Williams's Pastoral Symphony. And there's a further subtlety in the passage, which represents a vital aspect of Vaughan Williams's style. This is bi-tonality, or, more accurately, bi-modality, with the music suggesting two modes at the same time. I touched on it earlier in showing how Vaughan Williams combined different modes based on the white notes in the Fifth Symphony. But if the modes are used in different transpositions, taking in the black notes, you get more dissonant combinations, and this appealed to Vaughan Williams's sense of duality and instability. Just after the start of the Pastoral Symphony, pentatonic melodies on the oboe and solo violin, using only the white notes, clash gently with the predominantly black notes of the parallel chords underneath. The dark sub-text here makes you wonder how this profoundly spiritual work, clouded by the composer's war-time experience, could ever have been thought merely picturesque, or concerned with cows looking over gates.

So far we've looked at aspects of Vaughan Williams's style in fine detail, and I want to show how those primal elements work on a broader canvas. But before I do, I'd just like to touch on one further aspect of the composer's technique. It's an important one, and it relates Vaughan Williams to another twentieth century giant who used modes, but seems, perhaps for reasons of cultural snobbery, to have got away with it. I mean Bartók. After Vaughan Williams had combined strongly contrasting modes in a dissonant texture, the next, logical step was to invent modes of his own which were more dissonantly constructed. There's a fascinating one in his visionary choral work *Sancta Civitas*, completed in 1925. It starts out like the Lydian mode, with a sharpened fourth, and continues with the flattened sixth and seventh of the Aeolian mode.

Now savour the magnificence of the counterpoint he constructs from this synthesised mode. The voice parts pile in on each other until the very earth seems to shake. 'Lord God almighty, heaven and earth are full of Thy glory' sings the choir. But there's no easy emotion in these shouts of praise. The faith has been hard won, and Vaughan Williams is aware that it might need fighting for again. (Ex 4).

Ex 4: *Sancta Civitas*

© by Ursula Vaughan Williams.

Reprinted by kind permission of Faber Music Ltd, London.

Now to a longer section in which Vaughan Williams uses modal procedures to articulate a profound symphonic process. The Fifth Symphony reveals a vision of purity and serenity unique in twentieth century music. It opens with an idea of inspired simplicity which nevertheless depends on the subtlest of resonances.

Some people feel this passage to be bi-tonal: a D major horn call and a C major melody on the strings. Others, and I think rightly, hear it in the mixolydian mode on D – like D major but with a C natural, not a C sharp. Nevertheless, there is tonal ambiguity in the passage, because it's poised over a C, not the key note D. This produces quiet tensions, indicating that its serenity has not been easily attained. When quite suddenly mixolydian D becomes Dorian D, and all the F sharps become F naturals, the vision remains in focus but somehow expands. Modality, of course, is responsible. To go from major to minor like that in the tonal system would involve changing more notes: the sixth as well as the third degree of the scale would be flattened – a more dramatic and positive change of colour, no doubt; but it would have disrupted the contemplative feeling which only modal transition can sustain.

The C in the bass continues throughout this magnificent section. Next it underpins a paragraph in the Dorian mode on F, where the music darkens impressively. Then it becomes the keynote for a clinching passage in Dorian C. What gives this music its undisrupted visionary feeling is that the successive modes all have more vital notes in common than their counterparts in the tonal system. The C sharp, for instance, which would have been necessary to establish an opening in conventional D major, would have contrasted strongly with the C natural in the subsequent section in F. In the Dorian modes both D and F have C natural in their scales.

But at that point in the movement Vaughan Williams faces a problem. So far the music has floated seamlessly, achieving single-minded contemplation through modal subtleties. To have continued any longer would have been to risk monotony. The problem's solved by a masterstroke. No longer does the music slide imperceptibly between modes. It jumps un-expectedly into a key that seems worlds apart, E major (Ex 5) –

Ex 5: *Fifth Symphony*

traditionally the key of heavenly radiance. It's as if a magic casement has been opened onto a new, visionary landscape. The need to provide symphonic contrast, while remaining true to the processes of the contemplative mind are gloriously reconciled.

For many people that radiant music epitomises Vaughan Williams's art. But he's a composer who covered a wider range of feeling than almost any other 20th century master. Few since Beethoven have comprehended such hugely contrasted worlds as we find in Vaughan Williams's Symphonies Third, Fourth, Fifth and Sixth. I've often felt that the diametrically opposed viewpoints of Mahler and Sibelius are embraced by Vaughan Williams. Mahler's idea that a symphony should be all-encompassing is true of Vaughan Williams's Second and Sixth, while Sibelius' search for purity and logic is paralleled in the Englishman's Third, Fourth and Fifth.

The idea of modes being linked with a pure, lyrical world like that of the Fifth Symphony probably accords with many people's preconceptions. But that modality is at the basis of a violently disruptive work like the Sixth is less often spoken of. When the symphony's opening tumult dies down, it moves into an ironic jigg, based on one of Vaughan Williams's synthesised modes – a G minor which has a sharpened 4th degree of the scale, and a flat sixth and seventh (Ex 6).

Ex 6

It's perhaps also worth highlighting the rhythmic subtlety of this jigging music, which Vernon Handley conducts so imaginatively in his recording. Not just another folksy dance rhythm, as some might quip, but a complex, almost jazzy superimposition of triplet jigging in the accompaniment, and ordinary quaver jigging in the melody.

Next comes a poignant lyrical span which the jig keeps interrupting. The melody doesn't immediately reveal its secrets, but its modal shapes are continuously changing. We hear Dorian, Aeolian and Lydian elements, which give alternating major and minor inflections. Never did the composer articulate more movingly the great dilemma: that envisaging serenity is not quite the same thing as achieving it. It lends his art a profound humanity. There is here, and indeed throughout his later music, a serene insecurity which is one of the great contributions to 20th century music.

By now I hope I've suggested that the vast range of Vaughan Williams's music has very little to do with watercress and cowpats. The folk song element was very quickly transcended, and put to universal, visionary use. Which isn't to say that there are no folkloristic works in his output, or ironic references to folk music in his more ambitious works. Also many composers were influenced by such elements in his style, but lacked the bigness of vision to make of them what Vaughan Williams did.

However, it's becoming increasingly clear that Vaughan Williams has had a deceptively wide-ranging influence on much of significance that followed in his wake. He didn't merely spawn a school of pastoralists. Wilfrid Mellers in his outstanding book *Vaughan Williams and The Vision of Albion*[1] Links Vaughan Williams more or less directly with such composers as Maxwell Davies and even Birtwistle, as well as the likes of Rubbra, Howells, Hadley and Finzi.

Rubbra, for instance, is a perfect example of a composer of stature who was creatively influenced by Vaughan Williams, never slavishly reflecting him either in stylistic mannerisms or essential thought. Here's a passage from Rubbra's Second String Quartet which is utterly characteristic of his structural originality. Evolving and accelerating in a way that reminds us, perhaps, of Sibelius, the music suddenly achieves lyric incandescence. Harmonies include parallel motion which, as in Vaughan Williams, leads to instability, while the melody in the first violin slides from mode to mode, achieving something like the older composer's serene uncertainty. But it's all on Rubbra's own terms. (See Ex 7 on the following page).

That's hardly the music of skipping lambs or peasant song, modal though it is. Rubbra discerned, if only subconsciously, what Vaughan Williams was really about, and paid him the

1. Barrie and Jenkins, 1989.

compliment of relating to his modality at a profoundly creative
level. Another master, probably closer to Vaughan Williams in
his modal usage, though very much his own man, was Herbert
Howells. It was hearing the premiere of Vaughan Williams's
Tallis Fantasia at Gloucester Cathedral that helped determine
the seventeen year old Howells' creative path, and the two men
remained close friends.

Ex 7: Rubbra: *Second Quartet*

You can sense the shadow of the senior composer in much
of the modal writing of Howells' masterpiece *Hymnus Paradisi*,
but the rich, ecstatic textures don't quite encompass Vaughan
Williams's duality, yet Howells' command of extended
structure and his sustained intensity of emotion, matched only
perhaps by Delius among his English forebears, reveal a quite

special vision. There's a harmonic sensuousness that helps bind the polyphony and points key structural moments, and if there are not the varied levels of experience we find in Vaughan Williams, there is, in the magnificent Sanctus of *Hymnus Paradisi,* an interpenetration of the heaven-born music of the Latin text and the words of Psalm 121 "I will lift up mine eyes unto the hills". Heavenly and earthly protestations interact in visionary fervour.

Compared with Howells, even more so with Vaughan Williams, Patrick Hadley may be a lesser figure, but he commands a touchingly passionate range of feeling, and perhaps in his best works he shows, like Finzi, a little of Vaughan Williams's duality of expression. For Hadley, folk song still lived as a source of emotion, both elegiac and exuberant, and in *The Trees so High* he achieved the remarkable feat of generating the thematic material for a four movement symphonic work from a single folk song. If he lacked Vaughan Williams's symphonic scope, Hadley was still able to evolve a grand paragraph through modal technique.

It's often been said that any composer who didn't respond to the Second Viennese School's revolution automatically rendered him or herself anachronistic, which brings me to an important statement of Vaughan Williams's position in twentieth century music. Faced, like Schoenberg, with the need to forge a post-Romantic language which would move beyond established tonality, yet also somehow subsume it, he came to vastly different conclusions. Subsequent generations may have felt that he was backward looking in the light of Schoenberg's explorations, but no more so than Bartók, and Vaughan Williams, too, opened new doors for those who followed him. With today's broader temporal perspective, we can see that he found a way of encompassing his century's dilemmas and preoccupations. Vaughan Williams was, as Wilfrid Mellers points out, an example of Montaigne's 'Double Man', believing what he disbelieved, unable to rid himself of what he condemned. This lent him a many-sidedness, a breadth of vision and a humanity which will always sound fresh and contemporary.

VIII

John Huntley

The Film Music of Ralph Vaughan Williams

———◦◦◦———

IT IS DIFFICULT, IN THIS DAY AND AGE, TO IMAGINE, HOW a man near enough seventy years old could take on a new and demanding discipline like writing for the cinema. Much to the recorded annoyance of people like David Lean, "Smart" people still referred disparagingly to "the flicks" – not something that serious artists (especially serious composers) engaged in, unless they wanted to put their careers in the concert hall in jeopardy. Despite the occasional involvement of people like William Walton and Arthur Bliss, there were quite a group of composers whose careers in "Serious music" were to be damaged for the rest of their lives by involvement in the movies – William Alwyn, Benjamin Frankel, Arthur Benjamin. Ironically, it has taken fifty years (and their departure from the scene) for their chamber music, operas and symphonies to be played and occasionally recorded. Perhaps it was because his concert hall reputation could not be questioned that Vaughan Williams was able to do so much, not merely for his own obvious pleasure in being part of the film process but also because his work helped so much to gain respect for other practitioners.

There are varying accounts of how Vaughan Williams came into film music. According to Muir Mathieson, who had been asked to organise the music for a big war propaganda film to be directed by Michael Powell (with a generous budget) he had discussed the matter with, amongst others, David Lean, and was told that two main themes were required. The first was a powerful grand overture to suggest the sweep of the Canadian countryside and the second was for a sequence involving a vast co-operative farm, run by an emigre group in the heart of Canada. This seems to be the earliest reference to the possible "casting" for RVW. We know too that two colleagues from the Royal College of Music, Arthur Benjamin and William Alwyn, had now and then talked about the joys of film music to RVW. Muir said that he went down to Dorking to call on Vaughan Williams and found him a bit depressed because this was the height of the Blitz and the possible invasion of Britain by Germany and Vaughan Williams felt somehow he ought to be making a stronger contribution to the war effort. At the time he was going round the village with a hand cart, collecting scrap metal! It seems a bit unlikely but stronger things happened in wartime. So, instead of the caution that Muir was anticipating, when he outlined the plot of the film – *49th Parallel* (to be known in America as *The Invaders*), he found Vaughan Williams Positively enthusiastic.

It was all completely new for VW, even the timings:

when the film composer comes down to brass tacks he finds himself confronted with a rigid time-sheet. The producer says 'I want forty seconds of music here!' This means forty, not thirty-nine or forty-one. The picture rolls on relentlessly, like fate. If it is too short it will stop dead just before the culminating kiss; if it is too long it will still be registering intense emotion while the screen is already showing the comic man putting on his mother-in-law's breeches.[1]

Who could have described the basis of film music better than that. One of my jobs on later films was to liaise between composer and studio; I always began by quoting RVW! These restrictions might have seemed a source of great annoyance but not for this composer:

Film composing is a splendid discipline, and I recommend a course of it to all composition teachers whose pupils are apt to be dawdling in their ideas, or whose every bar is sacred and must not be altered. A film producer would

1. R. Vaughan Williams: 'Film Music IN *British Film Music*, edited by John Huntley. Skelton Robinson, nd (1947). All the quotations in this article are from this source.

make short work of Mahler's interminable codas or Dvorak's five endings to each movement.

To see Vaughan Williams at work during the recording sessions was always a joy. I remember him as, unlike some I could name, being humble about the whole film process – genuinely anxious to learn how it was done and what was required. One day on the recording studio, I recall him calling the third assistant sound mixer "Sir"! And how quickly he grasped the fundamentals of writing for the screen, even down to the acknowledgement that there were certain things a man born 25 years before the cinema was even invented could not do:

There are two ways of viewing film music: one, in which every action, word, gesture or incident is punctuated in sound. This requires great skill and orchestral knowledge and a vivid specialised imagination, but often leads to a mere scrappy succession of sounds of no musical value in itself. The other method of writing film music which personally I favour, partly because I am quite incapable of doing the former, is to ignore the details and to intensify the spirit of the whole situation by a continuous stream of music.

This chosen approach is supremely well illustrated in the overture to *49th Parallel*, the whole content of *Scott of the Antarctic*, the main theme from *Coastal Command* and much of *Loves of Joanna Godden*. In view of the subsequent success of the *Sinfonia Antartica* and the concert suite from *England of Elizabeth* (where the original film score was largely swamped by the commentary), the words of Vaughan Williams when he first started his film career are truly amazing:

Should film music have any value outside its particular function? By value I do not mean necessarily that it must sound equally well played as a concert piece, but I do believe that no artistic result can come from this complex entity, the film, unless each element – acting, photography, script and music are each in themselves intrinsically good.

Although in his early days, Vaughan Williams said he was not up to the close-synchronised technique (known in those days as "Mickey-Mousing" it) his work shows an increasing grasp of film devices and one is often surprised when he comes up with the sort of musical pointing-up such as Walton achieves in *Henry V* or *Richard III* The sudden dramatic appearance of the German U boat in Canadian waters at the start of *49th Parallel*, the penguins in *Scott of the Antarctic* or the unexpected sadness for an aircraft shot down over the Atlantic (even if he is a German) in *Coastal Command*. Again, the boundless ability of a seventy year-old to grasp and adapt to new ideas:

I soon found that the main stream flow of a musical idea can be modified (often at rehearsal!) by points of colour superimposed on the flow. For example, your music is illustrating Columbus's voyage and you have a sombre tune symbolising the weariness of the voyage, the depression of the crew and the doubts of Columbus. But the producer says, 'want a little bit of sunshine music for that flash on the waves'. Now, don't say, 'Oh well, the music does not provide for that, I must take it home and write something quite new'. If you are wise, you will send the orchestra away for five minutes (which will delight them). You look at the score to find out what instruments are unemployed – say the harp and two muted trumpets. You write in your flash at the appropriate second, you re-call the orchestra and the producer, who marvels at your skill in writing what appears to him to be an entirely new piece of music in so short a time!

All this suggests that Vaughan Williams thought film music was the best invention since sliced bread. But he was well aware of the snags:

Some years ago, I happened to mention to Arthur Benjamin that I should like to have a shot at writing for the films. He seemed surprised and shocked that I should wish to attempt anything which required so much skill and gained so little artistic reward. However, he mentioned my interest to Muir Mathieson and, one Saturday evening, I had a telephone call asking me to write some film music. When I asked how long I could have, the answer was ' 'till Wednesday'. This is one of the bad sides of film writing – the time limit.

One of Vaughan Williams's objections was taken seriously and since then, a number of composers are more and more being brought in right from the beginning – men like John Williams and Patrick Doyle. This message from Vaughan Williams actually got through:

When the photography is finished, when the dialogue and the barking dogs and the whistling trains and screeching taxis have been pasted on to the sound-track (I expect this is an entirely unscientific way of expressing it), then, thinks the producer, 'Let us have a little music to add a final frill'. ... The various elements should work together from the start. I can imagine the author showing a rough draft to the composer; the composer could even

sketch some of the music, and if it mutually approved of, the scenes could be
timed so as to give the music free play. Let us suppose, for example, that the
film contains a scene in which the hero is escaping from his enemies and
arrives at a shepherd's hut in the mountains. The compose finds he wants a
long theme to 'establish' the mountain scenery, but the producer says 'That
will never do; It would hold up the action'. And so they fight it out. Perhaps
the producer wins and the composer has to alter or modify his music, or the
producer is so pleased with the composer's tune that he risks-the extra
length.

This is exactly what happened on *Scott of the Antarctic*.
Vaughan Williams was given a script in advance and wrote the
big main theme with the wind machine effect and the echoing
female voice before the film was assembled. When recording
time came, the director (RVW calls him 'the producer') said
the opening music was far too long and the shots of the
Antarctic landscape too boring ("holding up the action"). But
the music director (Ernest Irving) insisted on Charles Frend
hearing the full Vaughan Williams score. Director Charles
Frend was so impressed that he actually did extend the visuals
to fit the music by asking for all the out-takes of the landscape
scene to be taken and re-cut so that the music was heard in full.
All of which led Vaughan Williams to say:

I still believe that the film contains potentialities for the combination of all
the arts such as Wagner never dreamt of.

IX

Jennifer Doctor

"Working for her own Salvation": Vaughan Williams as teacher of Elizabeth Maconchy, Grace Williams and Ina Boyle

———◦◦◦◦———

IN THE 1970S, THE COMPOSER ELIZABETH MACONCHY WAS asked to prepare a short talk about her studies with Vaughan Williams fifty years before for a BBC television programme. The following excerpt from the first draft of her script recalls the qualities that were fundamental to Vaughan Williams's unorthodox, but effective and inspiring, approach to teaching:

I first came to know Ralph Vaughan Williams in 1925. when I became a pupil of his at the Royal College of Music. He was in his early 50s and I was 18. It was the beginning of a friendship that lasted to the end of his life: – & perhaps the thing that strikes me most in looking back is how little he changed over all those years. Even his appearance remained almost unchanged. The large looming figure so familiar at the R.C.M. only became a little more stooped & the always rather shuffling walk a little slower. Otherwise he never grew old – & was just as he had always been with his lively sympathy & interest in other people & his quick enjoyment of a joke.

I was a pupil for 6 years. He was not a conventional teacher – & I find it difficult to describe his methods of teaching – his other pupils would probably find the same difficulty. But we should all agree that he was an inspiring teacher – by which I mean that he stimulated us to write better music than we should have done otherwise. And he set a standard of absolute musical integrity & complete & uncalculating devotion to music. He had little respect for the rules & conventional methods of teaching composition & never followed a formal scheme ...

He was very much alive to other people's music and to the experiments that were going on, even when he didn't like it, and always on the side of the young: he was ready to give advice & practical help to any young composer whose music he thought worthwhile, whether or not he was a pupil. His own pupils went back to him for criticism & advice & above all for encouragement to the end of his life – Few people can realise how much time he ungrudgingly gave.[1]

These memories have an immediate value today in providing us with a somewhat different perspective on a man who is now revered as one of the most important and influential British composers of this century. However, when one considers that these reminiscences were written by a woman who studied with Vaughan Williams in the 1920s – a time when British music was still in the initial stages of establishing a "post-renaissance" identity, and when women composers were relatively few in number – the positive and encouraging image of Vaughan Williams that is depicted here points to a deeper significance. In this paper, I will explore Vaughan Williams as a teacher not only of Maconchy, but of her two close friends, Grace Williams and Ina Boyle. Descriptions found in his students' writings and correspondence enable us not only to gain further insights into Vaughan Williams's pedagogical methods, but also into the highly significant role that he played in encouraging his women students to pursue careers as professional composers.

Vaughan Williams began to teach at the Royal College of Music in 1919 after finishing his war service. During these post-war years, the British musical scene underwent social and economic changes that fundamentally transformed traditional expectations. New technologies, such as the gramophone, film

1.   Elizabeth Maconchy, first draft of talk for BBC TV Omnibus Biography, undated. Maconchy's memories of Vaughan Williams's teaching also appear in "Vaughan Williams as a Teacher", *Composer*, no 2, March 1959, pp 18–20.

    I am very grateful to Nicola LeFanu, Marian Glyn Evans, Ursula Vaughan Williams, St Hilda's College, Oxford, the BBC Written Archives Centre (BBC WAC) and the Board of Trinity College Dublin for permitting me to quote from letters and other papers cited in this article. I would also like to thank Hugh Cobbe for his help with deciphering difficult passages in Vaughan Williams's handwritten letters.

and radio, brought art music to mass audiences, which had little, if any, previous experience of it.[2] In particular, John Reith's BBC, resolute in its aim to educate as well as to entertain, brought music to the British public on an unprecedented scale; radio broadcasts featured art music from the standard and contemporary repertories, with special emphasis on promoting British composers. By this time, it was no longer unheard of for British women to pursue successful careers as composers, especially in the sphere of song-writing.[3] Moreover, a few, such as Ethel Smyth, Rebecca Clarke, Dorothy Howell and Poldowski, gained recognition as composers of larger-scale works, intended for concert or stage performance. Thus, at the time that Vaughan Williams began teaching at the RCM, not only was interest in British music growing, but a number of women had already broken the ice as acknowledged composers of serious genres.

Perhaps it was this positive climate that encouraged a remarkable group of young women to study composition at the College in the 1920s. Maconchy met the Welsh composer Grace Williams there, as well as the Irish composer Ina Boyle, who visited the RCM on occasion for lessons. In addition, composers Elisabeth Lutyens, Dorothy Gow, Mary Chater, Helen Perkin and Imogen Holst attended the College during this period. As Williams later recalled, "most of us arrived at the Royal College of Music at the same time without knowing anything at all about each other, coming as we did from quite different backgrounds. ... it was very unusual that this should have happened in the late twenties."[4] In particular, Maconchy, Williams and Boyle remained in close contact in later years, and require more detailed introduction here.

Maconchy was born in 1907, one of three daughters of Irish parents who were living at the time in Hertfordshire. The family remained in England until 1919, when they rejoined

2. See Cyril Ehrlich, "New Directions", *The Music Profession in Britain Since the Eighteenth Century* Oxford, Clarendon, 1985, pp 186–208, and "The Marketplace" in *Blackwell History of Music in Britain*, vi: *The Twentieth Century*, ed. Stephen Banfield. Oxford, Blackwell, 1995, pp 46–8.
3. See Sophie Fuller, "Introduction", *The Pandora Guide to Women Composers: Britain and the United States, 1629 – Present*. Pandora, 1994, pp 17–20.
4. Williams, in interview with A J Heward Rees, "Views and Revisions", *Welsh Music*, v/4 (Winter 1976–7), p 7.

relatives near Dublin. Maconchy's parents had little interest in music; although she was given piano lessons and began to compose piano pieces at the age of six, she did not attend concerts or hear professional music performances while growing up.[5] Her father died of tuberculosis when she was 16, and her mother subsequently moved the family to London. Maconchy soon began her formal musical education at the RCM. She remained there for six years, studying piano and composition, first with Charles Wood, and from 1925, with Vaughan Williams; she also worked on orchestration with Gordon Jacob. During the 1930s, Maconchy established a reputation as a leading young British composer. After the war, her success continued, although not on the scale that she had achieved earlier. She is known especially as a chamber music composer, recognized particularly for her 13 string quartets, although she also received acclaim for her chamber operas, orchestral works, concertos and choral settings. Unusually, Maconchy never taught or became affiliated with an institution in a professional capacity. She preferred to work from her home in Essex, where she raised two daughters, the younger of whom is the composer Nicola LeFanu. Nevertheless, Maconchy strongly supported the development of British music and devoted much time to organizations such as the Society for the Promotion of New Music and the Composers' Guild. She continued to compose until the mid-1980s, and lived until November 1994.

Grace Williams was born in 1906, a year before Maconchy, in Barry, Glamorgan. She came from a musical family: her father was a school teacher who conducted a boy's choir (for which she was accompanist), her home overflowed with music and gramophone records, and her family eagerly attended concerts of visiting orchestras and went to London for the Proms. She went to Cardiff University in 1923 and took a B.Mus degree. In 1926 she continued her education at the RCM, like Maconchy studying composition with Vaughan Williams.[6] After finishing her studies, Williams taught at a

5. Maconchy, "A Composer Speaks", *Composer*, no 42, 1971–2, p 25.
6. "Grace Williams: a Self-Portrait", *Welsh Music*, viii/5 (Spring 1987), pp 7–16. Malcolm Boyd, *Grace Williams*, Composers of Wales, no 4. Cardiff, University of Wales Press, 1980.

girls' school in London. However, she never enjoyed this work, and after the war returned to Barry, where she lived until her death in February 1977. She worked as a free-lance composer, writing primarily for BBC schools programmes and also composing music for films. Recognized as one of the most important Welsh composers, Williams is perhaps best-known for her large-scale orchestral works and concertos, although she also fulfilled commissions for many choral pieces and wrote an opera.

Ina Boyle was born in 1889 in her family home near Enniskerry, in Ireland, and remained there in near-isolation throughout her life. She studied violin and cello as a child, and later went to Dublin for composition lessons; she also studied composition by correspondence with Charles Wood, a cousin. She did not formally attend the RCM, but came to London for lessons with Vaughan Williams in February 1928 and periodically during the 1930s. During these visits, she heard concerts, visited museums and acquired books, broadening her cultural awareness and knowledge. Throughout her life, she received her compositional inspiration from poetry, and her most significant works are for orchestra, for solo voice and chamber ensemble, and for chorus. Her isolation meant that she heard few performances of her music; nevertheless, she continued to compose until her death in March 1967.[7]

Although these three composers spent most of their adult years in remote locations in England, Wales and Ireland, their innate compositional talents were bolstered and encouraged throughout their lives by bonds that were forged in the 1920s at the Royal College of Music. These ties were enhanced in 1926 when Maconchy and Williams arranged for College composers to meet on a regular basis to share their music and ideas.[8] The meetings firmly established the practice among these composers of discussing and offering carefully thought-

7. Maconchy, *Ina Boyle* Dublin, Library of Trinity College, 1974. Also from an unpublished diary and the composer's handlist of works [Trinity College Dublin].
8. Maconchy reported on her progress in arranging the meetings in a letter to Williams, undated but written in 1926 [private collection].

out, constructive criticisms of each others' works, which was continued throughout their careers.

At the centre of this network and one of its binding forces was of course Vaughan Williams. As Maconchy's recollections revealed, Vaughan Williams's teaching method and commitment to his students' development set an example that profoundly influenced each student's way of thinking about his or her own compositions and those of his or her colleagues. In fact, this learning process replicates a pattern that had had a profound impact on Vaughan Williams's formative years. He recalled that a vital influence on his own educational development was a circle of friends who met at the RCM in the 1890s:

> The benefit that one obtains from an acadamy or college is not so much from one's official teachers as from one's fellow students. I was lucky in my companions in those days. Other students at the College were Dunhill, Ireland, Howard Jones, Fritz Hart, and Gustav Holst. We used to meet in a little teashop in Kensington and discuss every subject under the sun. ... I learnt more from these conversations than from any amount of formal teaching.[9]

In contrast to his own learning experiences, formal lessons with Vaughan Williams were apparently a source of inspiration for his students and directed their long-term approaches to music and to composition. His misgivings about structured teaching methods apparently led him to develop a unique and unconventional style. As Maconchy later recalled:

> The reason for [his] apparent lack of method was his distrust & rejection of ready-made solutions. All through his life he chose the difficult way of working out his own salvation! And this is what he encouraged his pupils to do – to think for themselves in their own musical language. Technical brilliance for its own sake he despised – he fully realised the importance of an adequate technique – For him the sole purpose of technique was how to give the clearest expression to one's musical ideas. This is something for which there is no formula & it can't be learnt at second-hand – out of books for instance: he hated text-books. He taught one to learn direct from the music of the past (from Bach in particular). He used to play the works we were discussing on the piano – often as piano duets (very odd performances

9. Vaughan Williams, "A Musical Autobiography", *National Music and Other Essays*, 2nd ed. Oxford: Oxford University Press, 1987, pp 185–6.

too – he took charge of the pedal & had a way of putting it down firmly at the beginning & only taking it up again at the end).[10]

Another student, Michael Mullinar, described his lessons in a short article published in 1926. Like Maconchy, Mullinar emphasized the way in which Vaughan Williams encouraged a student to discover his or her own compositional voice.

Dr. Vaughan Williams never forces his own ideas on you when giving instruction in composition. ...
He corrects all technical errors, of course. If your harmony does not seem to be going well in a definite direction, he asks you what you want it to do; and then, after you have told him (if you can) what you are trying to work out, he shows where the progression is doubtful or weak. ...
He queries all weak passages, and asks you to think over them for a few days, until you yourself arrive at the conclusion that they actually are weak. If after all you cannot realise that they are weak, and so cannot think his way, he does not wish them to be altered.
If he considers that a work which falls short of being satisfactory could possibly be improved, he will offer his ideas, but only as suggestions, and he will not allow you to adopt them unless you really feel that way and can make the ideas your own. ...
His leading advice is, 'That one must always write what one *feels*, and never what one thinks one ought to feel'. He directs you to be yourself, and it does not matter how old you are before you really find yourself.[11]

Jasper Rooper, who began his studies with Vaughan Williams in 1923, recalled that playing his composition exercises on the piano was an integral part of the lesson:

I used to look forward to each lesson as the great event of the week. He gave me very few exercises to do but encouraged me to produce something of my own each week. Each pupil was encouraged to play his work on the piano even if it was written for voices or strange combinations of instruments. He would listen – sometimes with his eyes shut as if he was asleep – on one occasion he was, but this was the composer's fault for writing soporific music. He would sometimes say 'I like that' and my whole world was full of joy. Other times he would express his displeasure in no uncertain manner.[12]

10. Maconchy, first draft of talk for BBC TV Omnibus Biography, undated.
11. Michael Mullinar, "Dr Vaughan Williams as Teacher", *The Midland Musician*, i/1, January 1926, pp 8–9.
12. Hugo Cole, "Vaughan Williams Remembered", *Composer*, no 68, Winter 1979–80, p 26.

Several students remembered, not surprisingly perhaps, the importance that Bach played in the learning process. According to Leslie Russell, who studied with Vaughan Williams between 1928 and 1931:

At my first lesson he studied my 'masterpieces' silently and with complete attention, throwing out a few questions and suggestions here and there; then, taking his pipe from his mouth he said 'Good. Now go away and write me some bad Bach' ... I can truthfully add that when I returned the next week and played my exercise he pronounced it to be 'good bad-Bach'.[13]

Russell also remembered the variety of subjects that were discussed at his lessons.

At [an] early lesson he warned me 'Remember, Russell, there is no such thing as Middle C' and we then discussed the colours of a single note of the same pitch when played by different instruments, or sung ... At yet another lesson we discussed his calculatedly outrageous statement that 'it wouldn't have mattered if Beethoven had never been born'. ... I recall yet another lesson at which we discussed that 'The great glory of Music is that it is absolutely useless'. I once asked him, after a lesson at which I felt that my efforts at composition were even more inadequate than usual, why he troubled to teach such mediocre pupils as myself. The reply, devastatingly candid, was that he hoped that, if he taught enough of us, one real good 'un would be discovered.[14]

Perhaps the most unusual source of information Vaughan Williams's teaching methods survives in a small, hand-written diary that was kept by Ina Boyle.[15] Although the diary entries are not in any way remarkable, they provide a record of each lesson that she had with "Dr VW" as she called him (unlike Maconchy and Williams, who always called him "Uncle Ralph"). Entries include comments about what pieces were worked on, what his main opinions were, and thoughts about other music that they had heard recently. Because Boyle only studied sporadically, when she came to London from her farm in Ireland, the sessions themselves may not have been typical compared to those of students whom Vaughan Williams taught regularly. Boyle brought a number of recently written

13. Leslie Russell; "Remembering Vaughan Williams", *RCM Magazine*, lxviii/3, 1972, p 80.
14. *Ibid.* pp 80–81.
15. The diary is in the Boyle Collection, Trinity College Dublin, TCD MS 10959.

pieces with her each time she came to London, and the lessons centred on discussions of them, rather than on composition exercises such as those recalled by Maconchy and Russell. Nevertheless, the Boyle diary is of interest today in that it provides specific details about what went on in one composers' lessons with Vaughan Williams.

In all, Boyle had 17 sessions with Vaughan Williams between 1928 and 1936. In her first seven lessons, all of which took place in February 1928, she and Vaughan Williams considered a Phantasy for violin and chamber orchestra, a Psalm for cello and orchestra, a Rhapsody for soprano and string quartet, her "Glencree" Symphony and several songs. Vaughan Williams's reactions to her pieces varied, some parts described as "scrappy" – a word that recurs again and again – but some receiving a more positive response. Comments about current musical events are interwoven into the discussion of her pieces, reflecting free-ranging conversation during the lessons. To give a few examples, the entry for 9 February focused exclusively on the first movement of her symphony and included several of Vaughan Williams's comments, set off in quotation marks:

Dr VW said it was too 'scrappy' & the development especially needed to be longer & more continuous. He said 'if people would only remember that what is wanted is not that they should take each theme & do something with it, but to make a continuous section, using perhaps only a phrase of one or two of the themes, which shall lead on & on till it comes back to the recapitulation'. He thought I had shortened my 'recapitulation' too much. He said 'it sounds as if it had been drastically cut down', & 'it is better to be too long than to be scrappy, – you must not be so afraid of "doing nothing" that is very important too'. He played it on the piano from my rough sketch which was almost illegible.

At the next lesson, on 11 February, their conversation was more varied, touching on a number of topics:

We went over the songs again & I showed Dr V.W. the copy I had made in the British Museum of Purcell's 'With sick & famished eyes', the same words I had set in 'Longing'. He said after looking at the Purcell 'that is rather a wonderful song' & he said he liked my setting too. ... He asked what I had thought of the Janáček 'Sinfonietta' the previous night, – he had heard it on the wireless & thought it scrappy. I said I had also been to hear Elizabeth Schumann & he said 'I am rather a heretic about E.S.' meaning, I think that

he thought her over-rated. He spoke of the coming Philharmonic concert, &
said he had not had a copy of Holst's new work …, 'Egdon Heath' yet, but
that Holst had played it to him from the M.S. Speaking of my song 'Blow,
blow thou winter wind', he said it was a difficulty when voice & piano started
together, as something must be done to give the singer his pitch, & it was on
the whole better that the composer should do it than the pianist. I said I
really wanted both to start together in this case, & he said 'then the pianist
must only "dab" a note as best he can'.

Perhaps the most personal entry was for 24 February, the
final session of the 1928 visit. Boyle worked very hard
preparing for the lesson, correcting the pieces that had been
discussed in previous meetings and renting a cello from Hill's,
in order to play her Psalm for cello and orchestra to Vaughan
Williams. As she later recorded, the performance was
something of a disaster:

I took the cello & Dr VW was most kind & said 'I can't play these things but
you know I will do my best' & got me a music stand which he said was very
old & would fall down if it was looked at. But I was so deadly nervous that
I could hardly play a note, – everything was out of tune & time, – it was a
perfect nightmare. I think Dr VW was aghast, but he was gentle & patient
beyond words & did everything to make it easy for me. He never said a word
about its being out of tune, though it must have been agonizing. He only
said, 'you are not always playing what you have written' & 'I think from
always being alone you have got into the habit of shortening long notes. You
ought to play with a metronome sometimes & test the things you write by it
to see whether you have written what you really want'. He then went over it
again bit by bit, altering anything that seemed necessary. At the end he said
'It does hang together better than I thought, I daresay it would be effective
if well played'. I felt so dreadfully sorry to have gone so utterly to pieces &
have asked him to listen to such a thing, yet in a way it was one of the most
helpful lessons I ever had, & I never felt more grateful to anyone than I did
for the consideration & sympathy he showed about it. He looked at the
revised things afterwards & said they were improved. We spoke of Holst's
'Egdon Heath' which had been played at the Philharmonic concert the night
before. Dr VW said that he had been rather doubtful about it beforehand,
but had liked it greatly when he heard it. He said it ought to have been
played twice to let people understand it better.

The previous entries have given some insight into Vaughan
Williams's views on the music of his contemporaries, notably
Janáček and Holst. Although Boyle did not record much
conversation about his own music, one entry, from 17 June
1933, refers to a performance of Vaughan Williams's opera,

and also to his advice about promoting herself as a composer:

I told him I had heard 'Hugh the Drover' the night before at the R.C.M. He said he was quite converted to Beecham as a conductor & that he had done wonders with the orchestra, only he thought he had taken parts rather too fast so that they could not get the words in. He said Beecham had only looked at the score for the first time about a week before the performance & that he had worked the performers terribly hard, but got a wonderful performance.

He asked 'What is this rumour about your ballet being done by the Carmargo Society' & when I said I had heard nothing definite he advised me to ring up the Secretary & ask for an interview about it. He said 'I always tell you young people that you must keep on sending your things to people even if they are sent back again & again, as how can they know about them unless you do. When Holst & I were young we sent works to Wood for about 10 years & he always sent them back, till at last one year he did one of mine & one of Holsts'.

He promised to write me an introduction to Mr Foss at the Oxford Press which I was very grateful for.

Boyle's diary depicts Vaughan Williams as a caring and careful teacher, who encouraged his shy pupil, but also dealt with her compositional problems honestly and directly. As the last entry reveals, Vaughan Williams believed that his job as teacher involved active promotion of his students in their compositional aspirations. Interspersed in the Boyle diary are his suggestions of potential publishers for her songs and of performers who might be interested in examining her scores. Jasper Rooper's recollections describe the lengths to which Vaughan Williams would go to secure students' music

He arranged performances of [their] works, informally in his own room or college concerts; he obtained commissions for them; he impressed on them the difficulties that would face them once they left the College ... He told Grace Williams: 'if you're going to be a composer you'll need the hide of a rhinoceros'.[16]

Again, Vaughan Williams himself provides a link between his dedication to his students' progress and his own educational experiences, recalling the brief period when he studied with Max Bruch in Berlin:

16. Cole, "Vaughan Williams Remembered", p 26.

I only know that I worked hard and enthusiastically and that Max Bruch encouraged me, and I had never had much encouragement before. With my own pupils now I always try to remember the value of encouragement. Sometimes a callow youth appears who may be a fool or may be a genius, and I would rather be guilty of encouraging a fool than of discouraging a genius. A fool, after all, may find his own salvation in artistic self-expression even though it means nothing to anyone else.[17]

In fact, Vaughan Williams continued to champion his students long after they ceased to study at the RCM. In a tribute to her teacher written in 1959, Maconchy described Vaughan Williams's unceasing dedication:

His own pupils continued to go back to him for criticism and advice and above all for encouragement for the rest of their lives ... He would travel miles to hear rehearsals of their new works, or invite the players to come to his house and play to him. He would listen with his head sunk on his chest, his eyes, half-dosed, bent on the score – missing nothing, though he appeared half-asleep. At the end of the piece he would perhaps make one or two small practical suggestions, and say something encouraging to the players about 'the difficult things these young composers expect you to be able to play': then rather tentatively ask if they would mind playing it all again! This second performance was usually twice as good as the first: though he had said little, the players were stimulated and enthusiastic, and felt that now at last they really understood the work.[18]

In 1931, Vaughan Williams asked Boyle whether she might be able to go abroad for further study and experience, but this was sadly not an option for her. His question may have been a reflection of the excellent experiences that other students of his had had on the continent – notably Maconchy and Williams, both of whom had followed their RCM years with European study. Maconchy left the RCM in 1929, when she was awarded an Octavia Travelling Scholarship. She used her award to go to Paris and Prague, where she had composition lessons with KB Jirák. During winter 1929, Maconchy heard that Williams, too, had been awarded an Octavia Travelling Scholarship[19] and the following spring, Williams went to Vienna. Of course, the two friends visited each other, Maconchy later remembering:

17. Vaughan Williams, "Musical Autobiography", p 187
18. Maconchy, "Vaughan Williams as a Teacher", pp 19–20.
19. Maconchy, letter to Williams, 3 December 1929 [private collection].

During that year I spent a week or so in Vienna with her, and she came for my first performance in Prague – what a support that was! We went three times to the opera in Vienna, as cheaply as possible: to *Mesitersinger, Die Entführung*, and *Salomé*, and we looked at pictures in the Kunsthistorisches and the Albertina, walked in the Wiener Wald, and even had coffee (we couldn't afford more) in the smartest Viennese cafe – where we smoked a cigar.[20]

This period was significant to Maconchy's development in that she received her first high-profile public performance, when her Piano Concerto was played by the Czech composer and pianist, Ervin Schulhoff, with Jirák conducting. This important event was well-received by the Prague critics and was given notice in the British press.

Foreign study was significant to Williams's development in a different way. In Vienna, she had lessons with Egon Wellesz, whose precise compositional instruction complemented Vaughan Williams's haphazard teaching style. She later described the differences:

[Wellesz] was marvellous, and had so different an approach from Vaughan Williams, who was the sort of personality to whom you could only take your best music. Vaughan Williams knew his limitations as a teacher though; he would say 'I know there's something wrong, but I can't put my finger on it', but Egon Wellesz could. He had a way of saying 'It begins to get weak at this point, so you will scrap from here onwards and re-write'. But then he'd been a pupil of Schoenberg, whose method this was.[21]

This precise approach clearly appealed to the detailed way in which Williams herself assessed both her own and others' music. Although Williams gained much from her studies with Vaughan Williams, unlike Maconchy she required a more structured approach to music, which was satisfied through her sessions with Wellesz. Nevertheless she always valued Vaughan Williams as a teacher and friend, and in later years returned to him for further advice and lessons.

After completing their European studies, Maconchy and Williams returned to Britain to pursue their careers. Although

20. Maconchy, "Grace Williams: a Symposium", *Welsh Music*, v/6 Summer 1977, p 18.
21. Williams, in interview with Rees, "Views and Revisions", p 8.

no longer students, they remained in close contact with Vaughan Williams, who continued to take an active interest in their compositional progress and accomplishments. Maconchy quickly gained recognition as a young composer of exceptional promise. In August 1930 the premiere of her orchestral suite, *The Land*, was given at the Promenade concerts, conducted by Sir Henry Wood, and the performance was a dazzling success. A few months later, her first publication appeared, three songs issued by Oxford University Press. Over the next two years, other works were performed in both public concerts and in BBC broadcasts. Although she contracted tuberculosis in 1932, she continued to compose; moreover, her compositions received frequent performances and were well-received by the press. In November 1933, Constant Lambert acknowledged: "There are regrettably few young composers of any personality in England to-day, but in Miss Elizabeth Machonchy [*sic*] and Mr. Benjamin Britten we have two whose future development should be of the greatest interest." [22]

In contrast, Williams was less successful in launching her compositional career. In November 1934, Vaughan Williams decided to use his influence to bring her music to wider attention. He contacted the BBC Music Department and offered to conduct a programme of orchestral works, which was to feature the first performance of a Williams Overture, as well as his own *Five Mystical Songs*, a Concertino by RO Morris, and two short pieces by Robin Milford. The broadcast was scheduled for 28 December,[23] but the orchestra's string section was thought to be inadequate for the Williams piece. Although Vaughan Williams reluctantly agreed that the Overture's performance might be postponed, he carefully protected Williams's interests – at the same time managing to cultivate those of another student:

I agree that if it is definitely settled that you put Miss Williams's Overture into the programme on January 16 it would be much better to take it out of my programme – but rather than that it should not be done at all I would

22. Lambert, "Matters Musical", *Sunday Referee*, 12 November 1933.
23. Correspondence in BBC WAC. RCONT1. Ralph Vaughan Williams, Artists, 1930–40, and RCONT1, Ralph Vaughan Williams, Composers, 1934–8.

prefer to do it even with the small number of strings – ... I feel that we ought to have something bright to take its place and suggest Comedy Overture ... by Elizabeth MacConchy [sic] ...[24]

In fact, Williams received two broadcasts from this effort since in addition to Maconchy's Comedy Overture, Williams's Two Psalms for voice and chamber orchestra were included in the Vaughan Williams programme. Williams's Overture received its first performance two weeks later in a broadcast conducted by Charles Woodhouse.

Despite this special opportunity, Williams, like most of her peers, found it difficult to gain recognition as a composer. Several of her colleagues, frustrated by the lack of performance opportunities, decided to take matters into their hands and mounted their own concert series: the Macnaghten-Lemare Concerts were launched in December 1931. Three or four recitals were given each season, presenting works by younger British composers, including Maconchy, Williams, Elisabeth Lutyens and Dorothy Gow, as well as Christian Darnton, Gerald Finzi, Benjamin Britten and Michael Tippett, to name only the most prominent.[25] The concerts generated a great deal of interest among British musicians, as well as in the press.

It did not go unnoticed that women's ideas, talent and energy dominated the scheme: the women organizers, the all-woman string quartet, the woman conductor, the many women performers, and the high proportion of programmes that were devoted to works by young women composers gave the series its impetus. At one orchestral concert on 4 February 1935, for example, all the contemporary works were by women: Maconchy was represented by her new ballet, *Great Agrippa – or the Inky Boys*, Lutyens by a setting for tenor, strings and horns, and Williams by her Suite for Chamber Orchestra. Several critics seized the opportunity to expose the gulf that lay between their expectations concerning femininity and the output of women composers. In the *Evening News*, for instance, William McNaught wrote:

24 Vaughan Williams, letter to Julian Herbage, 2 December 1934 [BBC WAC, RCONT1, Ralph Vaughan Williams, Artists, 1930–40].
25. For full programme details, see Sophie Fuller, "*Putting the BBC and T Beecham to shame ...*". *The Macnaghten-Lemare Concerts in the Thirties*. BMus thesis, King's College, London, 1988.

Miss Iris Lemare's orchestral concert at the Ballet Club Theatre last night was an interesting study of the young female mind of to-day.

This organ, when it takes up musical composition, works in mysterious ways. No lip-stick, silk stocking, or saucily-tilted hat adorns the music evolved from its recesses.

All is grim, intense, and cerebral. Sibelius himself is not more bleak and stark.[26]

The adverse reviews of Maconchy's ballet music incensed Williams, since it was a work she liked. She was particularly upset by Vaughan Williams's reaction to the piece, venting her anger in a letter to Maconchy written shortly after the performance:

Now – about Agrippa. I am completely baffled by the press & Uncle Ralph too. I don't think any of them really heard it – I mean heard right into it – or they would have grasped that apart from the brilliance of the scoring, the work is so *full* of invention …

Now Uncle Ralph is a dear, we all know, but he's got a great bee in his bonnet about one thing – he always turns his deaf ear to works which are brilliantly effective. Think of what he said about 'Sacre'! & even worse things about 'Wozzeck'.

I know they are far removed from his own particular genre & perhaps it is only natural that they mean little to him. He is *rhythmically* so far removed from them. – & I think perhaps he is rhythmically very far removed from Agrippa!! that is probably what upset him. He couldn't *really* have heard it as music or he wouldn't have said he so much preferred the [Comedy] Overture because *musically* I find the Overture & Agrippa have a lot in common. …

You mustn't bother your head any more, my girl, about writing safe scores. It doesn't become you. Besides it isn't necessary; your difficult things always come off best.[27]

It is interesting to consider Williams's complaint that their teacher "always turns his deaf ear to works which are brilliantly effective" in the context of Vaughan Williams's comments about the attitude of his own teacher, Parry, toward colorful orchestration:

I remember one day when I came in for my lesson I found a fellow student,

26. W[illiam] McN[aught], "The Mind of a Woman Composer", *Evening News*, 5 February 1935.
27. Williams, letter to Maconchy, undated [February 1935; private collection].

Richard Walthew, borrowing the score of the Prelude to Parsifal. Parry condemned it as the weakest of the Wagner preludes – 'mere scene painting' was, I think, his description of it He was always very insistent on the importance of form as opposed to colour. He had an almost moral abhorrence of mere luscious sound. It has been said that Parry's own orchestration was bad; the truth is, I think, that he occasionally went too far in his deliberate eschewal of mere orchestral effect.[28]

In fact, Vaughan Williams's own response to this particular Macnaghten-Lemare concert survives in a letter, in which he clearly explains his reservations about Maconchy's ballet, comparing it to her Comedy Overture:

Darling Betty

... I never said I didn't like Agrippa – but that I liked the overture better I can't help feeling that in Agrippa – there are certain stravynskyesque [sic] cliches which are not really you & are not worthy of you – they rather stood out &prevented my listening properly to the tunes – but I dare say that a 2d time the good wd come out & the framing fall into its proper background – but still I do feel that you are capable of so much finer thought than that Russian Monkey-brain & that you injure your real self by condescending to use any of his monkey-tricks. – But everyone else (even the Times) seemed to have liked it.

So you must forgive the old & ancient uncle for being stupid

Love from Uncle Ralph[29]

Although such a negative response to a Maconchy work was rare in the early 1930s, by the end of the decade, there was a noticeable shift in attitude against avant-garde compositional styles in Britain, which particularly affected Maconchy's reputation. Her music became victim to the increasing antipathy, attributable to the unstable social and political conditions, toward musical idioms that were "ugly", "cerebral", "dissonant" and, basically, "un-British". Even the BBC, which had previously performed her works regularly, failed to carry out promised performances.

As a performance platform, the BBC represented the single-most important means by which the British public, including Maconchy, Williams, Boyle and Vaughan Williams, could be aware of musical trends. By the late 1920s, the Corporation

28. Vaughan Williams, "Musical Autobiography", p 182.
29. Vaughan Williams, letter to Maconchy, undated [Maconchy Collection, St Hilda's College, Oxford].

had established a Europe-wide reputation for the performance of new music, transmitting works in the latest compositional styles. In effect, this vital medium played a central role in binding the circle of composers together over time: from the 1930s on, music broadcasts triggered immediate reactions from its members in the form of letters, discussing in detail personal reactions to performances and works, bemoaning the wireless reception – which was frequently unreliable – and continuing with news about what was going on in their lives.

With the declaration of war in September 1939, however, musical life in Britain came to a virtual stand-still. Reduced to a single wavelength, the BBC cancelled all scheduled music and initially fell back on cinema organ recitals as its mainstay of music programming. Given the vital role of the Corporation, as an employer, patron and music disseminator, this programming decision prompted Vaughan Williams to write a strong letter of protest to the BBC Director-General a month later:

It appears to me that one of the things we are fighting for is a free as opposed to a regimented culture. In that case we must prove that we have a culture worth fighting for.

I believe that in times of stress such as these when peoples' purpose & determination need special encouragement that only the best & most vital art is of any use – Anything else is enervating & discouraging and I believe that the 'ordinary man' will respond to the stimulus in a way which in normal times he possibly would not do.

It has, I think, been a great pain to many people to find that in the early days of the war it was apparently the opinion of your programme makers that the English people when their hearts & minds were strung up to great endeavour only wanted to listen to the loathsome noises of the so-called cinema 'organ'. Later on I admit the programmes began to get better, but to judge from this weeks 'Radio Times' things have taken a turn for the worse again & the so-called 'serious' programmes are filled with second-rate material which nobody wants.

In times like these when so many people are looking for comfort & encouragement from music, among them those who have probably never attended to music before, surely we ought to give them something that will *grip*. I believe that really great music, especially if it is familiar will grip everybody … Are we not missing a great opportunity which may never recur?[30]

30. Vaughan Williams, letter to the Director-General, 18 October 1939 [BBC WAC, R41/241: P.C.S./Ralph Vaughan Williams, 1939].

The war-time prohibition against adventurous music in fact favoured the more traditional and accessible style of Grace Williams. In summer 19391 the BBC had prepared for what Williams later called her first "big" broadcast,[31] featuring her newest orchestral piece, *Four Illustrations for The Legend of Rhiannon*. Although the engagement seemed doomed once war was declared, the BBC soon determined that 'it is a work of such general appeal that there is no need whatever to exclude it on the grounds o[f] there being only one wavelength.'[32] *Rhiannon* received its first performance on 24 October, shortly after Vaughan Williams had written his impassioned letter. This performance was the first of many BBC broadcasts of Williams's music that took place during the war and afterwards, many on the Welsh Regional programme, which firmly established her as a Welsh composer of the first rank.

Nevertheless, Maconchy's more dissonant and abrasive style led to few performances during the war years. Vaughan Williams attempted to reinterest the BBC in her music,[33] and sent his former student encouraging words, such as the following written in January 1944:

I do feel it very hard that you do not get your stuff done – Have you anything new you could send in to the proms? If so let md know *at once* & I will write to H.J..W[ood] ... – I have tried to persuade B.B.C. to do the Land again – but as usual they hedged.

I fear we must confess that you are not popular – I know though theoretically that is a very noble aspiration practically, it is galling.

But dearest Betty, you are still young – I was about 30 before I ever heard even a *song* of mine done in public – so your time may come – so push on and one day perhaps the key will turn in the lock.[34]

---

31. Williams, letter to C.B Rees, 6 May 1943 [BBC WAC, RCONT1, Williams, Composer, 1939–49].
32. Kenneth A. Wright, letter to Williams, 11 September 1939 [*ibid*].
33. Vaughan Williams, letter to Boult, undated [November 1943] and subsequent correspondence [BBC WAC, RCONT1, Maconchy, Composer, 1939-50]. Vaughan Williams's letter to Wood of 25 February 1944 [British Library, Add. ms. 56422, f.148] probably led to the performance of the Suite from Maconchy's ballet *Puck Fair* at the Proms on 5 August 1944 (my thanks to Hugh Cobbe for bringing this letter to my attention).
34. Vaughan Williams, letter to Maconchy, 18 February [1944] [Maconchy Collection, St Hilda's College, Oxford].

Once the war ended, Maconchy's situation did improve, as Vaughan Williams predicted it would, and her music gradually regained prestige and value, receiving performances, prizes and acclaim. In April 1950 Vaughan Williams once again exerted his considerable influence to put together a broadcast of "new or unknown orchestral works"[35] which included a symphony Maconchy had written between 1945 and 1948. When Ina Boyle heard of the concert, she expressed her pleasure and support, revealing also the lengths to which their teacher had been willing to go to secure this performance:

[I] rejoice that you are at last getting what you have deserved for so long, all the time you were doing dull household jobs for everyone … I guessed at once that the proposed V. Williams concert was for the sole purpose of bringing out your symphony, so you have, in a way, the best of both worlds now, the knowledge that he was prepared to back it, & that he will not now have to spend all it would have cost, it will yet be done by the best orchestra & A. Boult just the same.[36]

Although the broadcast elicited many enthusiastic responses, Vaughan Williams expressed reservations about the Symphony, describing it as "a little too hectic all the way through"[37] and the composer later withdrew the work.

Nevertheless the following years saw Maconchy return to the central arena of new British music. In 1951, her Concertino for Bassoon and Orchestra was first performed to rave reviews. Vaughan Williams was especially pleased with the performance, writing to her shortly afterwards: "Your work came as a great relief It had vitality and purpose. I won't say more after just a first hearing without seeing the score. You are getting performed at last, I am so glad".[38] Furthermore, in July 1953 it was announced that Maconchy's overture, *Proud Thames*, had been awarded the first prize in the London County Council "Coronation Overture" competition, leading to a prestigious performance of the winning work at Royal

35. Vaughan Williams, letter to Maconchy, 30 November 1949 [*ibid.*].
36. Boyle, letter to Maconchy, 11 January 1950 [Boyle Collection, Trinity College Dublin].
37. Vaughan Williams, letter to Maconchy, 17 May 1950 [Maconchy Collection, St Hilda's College, Oxford].
38. Vaughan Williams, letter to Maconchy, 28 February 1951 [*ibid.*].

Festival Hall. From this time, Maconchy was regarded as a British composer of significance.

Despite their successes, Maconchy and Williams certainly never achieved the international renown of Vaughan Williams, or even of their British contemporaries, notably Britten, Tippett, and perhaps even Lutyens. Moreover, Ina Boyle's music is rarely played, the little we know of her and her compositions due primarily to Maconchy's belief and encouragement of her friend's talents during Boyle's lifetime and her efforts to establish a lasting legacy after Ina's death. Nevertheless, this circle of friends achieved something that had been virtually unknown for British women of previous eras: they all aspired to compose large-scale concert works and continued to do so throughout their lives. Having chosen to study at the Royal College of Music in the 1920s, they found there in their remarkable teacher, Ralph Vaughan Williams, a friend and mentor, who gave them the technical knowledge, the confidence and the practical support to achieve their individual goals. When Maconchy left the College in 1929, Vaughan Williams wrote on her final report:

> Very sorry to lose her
> – but I can teach her no more
> – she will work for her own salvation & will go far.[39]

Vaughan Williams's vision and encouragement enabled Maconchy, Williams and Boyle to do exactly that.

39. "Royal College of Music: Teachers' Terminal Report", Midsummer Term, 1929 [Maconchy Collection, St Hilda's College, Oxford]

X

Stephen Banfield

Vaughan Williams and Gerald Finzi

━━━◦◦◦◦━━━

W HEN RALPH VAUGHAN WILLIAMS RETURNED FROM the First World War to find himself along with Holst, the musical man of the moment, projected through one of those sudden culture shifts into a position of seniority and authority, he could expect to attract disciples. He soon did, and the young Gerald Finzi, thirty years his junior and tied to the apron-strings of a widowed Jewish mother in Harrogate, was a model one. From this beginning a rather remarkable relationship developed, and I should like to chart its course more or less chronologically, and follow that with a number of general points.

Picture, by way of comparison, the young Brittenite after the Second World War; the SPNM groupie rallying to the cry of 'Maxwell Davies' in the mid-1960s; or the schoolboy or -girl subscribing to NMC records and following the progress of Weir, Martland, MacMillan and Turnage today. We need such flawed analogies if they can shock us into grasping that, in attaching himself to the pastoral school of Vaughan Williams in the early 1920s, Finzi felt sure he was getting straight into the iconoclastic heart of British contemporary music. 'By the way,' he wrote to an older, cosmopolitan friend, Vera Somerfield, in 1923,[1] 'it was most amusing to see a Nation &

---

1. Gerald Finzi, letter to Vera Somerfield, September 1923. Most of Finzi's surviving correspondence is in the Bodleian Library and exists only in photocopy, the original letters having been destroyed by fire

Atheneum critic saying "I distrust romantic rustics, folk songs, folk dancing, madrigals ..."!! I distrust the theatre, I distrust sonatas, I distrust symphonies.' He bludgeoned her repeatedly with his artistic manifesto. A nationalist credo above all, its Bible was the new periodical *Music and Letters* which began in 1920, its saviours Holst and Vaughan Williams, its high priests and their learning the other constituencies that appeared in those early issues of the journal – Cecil Sharp and folksong, Plunket Greene and English art song, R O Morris and Tudor counterpoint, Violet Gordon Woodhouse and early keyboard instruments. "Now that Holst is recognised," Finzi told Somerfield,

> I expect you'll find many people wanting to make him out German. In 'Music & Letters' (no 3 July 1920) there's an article on Holst ... by Vaughan Williams. This is what he says: you may as well learn it by heart.
>
> > 'and it may be well to add here that "in spite of all temptations" which his name may suggest, Holst "remains an Englishman"[;] on his mothers and grandmothers side he is pure English; on his father's side there is Swedish blood, but the Holst family came to England from Russia, where they had long been settled, more than a hundred years ago. There is a good deal of unclear thinking prevalent on the subject of race and nationality. Every one is to a certain extent of mixed race' etc etc.
>
> So you see Holst is no more German than Grieg was Scotch (His Grandfather was a Scotsman)[.] Please propogate [*sic*] 'Music & Letters' as I'm told its in a bad way.[2]

Finzi was virulently on his guard against accusations of either degeneracy or parochialism that might attach to this new religion of British music. Buttonholing Somerfield again, he wrote:

> ... your eyesight failed you in the vision of young students from the RCM – spectacled & weedy. What about those who are so like other people that you don't know that they are students? Musicians have a tremendous record When your athletics are slipping into the grave at 40 with ruined hearts, Parry gets well over 70. Stanford & Elgar are nearly there: (R.V.W will get to 80.) Verdi & Byrd were nearly 90. Wagner, Tallis, Gluck, Handel, Cherubini, to take a few at random, all over 70. True, Schubert, Chopin, Weber, Purcell, died of consumption but what about the thousands who are dying of it every day
>
> Tennis players included!

2. Gerald Finzi, letter to Vera Somerfield, 24 November 1920.

Holst, for instance, composes in the summer holidays! The rest of his time is a rush between St Pauls Girls School & Morley College, The R.C.M & private teaching, half a dozen district choirs & lectures at the most insignificant schools all over England This from a constitutionally delicate man.

I don't think you have the least conception as to what Art is. Art is ordinary conversation & like speech is to bring affinities into spiritual contact. This is quite straight forward.[3]

He was still only twenty-one when he wrote this, and while lacking anything much in the way of a professional portfolio-- no formal education, but a training of sorts under Bairstow and Ernest Farrar) – if he could muster such passionate articulation at that age, it was not surprising that in time he should become a special friend of his hero.

Farrar had set him up, telling his fifteen-year-old adolescent pupil about the fresh young composer on the London scene remembered from his own RCM days. Farrar had got to know Vaughan Williams personally at that time, and Vaughan Williams was to see the connection come full circle nearly half a century later when he was staying with the Finzis at Ashmansworth after the first public performance of his *Oxford Elegy*. On that occasion Joy Finzi, Gerald's wife, wrote in her journal:

G referred to [the] fact that he had used a quotation from the Matthew Arnold poem in a very early orchestral work Harnham Down (now a bungalow village!). VW seemed amazed that G knew about this work which had been discarded nearly 40 years ago. He had incorporated some of its material into the new work. Later he posted G the early MS of Harnham Down for G to look at. G found it all rather touching, & remembered Ernest Farrars enthusiasm for it round about 1916. Then VW was the rising young composer & the order of the day was 'out-of-door' music, Whitman, Norfolk jackets, pastoral impressions. It all seems so far away & though the beauty of these musical counterparts of the English water colour school will one day be re-felt, for the present it is a turned page. Harnham Down has something of the VW we know in it, but has a good deal of amorphous impressionistic harmony which has long ago been discarded from his vocabulary.[4]

Finzi took his mother to see Vaughan Williams's birthplace

---

3. Gerald Finzi, letter to Vera Somerfield, 22 January 1923.
4. Joy Finzi, journal entry, 19 July 1952. Joy Finzi's journals are in the possession of Christopher Finzi.

at Down Ampney while they were on holiday in the Cotswolds in March 1921, prior to moving to the region the following year. 'His father had the living about 40 years ago,' he explained to Somerfield,

so we rang the vicarage bell & delighted the vicar by telling him that the house was the birthplace of a celebrity. (He hadnt even heard of R.V.W!) Mother had tea with a dear little aged hunchback aunt who kept house for her nephew, while I was shown over the house from top to bottom so that there c^d be no chance of missing the room where our hero was born! Many will make the pilgrimage but we are the first!![5]

This seems fairly precocious for a young man not yet out of his teens, and must surely have been partly an extension of hero-worship of Farrar, killed in action in 1918.

As for Vaughan Williams's music, there is plenty of internal evidence of its assimilation by Finzi at this time, probably score by score as they were issued, and I shall say a little about that at the end, though this paper is more about the friendship of the two men. But how many Vaughan Williams performances he managed to hear before his move to London in 1926 at the age of twenty-four is difficult to determine. He may have gone to one of the first of the *Pastoral Symphony* in London early in 1922, and his much later description, in an article on Howells, of the 'pastoral whatnots by younger composers' that followed in its wake was probably meant to include himself. He knew the *London Symphony* before he was twenty[6], and said it belonged to Vaughan Williams's "great period".[7] And he went to most of the Three Choirs Festivals in the first half of the 1920s, finding Vaughan Williams "as glorious as usual" at Worcester in 1923.[8]

This reference may have been to the man rather than his music, since the only Vaughan Williams performed that year was 'Lord, thou hast been our refuge', but what he meant by

5. Gerald Finzi, letter to Vera Somerfield, 4 April 1921
6. At least, he said he did. This could have been by repute only, for he and his mother were not in Harrogate at the time of its early performance there [see pp 94–5]. However, the symphony was published in 1920, by which time it had received several further performances, in London and Bournemouth.
7. Gerald Finzi, letter to Vera Somerfield, 24 November 1920.
8. Gerald Finzi, letter to Vera Somerfield, 7 September 1923.

it, and whether or when he met Vaughan Williams during this time, is unclear. A letter he wrote the older composer in November 1923 makes no acknowledgement of previous contact, yet somehow he elicited his criticism of a song he had composed in January 1923, a setting of Hardy's "Only a man harrowing clods" that later became the third movement of his *Requiem da camera*. We know this because he annotated an alteration on the manuscript as being Vaughan Williams's suggestion. The letter was about permission to quote the folksong "The truth sent from above" in his Christmas anthem "The brightness of this day", basically a three-verse harmonisation of it. Vaughan Williams and Mrs Leather of Weobley had collected the tune in Herefordshire, and as so often in Finzi's life, there was a sequel many years later when he and Joy and Ralph and Ursula Wood drove out to see Weobley during the 1949 Hereford Festival.[9]

To what extent Vaughan Williams took note of the name and the man Finzi at this early stage is another unknown. He certainly did him a good turn, however, for he was one of the adjudicators of the 1924 Carnegie music awards, along with Hugh Allen and Dan Godfrey, and marked Finzi's *Severn Rhapsody* "A-, well worth doing".[10] It got published and performed, and Ursula Vaughan Williams in her biography implies that her husband's knowledge of Finzi began with this submission.[11]

Speculation ends as we reach the second phase of the relationship. Finzi undertook a course of study with R O Morris in London in mid-1925 and moved to the capital the following January, continuing to consult Morris as an informal pupil, junior colleague and friend for several years afterwards; Morris was in fact the hub of his professional circle, which soon included Howard Ferguson, Arthur and Trudy Bliss, Edmund Rubbra, Robin Milford and others. Morris and Vaughan Williams, as is well known, had married two sisters of the formidable Fisher family and even lived in the same

9. U Vaughan Williams: *RVW: a biography of Ralph Vaughan Williams*. Oxford University Press, 1964, p 294.
10. Carnegie UK Trust Archives, Scottish Record Office, Edinburgh.
11. U Vaughan Williams, *op cit*, p 196.

house, 13 Cheyne Walk, Chelsea. Finzi ensconced himself not far away, near Sloane Square, and there was a good deal of trafficking in cats (and their photographs) as well as scores between the two abodes.

In November 1927, perhaps at Morris's prompting, Vaughan Williams asked to take a second look at the score of Finzi's Violin Concerto, his first major work completed in London. Written for Sybil Eaton, it had had an incomplete and unsatisfactory performance, conducted by Sargent, in May 1927, before which Finzi had consulted Vaughan Williams, who now decided he wanted to conduct it at a Bach Choir concert in Queen's Hall in February 1928. (He performed Milford's Double Fugue for orchestra on the same occasion, though this was not a premiere.) It was potentially Finzi's big break, though it led to as much agonising and constipation as empowerment, for the composer was not happy with the work and withdrew it. However, there can be little doubt that Vaughan Williams had faith in Finzi's potential and was not "just being kind", perhaps unlike Morris who, for all his support and friendship, according to Howard Ferguson[12] did wonder whether Finzi, never a musician with natural fluency and in no sense an executant, would make the grade. At the last rehearsal of the concerto, as Eaton related to Finzi's mother, Vaughan Williams

made a speech to the orchestra saying that he very much wanted the work to go well, for although the composer from youth & inexperience had miscalculated his effects in places he liked the work, & believed that he (G.) w^d do great things some day.[13]

"Was'nt [*sic*] that nice?" she added.

Finzi was still in awe of Vaughan Williams, who towered above him in physical as well as artistic stature. Shortly before going into a sanatorium (which he dubbed "The Caliphate") for several months with suspected tuberculosis in the spring of 1928, he wrote to Ferguson:

Perhaps I shall just manage to do a two part invention in The Caliphate, for as V.W. said the other day, we can all compose away from a piano, but it

12. Conversation with the author, 28 March 1991.
13. Sybil Eaton, letter to Lizzie Finzi, 6 February 1928.

sounds quite different when we play it! I told him, by the way, and he asked rather significantly if I sh^d be allowed visitors. But that is too much to hope for.[14]

It was too much to hope for, though Morris and the Blisses did visit him there. Nevertheless, an important friendship gradually matured and equalised, probably with ambition and determination on Finzi's part behind his diffidence. The diffidence in any case may not have been apparent, for he was an urgent and lively conversationalist in sympathetic company, though against this must be weighed Adeline Vaughan Williams's rather severe and remote presence, which probably inhibited him until Joy came on the scene.

For Finzi, Vaughan Williams's music would always remain a vital fixed point, probably the most important of all on his compositional horizon insofar as it was contemporary, as the following comments in a letter to Ferguson as late as 1939 testify:

I listened in to the Bloch [Violin Concerto] & liked it v. much. It's easy to imagine posterity finding a style of the age & giving V.W. & Bloch as examples, whereas you c^d never find it say, between Bax & V.W. Bloch's music always (no, not always) strikes me as being extraordinarily English! The slow mvt of the Concerto Grosso, the 4tet, the sacred service, this work might almost be written by V.W's brother. (musical brother, not blood!) & if one finds probably by suggestion, slight oriental turns, what c^d be more oriental than 'Flos Campi'. Of course, biblical is the word, not oriental, but you'll know what I mean.[15]

He kept closely abreast of Vaughan Williams's later development, for he not only went to virtually every first performance but was very soon among the select few invited to the celebrated piano and two-piano run-throughs of new works, and over the years probably heard more of these than any other person except the composer. At the same time, while never less than fully committed to the older man and his music, he became critical and discriminating in his reactions. When he heard an early playthrough of *Job* and portions of *Sir John in Love* at Morley College in 1928 he felt that the latter contained "the worst music VW has ever written", though the

14. Gerald Finzi, letter to Howard Ferguson, probably 9 or 10 April 1928.
15. Gerald Finzi, letter to Howard Ferguson, 10 March 1939.

former was "quite another matter ... the beginning and the end ... as lovely as the loveliest parts of Flos Campi", as he told Ferguson.[16] He profoundly admired the Fourth Symphony, whose two-piano run-through at St Paul's Girls' School on 6 January 1932 must have been a red-letter day for him. As for the Piano Concerto, which he had first heard in similar fashion a few months earlier, he was more charitable about it than some of his friends, including Rubbra, when he wrote to Ferguson in August 1933:

I listened-in to V.W's piano con: & still felt the same about it. The middle of the slow mvt is as lovely as ever & the chromatic fuge [sic] magnificent, though much too short (however, he says he's going to lengthen it) but the shape of the last mvt & the material of the first, most unsatisfactory. The chief thing about it is a certain royalty which is in a lot of Job & the Sym. (which he's now scoring).[17]

Particularly interesting is Finzi's reaction, in a letter to Ferguson, to an early run-through of the Fifth Symphony on 16 December 1941:

I had one of V.W's characteristic little notes to say that there was a run-through of his new Sym: on two pianos at Trinity college, with Foss & Alan Richardson playing, 'to see whether he liked it well enough to go on with it. Your criticism w^d be valued' !!! There was noone else there, beyond Colles & the two pianists' wives, & needless to say the 'sketch' which he mentioned in his letter proved to be the finished work, scored & all. It's got both heavenly magnificent stuff in it, though on the whole, I sh^d not say that it was quite up to the Pastoral or no 4. It's a much more reasonable work. After all, the excessive contemplation of the Pastoral or the Royal fury of no 4 does not make for a reasonable work in either case. This one is better balanced from that aspect, but possibly loses from the defects of its virtues. 4 mvts, a prelude, Romance, Scherzo & passacaglia. Dedicated, in a rather flowery dedication (which I do hope he'll scrap) to Sibelius. The scherzo is very much like the scherzo of no 4 & some of the tunes in the work are taken from an unfinished opera 'The Pilgrims Progress'. That sounds interesting. I find it difficult to imagine what is left of The Pilgrim's Progress after the Shepherds episode has been taken out.[18]

The better-chronicled run-through was not until just over a year later, so what was Vaughan Williams doing with the symphony in the meanwhile?

16. Gerald Finzi, letter to Howard Ferguson, probably 9 or 10 April 1928.
17. Gerald Finzi, letter to Howard Ferguson, 23 August 1933.
18. Gerald Finzi, letter to Howard Ferguson, 23 December 1941.

On his part, Vaughan Williams began strongly to admire the younger man's music, particularly his word-setting. After hearing a broadcast of the Hardy cycle *A Young Man's Exhortation* he told Finzi, in an undated letter:

I want to give a lecture one day on the English song – showing how you & Gurney & Robin & one or two others have at last found the musical equivalent of English poetry[–]only that w^d mean an intensive study of all your songs which my natural laziness boggles at[.]

He loved *Dies natalis* too: "the nuisance was that it set me thinking of all my sins of omission," he wrote after an early broadcast of it in December 1943.[19]

Ralph and Adeline had gradually adopted Finzi, no doubt responding to a combination of his patrician warmth and energy and his constant potential for becoming a lost soul in London if not watered and nurtured appropriately (for he came close to a nervous breakdown more than once during his bachelor years). He shared their box in the theatre at *Job* in London in 1931, by which time he had for some while been going down to Dorking to play tennis at The White Gates and stay overnight as an escape from the city. He also house- and cat-sat for them there for the same reason for a week at a time in May 1931 and 1932. By 1932 he had met the love of his life, Joy, and seems to have been eager for them to meet her, which they did in March 1933 while he was staying with her in Sussex, not too far from Dorking, in a kind of trial cohabitation before they agreed to get married. Perhaps her sister Mags went too, as chaperone, or just as companion, for Ursula states that by the time of the wedding Ralph had met the two girls "often" and enjoyed playing tennis with them.[20] Joy was a highly charismatic character, and she must have broken any remaining ice where Adeline was concerned: the Vaughan Williamses agreed to be the witnesses – sole witnesses except for Mags – at the Finzis' wedding on 16 September 1933, which took place at the Dorking registry office. It was not the first time Finzi had elevated an adoptive

19. Ralph Vaughan Williams, letter to Gerald Finzi, 23 December 1943.
20. U Vaughan Williams, *op cit*, p 196.

family above his biological one, and Joy seems to have been happy enough to go along with the principle.

Would Vaughan Williams have done this for any one of his younger associates to whom he was by now irredeemably "Uncle Ralph"? Or was his friendship with Finzi already unique? I am inclined to the latter view, though it has to be remembered that none of Finzi's mature compositions had yet appeared and it is not even certain that Vaughan Williams preferred them to his early ones when they did. Whatever the truth, Vaughan Williams certainly enjoyed the avuncular role as the wedding approached, though an accident threatened to upset the arrangements, as the following letter indicates:

> The White Gates,
> Westcott Road,
> Dorking
> July 7

Dictated

Dear Gerald

The following facts are true –
    (a) I fell into the brook.
    (b) I broke my ancle [*sic*]
    (c) I mayn't put my foot to the ground for a month.
But –
    (a) I have no pain
    (b) I am quite well
    (c) I was not drunk at the time.
Don't wait to examine those registry steps till my foot is well – but come over one day – both of you – and see us.
I find that Ellen has reported about the steps as follows –
There are none.
Mayn't I play the harmonium?

Ys RVW

Ursula's account of the wedding, which took place while The White Gates was being extended, cannot be bettered:

Both [Ralph] and Adeline had become very fond of Gerald, they admired his music, his great knowledge of English poetry, and his love of the countryside, and Joy with her many talents seemed a perfect companion for him. So they welcomed the idea of the wedding as one they could wholeheartedly approve. On their side, the 'young people' as Ralph always called them, felt that 'Uncle Ralph and Aunt Adeline' were the friends they would like to have at their marriage. They did not know how amused Ralph and Adeline were when Joy, given her marriage lines by the Registrar, said matter-of-factly that she would put it away with her dog licence. They all sat among the dust sheets for coffee and cakes, then went their respective ways. But Ralph and Adeline were greatly touched when two little maple trees arrived for the garden as a present from the young marrieds to the long married.[21]

The dog licence story was not Joy's only piece of dotty behaviour that day. She herself said that when the Registrar asked 'Who is the bride?' she looked around the room for her.[22]

Ralph was always candid and blunt in his comments, often with a calculated frisson of unorthodoxy. ("It is delightful to hear of VW's remark about not being able to tell whether a movement ended in the same key. That is really encouraging!" William Busch wrote to Finzi in October 1940.)[23] Some of this comes through in Ralph's letters to Finzi (the other side of the correspondence does not survive). That is, it does once they can be deciphered – one has a vivid mental picture of the whole family sitting around the breakfast table excitedly trying to do so, for his handwriting was the worst ever. But his laconic brevity tended to cancel out the plain speaking in terms of real self-revelation. What are we to make of this cryptic request in a letter of 25 July 1937?

Now another subject
Could you send me a complete list of all gramophone records, pfte duet or solo arr[ts] of Sibelius symphonies
I want these
    (a) because, as you know, I can't read a full score
    (b) because, being no longer able to compose, and having by my
        mode of life unfitted myself for any useful occupation I think it is
        time I learnt something about music[.]
We passed through Aldbourne the other day where
    (a) Hon: bought an ice
    (b) we failed to spot your house
My love to Joyce

Against this apparent openness, and reminded by his comment about passing through Aldbourne, one has to

21. U Vaughan Williams, *op cit*, pp 196–7.
22. Joy Finzi, conversation with the author, 30 October 1990.
23. William Busch, letter to Gerald Finzi, 15 October 1940.

remember that Adeline's personality and severely arthritic condition put a strict limit on equality and reciprocality of hospitality between the two couples. I do not think she ever visited the Finzis, though they often visited her, which means that Dr and Mrs (first) Vaughan Williams must have been just about the only couple among their close friends not to have stayed in the guest room at Ashmansworth, which Ralph, who did stay there on his own and later, many times, with Ursula, used to say had the best view in the world along with Mycenae. Joy kept the geographical lines of communication open by sending Adeline cowslips from Aldbourne with monotonous regularity. Ralph advised Gerald on all matters to do with his amateur orchestra, the Newbury String Players (founded in 1940), from how to get around petrol rationing to how to acquire and benefit from a professional leader, and was eventually persuaded to come and conduct them and the massed choirs in the Newbury Festival of 1945. He was impressed, and perhaps not only by the musical standards Gerald had managed to squeeze out of them – they performed his *Tallis Fantasia*, against his initial advice – for he wrote a few months later: "I enter a strong protest against your excellent orchestra which includes several young & lovely women (including your own wife) being described as 'old ladies'[.]" [24]

In 1936, Gerald had sent Ralph a copy of his newly published set of Hardy songs, *Earth and Air and Rain*, with justified pride and the resolve that from now on there would be "no more songs" for a while. "What is it going to be[?]" Vaughan Williams asked, adding: 'You must remember what was said about Madame d'Arblay[: ']that she must see that the works of art kept pace with the works of nature[.']" [25] Finzi had every intention of making the works of art keep pace with the works of nature – his two new-born sons – and was knuckling down to serious work on his magnum opus, the setting of Wordsworth's "Immortality" Ode for tenor, chorus and orchestra. He meant to dedicate this to Vaughan Williams, proof enough of the strength of feeling in the relationship and importance of the older composer's influence, and may already

24. Ralph Vaughan Williams, letter to Gerald Finzi, 3 August 1945.
25. Ralph Vaughan Williams, letter to Gerald Finzi, 23 November 1936.

have planned it for Vaughan Williams's 70th birthday in 1942. But the Second World War and other circumstances intervened and Finzi, disappointed, had to settle for offering him a Shakespeare song cycle, *Let Us Garlands Bring*, instead. Adeline kept careful tabs on the affair by persuading Finzi to remove the word "70th" from the dedicatory title page. Finzi sketched the beginnings of a setting of "Crabbed age and youth" which may have been intended for this cycle, perhaps it was as well that it never got anywhere, with its refrain line of "Age, I do abhor thee". *Let Us Garlands Bring* was performed by Robert Irwin and Howard Ferguson at a National Gallery lunchtime concert devoted to Vaughan Williams, and rather set the seal on the pre-eminence of Finzi amongst Vaughan Williams's composer friends, since he was the only one to share the platform with him at this focal event and it was Joy and Gerald who threw the lunch party afterwards – a lavish gesture in wartime. There was a BBC concert of brief tributes by others in the afternoon, but Finzi's cycle stayed in the forefront with its own broadcast, with strings, a few days later.

After this, the dedication of *Intimations of Immortality* was deflected to Adeline, who survived long enough to hear it broadcast in 1950 but died the following year. In the meantime Ursula Wood, a poet, had become a friend of both Vaughan Williams and, through him, of the Finzis, whom she first met at the 70th birthday concert shortly after the sudden death of her first husband. For the rest of her life Joy was particularly close to Ursula. Gerald introduced her to Gilmour Jenkins, his boss at the Ministry of War Transport (where he worked as a civil servant during the war), and since this made for a tight circle of friendship almost without Vaughan Williams, it is easy to see why after Adeline's death a wonderful new lease of life was enjoyed by all parties, with Ralph growing younger by the day at its centre. He eventually married Ursula, of course, and then at last the two couples could get out and about together, staying at each other's houses – the Vaughan Williamses exchanging the increasingly dowdy and unloved White Gates for an extremely smart flat in Regent's Park – and partaking of huge, lively house parties, organised with characteristic grace and efficiency by Joy, at the Three Choirs Festival, which became a focus for their social life after the war. Photos of Gerald and Ralph together at these festivals really do make of their friendship something to celebrate, and there survives a particularly good back view of them marching off somewhere conspiratorially, Gerald brisk, lively and short as ever, Ralph shambling along with walking stick and hearing aid. The story is well known of how the Finzis took the Vaughan Williamses up Chosen Hill, to see the setting of one of Gerald's pieces and youthful experiences, during the 1956 Three Choirs Festival (which was their last one as well as the Finzis'): he caught his death there from the sexton's children in the form of chicken pox, from which Hodgkin's Disease had destroyed his immunity, and died only three weeks later, by which time Ralph and Ursula were on holiday in Majorca. Rather than dwell on this, perhaps the best way to savour the great flowering of conviviality that all four of them enjoyed in the 1950s is to quote from Joy's journal entry for 7 December 1951:

To Oxford for the 1st performance of Wellesches [sic] opera Incognito[.] Met V.W & Ursula for dinner before. Dent was there also. Long opera over 11.30 – home [to Ashmansworth] by 12.30. Ovaltine & bread & cheese in the kitchen warmth & then sat over the wood fire talking. Cats perched on V.W – at 3.30 he said 'I hope I am not keeping you young people up'[.] He was first up next morning & walking out to see the day while I made breakfast. Went home after lunch.

So much for the chronicle; now for the general points. I have five. The first is that the influence of Vaughan Williams's music on Finzi's is so obvious that I have not thought it necessary to dwell on it. It can, I believe, be expounded chapter and verse in many instances, from Finzi's earliest compositions onwards; but in those early works it is perhaps Holst whose idiom stands out the more and proves a more flexible tool with which he can work. Nor is it necessarily the whole of Vaughan Williams's style that one notices in Finzi: the rapt diatonicism, slow of pace, heavy of texture, lucid and sometimes austere in effect, is what gets taken up most pervasively. It is the Bachian side of both composers with which we are dealing here, very much a specific residue of the mid-1920s (Vaughan Williams's *Concerto accademico* was a particular influence on Finzi, coming at the time of the young man's own Violin Concerto). And that diatonicism, with its modal tendencies, is only a part of Finzi's style, just as it is only a part of Vaughan Williams's, though it is often taken for the whole in both cases. They are very much farther apart when they move beyond it, which Finzi had to do – in my view, with the help of Bliss and the continental romantics rather than more pastoral models – in order to mature, though I think he did take in the furious chromaticism of Vaughan Williams's *Job* and Fourth Symphony, for it is given out again occasionally.

This leads to the second observation, which is that they gave and received mutual advice and criticism but it was not always to the point. Vaughan Williams seems to have responded to the musical personality of the young Finzi but did not necessarily understand the older Finzi's stylistic imperatives. He didn't like the Grand Fantasia, whose passionate, romantic use of minor-key chromatics represents probably the biggest single breakthrough in Finzi's idiom. Nor was he particularly enthusiastic about the Oboe Interlude, Finzi's first mature publication. "I went right through it twice yesterday – I like it[.] Rather different perhaps from your style as I know it – but all you all the same (including some 'wrong notes'!)" he commented in August 1936 on receiving the score.[26] Other technical points made on receipt of Finzi's scores rarely strike one as going to the heart of the matter, either in appreciation or censure. Nor am I quite sure why he felt Finzi needed the lecture he gave him in March 1945 when he was sent the score of *Farewell to Arms*. "Don't call it 'small beer'," he wrote,

because it isn't & you know it isn't. If you did think so you ought not to have published it[.]

But I hope you have a pride in your own work--which is quite a different thing from the modesty which sees the vast difference between the final result & what we all feel of our work it <u>might</u> have been – so don't <u>denigrate</u> your own work[.][27]

26. Ralph Vaughan Williams, letter to Gerald Finzi, 16 August 1936.
27. Ralph Vaughan Williams, letter to Gerald Finzi, 13 March 1945.

On the other side, Finzi knew perfectly well that Vaughan Williams used to court his friends' criticism at the new works' playthroughs only to ignore it entirely. Here is Joy's journal account of that of the Eighth Symphony in April 1955:

Lovely spring day[.] Up to London to hear first private, run through of V.W's new symphony[.] He has been working on this about a year, but has kept it secret tho' we have known about it most of the time. He had asked Howells, Bliss (Arthur & Trudy) Rubbra, Frank Howes, Scott Goddard (these two personally not as representatives of the press) Alan Frank & ourselves. Roy Douglas, who had done the vetting & copying played it through twice. V.W in fine form & playing his usual little game of pretending that he wanted our criticism. He said he didn't know whether it was the product of intellect & without any real impulse behind it, but it is quite clear that the only criticism in which he is interested is that which co-incides with his own doubts. There was one section [of] the 1st mov which E.R, A.B, H.H & G.F all independently agreed was a dead patch. It turned out to be a passage which he had only recently re-written. We asked to hear the earlier version & all agreed that it was better than the last. V.W agreed that he might re-write it. But when all the others had gone he seemed to suggest that he wdnt alter it at all.[28]

Nevertheless, Finzi must have felt flattered when Vaughan Williams asked him to go through the *Pilgrim's Progress* libretto, which he did, responding with detailed support and criticisms in November 1945 (he strongly disliked Bunyan's reappearance in the Epilogue, and feared "Something of the same effect if, after the end of 'Neptune', you heard 'Chocolates & Cigarettes' ").[29] It was not the only time Vaughan Williams solicited written criticism from him, the most dramatic – and touching – coming after the failure (which they both acknowledged) of *The Sons of Light* (1951) and probably precipitated by thoughts or discussion of retirement at the age of 80, which he had just reached. He wrote to Finzi: "I want you, and my other friends, to tell me, like the policeman did to Mrs Sheldon Amos at Piccadilly Circus, when I ought to go home as being too old for this job. This probably will not prevent me going on writing but I can keep it all confidential."[30] Now it was Finzi's turn to administer a lecture:

28. Joy Finzi, journal entry, 11 April 1955.
29. Gerald Finzi, letter to Ralph Vaughan Williams, 5 November 1945, quoted in Joy Finzi's journal.
30. Ralph Vaughan Williams, letter to Gerald Finzi, 19 October 1952.

Strictly speaking you never wrote a bad work (once you got started) whilst you had to struggle to write, though [you] wrote immature works. After 1920 or thereabouts, when your technique began to get working, you wrote quite a number of unmemorable works. King Cole, for instance and The Poisoned Kiss, isn't really one of your best works; yet, these were works written amongst your major works ... and you would hardly have asked at the time 'shall I stop writing'.

Anyhow, it's a good job you didn't!

S.O.L. will take its place with Old King Cole and a few other things, to be looked at by the more curious and enterprising minds of the future who want to know something more about you than the obvious. I should leave it at that and get on with the next work.[31]

One has to read between the lines of this exchange. Gerald, who had a puritanical side, was rather disapproving of Ralph's second creative youth with Ursula (who had written the *Sons of Light* libretto), and perhaps unconsciously jealous of it, for he knew that he himself would never reach that age. He was extremely reluctant to admit the virtues of Ralph's compositions of the 1950s; and there were certainly tensions between Gerald and Ursula.

My third point is that Finzi probably remained slightly overawed by Vaughan Williams not just throughout his journeyman career but throughout his life, regarding him as an object of intimate affection but also "one about whom most of us feel as Morley felt about Byrd, 'never to be named without reverence' (or words to that effect)," as he wrote to Bliss as late as 1942.[32] It was not always a matter of respectfulness, since on the occasion just discussed this was the one thing not wanted. But it was also that relations between individuals, and married couples as well, were more formal in those days, at least with older people (those of a 19th-century generation), so it is difficult to tell exactly how to judge their modes of address, though one should try, because they were carefully selected. Vaughan Williams only went from heading his letters "Dear Mr Finzi" to heading them 'Dear Gerald' when Finzi announced his engagement, after which Adeline, who had also addressed him as "Dear Mr Finzi", wrote to "Dear Joyce"

31. Gerald Finzi, letter to Ralph Vaughan Williams, 20 October 1952.
32. Gerald Finzi, letter to Arthur Bliss, 9 October 1942. BBC Written Archives.

instead. He signed off, as a colleague, "Yrs/RVW", only using his "Uncle Ralph" designation when writing to Joy as well – that is, until the *Sons of Light* soul-baring, when he became "Uncle Ralph" in a letter to Gerald alone (unless this was because he was now engaged to Ursula). Touchingly and uncannily, only in his very last letter to Gerald, dating from June 1956, did he sign himself simply "Ralph". Almost none of Finzi's letters to Vaughan Williams survive, but we do know that he was addressing him as "Dear Uncle Ralph" by 1935.

The fourth point must probably remain somewhat opaque. Finzi's was a confessedly minor musical talent, and his rural seclusion, small output, antiquarian and scholarly interests and general uncompetitiveness – for his avoidance of formal education was by desire, not lack of opportunity – bespeak the small man attaching himself to the great one in his dealings with Vaughan Williams. This is a curious form of power relations, for it frequently works, and in any case the larger or senior person can do nothing about it short of rejection. But it becomes a form of ambition in itself: to go round the back of normal institutional procedures and conventional relations into personal collegiality.

So was Finzi Vaughan Williams's Boswell? I don't think so, because it was surely a more equal relationship than that, as this account has shown. Perhaps the key to the equality lay in Finzi's naturally patrician outlook, for just as Vaughan Williams belonged to the network of high-achieving eighteenth- and nineteenth-century families that has been called the intellectual aristocracy, so did Finzi hail from a long and venerable line of Jews who on his father's Sephardi side had accomplished a great deal on the continent ever since the, fourteenth-century and, more to the point, on both sides securely rode the waves of liberalisation and assimilation in nineteenth-century Britain. This was the facet of his background that he chose, perhaps understandably, to close off, but my point is that his attitudes throughout life seem to have taken for granted, perhaps unconsciously, that he should himself be a responsible and empowered liberal citizen who helped and expected to get things done, just like Vaughan Williams. Underneath the modesty he knew who he was.

Indeed, he was almost as adept as Vaughan Williams at fulminating against injustices – John Amis describes him as having looked like a kind of walking *Manchester Guardian*.[33] He wrote to newspapers, gathered signatures, helped struggling young composers (plus old ones – lobbying the powers that be to get *The Pilgrim's Progress* on – and undervalued dead ones such as Parry), told the government or the populace how it should be treating its artists, and above all stood up for the amateur in musical life. With this agenda to share they got on well and equitably enough.

But Finzi was nearly thirty years younger than Vaughan Williams, and the final point must be to ask whether he took the place of the son he and Adeline never had. Butterworth, more like a brighter, younger brother, perhaps, had fulfilled a unique critical role in Vaughan Williams's life, one that was indefinably but strikingly different from Holst's, and insofar as anyone could replace Butterworth after his death on the Somme in 1916 Gerald Finzi probably did. His own son Christopher even became a kind of great-nephew. It would be good to know why Adeline and Ralph Vaughan Williams never had children – no-one ever seems to ask – just as it would be good to be able to trace how, when and why Vaughan Williams began to be known generally as 'Uncle Ralph', the implication being that with his so-called nieces he stopped being a real, inflammable sexual presence and became a wise and harmless, if flirtatious, elder. (He was a notoriously difficult sitter and Joy Finzi somehow worked her magic on him to accomplish two superb pencil portraits.[34]) When did he make this generational shift? Was it painless and gradual, or agonised and precipitated? Where was Finzi at the time? The question is the more urgent because we do know that Finzi was in a precise and special sense Vaughan Williams's heir. In June 1949, a few months after the death of his brother-in-law R O Morris, Vaughan Williams wrote to Finzi as follows:

In my will which I made a few years ago I appointed Morris and Bliss as my literary executors. I should feel so happy if you could now undertake it with Arthur Bliss.

33. J Amis: *Amiscellany: my life, my music*. Faber, 1985, p 84.
34. *See* J Finzi: *In That Place: the portrait drawings of Joy Finzi*. Marlborough, 1987.

Your duties would be to look at all my unpublished manuscripts and decide what is to be done with them ie – either to be destroyed – kept in manuscript or published. All that you think ought to be published will be handed over to the Butterworth Trust to whom I am leaving all my copyrights and royalties.

I do hope you will do this for me.

Perhaps you will like to know also that I am leaving you Beethoven's tuning fork which was left to me by Gustav Holst to be passed on to anyone I considered worthy.[35]

Presumably Finzi agreed to the responsibility and accepted the privilege. But the sad thing is that he died first, and thus never reaped the symbolic reward of the old man's blessing.

35. Ralph Vaughan Williams, letter to Gerald Finzi, 5 June 1949.

APPENDIX A

Vaughan Williams's own programme note for the third performance of
A London Symphony*, given by the Bournemouth Municipal*
Orchestra conducted by Dan Godfrey on 11 February 1915.

It has been suggested that this Symphony has been misnamed, it should rather be called "Symphony by a Londoner". That is to say it is in no sense descriptive, and though the introduction of the "Westminster Chimes" in the first movement, the slight reminiscence of the "Lavender cry" in the slow movement, and the very faint suggestion of mouth-organs and mechanical pianos in the Scherzo give it a tinge of "Local colour", yet it is intended to be listened to as "absolute" music. Hearers may, if they like, localize the various themes and movements, but it is hoped that this is not a necessary part of the music. There are four movements: – The first begins with a slow prelude; this leads to a vigorous allegro – which may perhaps suggest the noise and hurly of London, with its always underlying calm. The second (slow) movement has been called "Bloomsbury Square on a November afternoon". This may serve as a clue to the music, but it is not a necessary "explanation" of it. The third movement is a nocturne in form of a Scherzo. If the hearer will imagine himself standing on Westminster Embankment at night, surrounded by the distant sounds of the Strand, with its great hotels on one side, and the "New Cut" on the other, with its crowded streets and flaring lights, it may serve as a mood in which to listen to this movement. The last movement consists of an agitated theme in three-time, alternating with a march movement, at first solemn, and later on energetic. At the end of the Finale comes a suggestion of the noise and fever of the first movement – this time much subdued – then the "Westminster Chimes" are heard once more: on this follows an "Epilogue", in which the slow prelude is developed into a movement of some length. This Symphony received its first performance at Mr F B Ellis' concert, in London, last March.

R V W

APPENDIX B

A LONDON SYMPHONY: A BIBLIOGRAPHY

George Butterworth:

- Programme note for the first performance of *A London Symphony*, Queen's Hall, March 27 1914 (10 pages with 27 music examples)
- 'Vaughan Williams' "London" Symphony', *The RCM Magazine*, Vol 10 No 2 Easter Term 1914, 44–6, reprinted in *George Butterworth 1885–1916*, privately printed 1918, 95–6

Ralph Vaughan Williams:

- Programme note for the first performance of the reconstructed score, Bournemouth, February 11 1915 (As the *Harrogate Times* review makes it clear, this note was earlier used for the Harrogate performance, although a copy of that programme has not been located.)
- in 'A Musical Autobiography' in Hubert Foss *Ralph Vaughan Williams*, Harrap 1950, 37, and reprinted in *National Music and Other Essays*, OUP 1963, 193
- in *George Butterworth 1885–1916*, privately printed 1918, 92–4
- *Music & Friends: seven decades of letters to Adrian Boult from Elgar, Vaughan Williams, Holst, Bruno Walter, Yehudi Menuhin, and other friends*, annotated by Jerrold Northrop Moore. Hamish Hamilton, 1979, pp 27-8, 30–1

H. C. Colles:

- 'The "London" Symphony', *The Times* review dated 8 May 1920, reprinted in *Essays and Lectures*, OUP 1945, 89–91

Percy A. Scholes:

- 'A Gramophonist's Guide: IV – The First Movement of Vaughan Williams' "London Symphony" as played by the London Symphony Orchestra under Sir Dan Godfrey [Columbia Ll 507-8]' (with 6 music examples and a list of the cuts made for this abridged version), *The Gramophone* November 1924, 197-9, reprinted in *The Second Book of The Gramophone Record*, OUP 1925, 147–153
- Review of Sir Dan Godfrey's recording of *A London Symphony*, *The Gramophone* April 1926, 527
- 'A London Symphony', a detailed description of the work in conjunction with Sir Dan Godfrey's recording for Columbia (with 24 music examples), *The British Musician* December 1926, 149–156

A. E. F. Dickinson:

- 'A London Symphony', in *An Introduction to the Music of R Vaughan Williams*, detailed analysis with 26 musical examples, 'The Musical Pilgrim', OUP 1928, 32–51

- in *Vaughan Williams*, detailed discussion of *A London Symphony* and its revisions with 19 music examples, Faber 1963, 189–208

Bernard Shore:

- Vaughan Williams' "London Symphony" ', in *Sixteen Symphonies* (general description with 51 music examples), Longmans 1949, 287–303

Humphrey Jennings:

- 'Working Sketches of an Orchestra', description of a rehearsal and concert with Vaughan Williams conducting *A London Symphony*, February 21 1949, in Hubert Foss and Noel Goodwin *London Symphony: Portrait of an Orchestra*, Naldrett Press 1954, 241–4

Scott Goddard:

- 'No 2, The London Symphony' (with 9 music examples), in *The Symphony* ed. Ralph Hill, Penguin 1949, 366–8 & 383

Bernard Herrmann:

- 'Vaughan Williams' London Symphony', in Letters to the Editor (concerning section cut from 1920 version), *The Musical Times* January 1959, 24

Michael Kennedy:

- *The Works of Ralph Vaughan Williams*, detailed analysis of different versions, etc., OUP 1964, 136–141, 462–8 & 710–1

Sir Adrian Boult:

- 'The London Symphony', concert interval talk in July 1965, reprinted in *Boult on Music* ed. Martin Anderson, Toccata Press 1983, 65–72

- in *My Own Trumpet*, Hamish Hamilton 1973, 34–5

APPENDIX C

BIBLIOGRAPHY TO CHAPTER VI (DUNCAN HINNELLS)

The following list of sources support the discussion in Duncan Hinnells's study (pp 118–163), from which reference is made using the "Harvard" system (ie author and date). Place of publication is only given if not London.

1. Abercrombie, L (1933) *A Plea for the Liberty of Interpreting*. Oxford, Clarendon Press.
2. Boyes, H (1993) *The Imagined Village: culture, ideology and the English folk revival*. Manchester, Manchester University Press.
3. Cohen, H (1936) *Music's Handmaid*. Faber & Faber.
4. – (1969) *A Bundle of Time: the memoirs of Harriet Cohen*. Faber & Faber.
5. Dahlhaus, C (1989) *Between Romanticism and Modernism: four studies in the music of the later nineteenth century*. Berkeley, University of California Press.
6. Day, J (1961, rev ed 1975) *Vaughan Williams*. Dent.
7. Dickinson, A E F (1963) *Vaughan Williams*. Faber & Faber.
8. Doctor, J R (1993) *The BBC and the Ultra-modern Problem: a documentary study of the British Broadcasting Corporation's dissemination of Second Viennese School repertory, 1922–36*. PhD Thesis, Northwestern University.
9. Ehrlich, C (1989) *Harmonious Alliance: a history of the Performing Right Society*. Oxford University Press.
10. – (1991) "Glock's War on the provincial" *Times Literary Supplement* 3 May 1991 p 16.
11. Foreman, L (1983, rev 1988) *Bax: a composer and his times*. Scolar Press.
12. – (1987) *From Parry to Britten: British music in letters 1900–945*. Batsford.
13. – (1992) *Farewell, My Youth, and other writings by Arnold Bax*. Aldershot, Scolar Press.
14. Foss, H (1950) Ralph Vaughan Williams. Harrap & Co.
15. Frogley, A (1986) "Hardy in the Music of Vaughan Williams" *Thomas Hardy Journal ii*, 3 October 1986 pp 50–5.
16. – (1987) "Vaughan Williams and Thomas Hardy: 'Tess' and the slow movement of the Ninth Symphony" *Music & Letters 68* No 1 January 1987 pp 42–59.
17. – (1989) *The Genesis of Vaughan Williams's Ninth Symphony: a study of the sketches, drafts and autograph scores*. D Phil Thesis, Christ Church, Oxford.
18. – (1993) "H G Wells and Vaughan Williams's A London Symphony: politics and culture in fin-de-siècle England" *Sundry Sorts of Music Books: essays on the British Library collections* edited by Paul Banks. The British Library.
19. – (1996) "Constructing Englishness in Music: national character and the reception of Ralph Vaughan Williams" *Vaughan Williams Studies* edited by Alain Frogley. Cambridge, Cambridge University Press pp 1–22.

20. Glock, W (1991) *Notes in Advance: an autobiography in music.* Oxford University Press.
21. Greene, R (1995) *Holst: The Planets* Cambridge, Cambridge University Press.
22. Harrington, P (1989) "Holst and Vaughan Williams: radical pastoral" *Music and the Politics of Culture* edited by Christopher Norris. Lawrence and Wishart.
23. Hepokoski, J (1993) *Sibelius Symphony No 5.* Cambridge, Cambridge University Press.
24. Hobsbawm, E *and* Ranger, T (1983) *The Invention of Tradition.* Cambridge, Cambridge University Press.
25. Howes, F (1937) *The Later Works of R Vaughan Williams.* Oxford University Press.
26. – (1954) *The Music of Ralph Vaughan Williams.* Oxford University Press.
27. – (1966) *The English Musical Renaissance.* Secker & Warburg; New York, Stern & Day.
28. Kennedy, M. (1964) *The Works of Ralph Vaughan Williams.* Oxford University Press.
29. – (1982) *A Catalogue of the Works of Ralph Vaughan Williams.* Revised edition, Oxford University Press.
30. – (1987) *Adrian Boult.* Hamish Hamilton.
31. – (1995) "This Concerto is a Masterpiece" *Journal of the RVW Society 4* November 1995 pp 8–9.
32. Kerman, J (1980) "How we got into analysis, and how we get out" *Critical Inquiry* 6 pp 311–31.
33. Kramer, L (1990) *Music as Cultural Practice.* Berkeley, University of California Press.
34. Meller, W (1989) *Vaughan Williams and the Vision of Albion.* Barrie and Jenkins.
35. Nattiez, J (1990) *Music and Discourse: towards a semiology of music.* Princeton University Press.
36. Onderdonk, J (1996) "Vaughan Williams's Folksong Transcriptions: a case of idealization?" *Vaughan Williams Studies* edited by Alain Frogley. Cambridge, Cambridge University Press pp 118–138.
37. Pakenham, S (1957) *Ralph Vaughan Williams: a discovery of his music.* Macmillan.
38. Peacock, A and Weir, R (1975) *The Composer in the Market Place.* Faber & Faber.
39. Rodden, J (1989) The Politics of Literary Reputation: the making and claiming of *"St George" Orwell.* Oxford University Press.
40. Scannell, P and Cardiff, D (1991) *A Social history of British Broadcasting Vol 1: Serving the Nation, 1922–1939.* Oxford, Basil Blackwell.
41. Threlfall, R (1975) "The Final Problem and Vaughan Williams' Piano Concerto" *Music Opinion* February 1975 pp 237–8.
42. Treitler, L (1991) "The Politics of Reception: tailoring the present as a fulfilment of a desired past" *Journal of the Royal Musical Association 116* pp 280–98.

43. Vaughan Williams, R (1963, rev 1986) *National Music and Other Essays*. Oxford University Press.
44. Vaughan Williams, U (1964) *R V W: a biography of Ralph Vaughan Williams*. Oxford University Press.
45. Vaughan Williams, U *and* Holst, I *eds* (1959) *Heirs and Rebels*. Oxford University Press.
46. Whittall, A (1987) "The Theorist's Sense of History: concepts of contemporaneity in composition and analysis" *Journal of the Royal Musical Association 112* pp 1–20.
47. – (1996) "Symphony in D Major: models and mutations" *Vaughan Williams Studies* edited by Alain Frogley. Cambridge, Cambridge University Press, pp 187–212.
48. Young, P (1953) *Vaughan Williams*. Dennis Dobson.

CONTRIBUTORS

Stephen Banfield is Elgar Professor of Music in the University of Birmingham. His books include *Sensibility and English Song* (1985), *The Blackwell History of Music in Britain* – Vol 6 *The 20ᵗʰ Century* (1995), and *Gerald Finzi – an English composer* (1998).

Jeremy Dibble is Reader in Music and Chairman of the Board of Studies in Music at Durham University, and author of *Sir C Hubert H Parry: his life and music* (1992).

Jennifer Doctor is Musicologist at the Britten-Pears Library in Aldeburgh, previously editor for 20ᵗʰ-Century composers for the revised *New Grove Dictionary*. She has carried out extensive research in the BBC Archives, and is preparing her Doctoral thesis, *The BBC and the Ultra-Modern Problem … 1922–36* (1993), for publication. Since 1992 she has been responsible for the Maconchy archive at St Hilda's College, Oxford.

Lewis Foreman, a freelance writer, is Music Trustee of the Sir Arnold Bax Trust. His many books on music include *Bax – a composer and his times* (1983, 1988) and *From Parry to Britten – British music in letters 1900–1945* (1987).

Andrew Herbert is a post-graduate tutor in music at the University of Birmingham, and has recently completed his Doctoral thesis *The Musical and Intellectual Development of Ralph Vaughan Williams*.

Duncan Hinnells made his first CD recording as a conductor with Verdi's *Il Trovatore* in 1994. He is currently completing doctoral research at Oxford on the relationship of Vaughan Williams with the Oxford University Press and the BBC. He is author of *An Extraordinary Performance* (1998), the history of the OUP Music Department.

John Huntley was assistant to Muir Mathieson at Denham Studios and took part in recording sessions with Vaughan Williams, Walton, Bliss and others. He was the author of *British Film Music* (1947) and joint author of *The Technique of Film Music* (1957, 1975) and is now a freelance lecturer and film historian.

Tony Kendall is well known for his songs, poetry and stories of old Essex. He has made a succession of well-received folk-song CDs, including "Rose of Essex", "Closer to the Heartland", and his programme of Vaughan Williams's Essex folksongs "A Bicycle Ride with Vaughan Williams".

Stephen Lloyd is author of *H Balfour Gardiner* (1984), *Sir Dan Godfrey Champion of British Composers* (1995) and *Fenby on Delius* (1996). Between 1980–95 he edited the Delius Society Journal, and has recently completed a book on Sir William Walton.

Anthony Payne, composer, critic, and author of *Frank Bridge, Radical and Conservative* (1984) and *Arnold Schoenberg* (1968), has recently been acclaimed for his performing edition of Elgar's Third Symphony.

Index

The index largely concentrates on works, names and places, although with a spread of more general matters that impinge on Vaughan Williams and his work. Music by Vaughan Williams is entered directly under the name of the work, the symphonies in numerical order under "symphony". Folk songs and films are also entered under their specific titles. All other music, books and works are entered under the name of their composer or author. Thus *Siegfried Idyll* appears under Wagner. Where the textual reference is small, the name of the composer/author is indexed but the title of the work in question does not necessarily appear in the index. The definite and indefinite article have been omitted in the majority of entries. Plate numbers are in *italic*.